HOLISTIC MISSION THROUGH MISSION PARTNERSHIP: AN INSTRUMENTAL CASE STUDY IN LA CEIBA, HONDURAS

Enoch Wan & John Jay Flinn

Relational Paradigm Series of CDRR

Holistic Mission Through Mission Partnership:
An Instrumental Case Study in La Ceiba, Honduras

Enoch Wan & John Jay Flinn

Cover designed by Mark Benec

ISBN: 978-1-954692-03-9

All rights reserved. Except for brief quotations in critical publications or reviews, no part of this book may be reproduced in any manner without prior written permission from the publisher or author.

Scriptures for this book were taken from the HOLY BIBLE, NEW INTERNATIONAL VERSION ®, NIV ® Copyright © 1973, 1978, 1984, 2011 by Biblica, Inc. ®. Used by permission of Zondervan Publishing House. All rights reserved.

CDRR (Center of Diaspora & Relational Research) @
https://www.westernseminary.edu/outreach/center-diaspora-relational-research

Western Academic Publishers

TABLE OF CONTENTS

- LIST OF FIGURES v
- List of Tables vii
- **Chapter 1 INTRODUCTION** 1
  - 1.1 Purpose of the Book 1
  - 1.2 The Background of the Book... 1
  - 1.3 The Definition of Key Terms... 3
  - 1.4 The Organization of the Book... 5
- **Chapter 2 Evangelical holistic mission and mission partnership: past and present** 7
  - 2.1 Introduction 7
  - 2.2 Holistic Mission – Description, Nature, and Scope 7
  - 2.3 Holistic Mission Partnership – Description, Nature, and Motivations 35
  - 2.4 Summary... 64
- **Chapter 3 The making of a partnership** 67
  - 3.1 Introduction 67
  - 3.2 Mission Partnership Further Defined..................................... 67
  - 3.3 The Context and the Beginnings 69
  - 3.4 Common Vision 72
  - 3.5 A Summary of the Relational Paradigm 75
  - 3.6 Partner Member Relationships 76
  - 3.7 Mutuality and Interdependence 81
  - 3.8 Working Through Cultural Issues with Sensitivity, Patience, and Grace 83
  - 3.9 Summary... 89
- **Chapter 4 Partnership as a facilitator for holistic mission**.......... 91
  - 4.1 Introduction 91
  - 4.2 Holistic Mission... 92
  - 4.3 Missional Relationships in Mission Partnerships 99
  - 4.4 Practical Benefits to Mission Partnership 103
  - 4.5 Spiritual Formation through Mission Partnership Relationships 105
  - 4.6 The Importance of Spiritual Formation to Mission Practice 121
  - 4.7 Attesting to a "New Reality" 123
  - 4.8 Summary.. 125

Chapter 5 Missiological Implications 127
   5.1 Introduction 127
   5.2 A Broadened Missiological Perspective 127
   5.3 Implications of the Church – Non-Church Partnerships.... 128
   5.4 Partnering in the U.S. Context 131
   5.5 Implication of Partnership Relationships on Discipleship...132
   5.6 Summary... 134
Chapter 6 Conclusion 135
APPENDIX 1 RESEARCH DESIGN AND METHODOLOGY 139
   Introduction.. 139
   Methodological Design 139
   Integrative Research Approach 139
   Role of the Researcher 140
   Data Collection... 140
   Data Interpretation and Presentation 143
   Ethical Considerations 143
Bibliography 145

LIST OF FIGURES

Figure 1. – Missiological Responses to the Plight of the "Poor" 14
Figure 2. – Recursive Learning Cycle.. 28
Figure 3. – A Relational Understanding of Poverty 31
Figure 4. – Transformed Relationships...33
Figure 5. – Integrated Approach of Holistic Christian Mission in Practice..100
Figure 6. – Total Health Partnership Missional Relationships.............. 101
Figure 7. – Transformation and Mission 122
Figure 8. – Total Health Logo 124
Figure 9. – Convergence of Multiple Data Sources into Thematic Conclusions.. 141

List of Tables

Table 1. – Social Service vs. Social Action 21
Table 2. – Mediating Factors in Cross-Cultural Mission Partnerships .. 54
Table 3. – How Cause Shapes Response 56
Table 4 – Programmatic Partnership vs Relational Christian Partnership 68
Table 5 – Aspects of Relational Partnership vs Programmatic Partnership 69
Table 6. – Partnership Within the Trinity 77
Table 7. – Mission Partnership Roles and Responsibilities 78
Table 8. – Partnership in Light of the Trinity 79
Table 9. – Shared Economic Responsibilities for La Ceiba Clinic Operation 82
Table 10. – Latin American – U.S. Cultural Differences 85
Table 11. – Practical Partnership Benefits 103
Table 12. – Holistic Medical Mission Weaknesses Mitigated by Partnership 104
Table 13. – Bible Verses Supporting Christian Action of Compassion ... 116
Table 14. – Examples of Otherness 117
Table 15. – Wan's Way of Integrative Research ("STARS") 140

CHAPTER 1

INTRODUCTION

Purpose of the Book

This book is the product of a case study that examines how Total Health (a U.S. based medical missions organization) and the Great Commission Latin America (GCLA) church in La Ceiba, Honduras created a mission partnership model that integrates compassionate medical care with ongoing spiritual care and spiritual formation to serve the La Ceiba community and its residents. The purpose of the case study is to gain missiological insights and understandings about achieving holistic mission through partnerships between churches and non-church organizations by describing and examining the mission partnership between Total Health and the GCLA church in La Ceiba, Honduras as an instrumental case study.

The Background of the Book

Recognizing the plight of the economically and spiritually impoverished community of La Ceiba, Honduras led two men to convergent desires to follow God's prompting to do their part to minister to the people of that community. One is the pastor of a small evangelical church in the GCLA organization, and the other, a young U.S. Christian doctor with a heart for mission.

In 2004, Total Health was formed as a U.S. based medical mission organization to work specifically in the community of La Ceiba, Honduras alongside the local church. Noted missiologist Lesslie Newbigin (1909–1998)[1] writes, "word and act belong together. The word is essential because the name of Jesus cannot be replaced by anything else... the deed is equally essential because the gospel is good news of the active presence of the reign of God."[2] Proclamation, though essential and central to the message, need not be the first act of mission. Newbigin explains that proclamation in the New Testament, both from Jesus and in the Book of Acts, generally follows an act of healing, compassion, or power. Newbigin notes that these acts represent a "new reality" that elicits questions for which only the gospel is the answer.[3]

The story in John 9 of Jesus healing the man who had been born blind shows just how powerful a new reality can be at generating questions that require a gospel

---

[1] Lesslie Newbigin was a British theologian, missiologist, missionary and author. He spent much of his career serving as a missionary in India and became affiliated with the Church of South India and the United Reformed Church. He became one of the Church of South India's first bishops.
[2] Lesslie Newbigin, "Cross-currents in Ecumenical and Evangelical Understandings of Mission," Vol. 6 (4), (1982), *International Bulletin of Missionary Research,* 148.
[3] Lesslie Newbigin, *The Gospel in a Pluralist Society* (Grand Rapids: Erdmans, 1989). See pages 128–140 for biblical analysis and support for his assertions that gospel proclamations follow questions about acts and deeds that in turn generate questions about a "new reality" observed by the crowds.

response. After being healed by Jesus, the man returned home. Upon his return, his new reality subjected him to questions from his neighbors, his family, and the religious leaders. Though he had not yet seen Jesus, he could testify that it was Jesus who had healed him.

Verse 25 reflects his powerful testimony to the Pharisees when he says, "Whether he is a sinner or not, I don't know. One thing I do know. I was blind but now I see." This is a powerful example of how the new reality of a transformed Christian life leads to questions only the gospel can answer. This pattern is replayed throughout Jesus' teachings. It must be understood as Newbigin points out, "The works by themselves did not communicate the new fact. That had to be stated in plain words: 'The kingdom of God has drawn near.'"[4]

The newly formed Total Health organization began working collaboratively with the church in La Ceiba to open and operate a primary healthcare clinic in the community. The clinic has since become a beacon of hope in a poverty-stricken, economically oppressed area of the world. The partnership has worked in such a way that the community looks at the clinic not as something brought to them by the North Americans but rather as their community clinic, where they can go to receive care and get well. The clinic is situated next to the church and the clinic workers are all Christians and members of a church, most as members of the La Ceiba GCLA church. It is an example of where the patients can go and see Jesus in the lives of those serving them. The patients not only hear the gospel, they also see it in action. As a result, not only is the community becoming healthier physically, the church has now grown to more than 1,000 members. These partners have established a working example of a Christian mission partnership that achieves holistic mission.

Jay Flinn was a member of the board of directors of the newly formed Total Health organization. During his theological and missiological studies Flinn was exposed to Newbigin's (and others') thoughts related to the inseparability of word and deed, of proclamation, and of social action. This holistic model of mission was intriguing given the Flinn's involvement in Total Health and other areas of mission in Latin America. He also began to realize the transformation that was occurring in his life as a result of the various relationship experiences occurring throughout the mission partnership.

There is both a vertical dimension and a horizontal dimension to the Christian faith and Christian mission. Enoch Wan, Director of the Doctor of Intercultural Studies program at Western Seminary, emphasizes a dynamic vertical relationship theme in a paradigm he calls "relational realism." He writes that "reality is primarily based on the vertical relationship between God and the created order and secondarily horizontal relationship within the created order."[5] Wan suggests that this relationship paradigm emphasizes a relational network that transcends culture, "trans-culturally relevant," making it an essential element to cross-cultural partnership relationships.[6]

Wan and Mark Hedinger, Executive Director of CultureBound, use this relational realism paradigm to construct a framework for relationally training intercultural missionaries. As part of developing this training methodology, they identify and

---

[4] Newbigin, The Gospel in a Pluralist Society, 132.
[5] Enoch Wan, "The Paradigm of 'Relational Realism.'" *Occasional Bulletin of the Evangelical Missiological Society*, Spring 2006, 1.
[6] Wan, 2.

examine the key relationships, both vertical and horizontal, that are important in training intercultural workers.[7] Though their relational framework is focused primarily on training intercultural workers, this framework leads to questions about what relational transformative learning and discipling might be occurring throughout the various relationships in a holistic mission model such as described herein.

Mission is often described as the work that God is doing through the mission workers in the lives of the mission recipients. To put in terms of the Total Health example, it is the spiritual and physical work that is being done in the lives of the clinic patients. However, what is lost in this description is the work that God is also doing in the lives of the mission workers at the same time.

It is this thought that was the catalyst for the case study that formed the basis of Flinn's doctoral dissertation and now the basis for this book. Can a mission partnership, through its various missional relationships, offer unique opportunities for transformation, not only of the targeted population to be served but of the partnership members and its participants as well? The dissertation case study uses the Total Health mission partnership with the La Ceiba GCLA church as a case to evaluate the potential of Christian mission partnerships to facilitate the achievement of holistic mission.

It is the prayer of the authors that this book will broaden the perspective of holistic mission and the related manner in which Christian mission partnership can facilitate the achievement of the mission. The biblical call to be His witnesses and make disciples formed in the likeness of Jesus has never been more important. We pray that the examples used in this book illustrate the relational nature of Christian mission partnership that fit into this broadened perspective of holistic mission.

We also pray that this book will create a willingness and desire for Christians to move past cultural differences and misunderstandings to a more partnership oriented mission philosophy. The holistic mission needs of the global world cannot be met by people or organizations working in isolation. It is our prayer that this book is an example of how mission leaders, empowered by a vital relationship with the Triune God, can look beyond a view of their own ministries, asking how their gifts might be used in partnership with others to facilitate even greater missional gains and fruit that will last.

The Definition of Key Terms

The terms and phrases listed below will be expanded upon in later sections of this book and are used in this book with specific intended definitions.
- Case Study: A qualitative research study approach that "investigates a contemporary phenomenon in depth and in its real-world context."[8]
- Instrumental Case Study: A qualitative research study of a specific case in order to provide insights and understanding into more than just the case being

---

[7] Enoch Wan and Mark Hedinger, *Relational Missionary Training* (Skyforest, CA: Urban Loft, 2017). Pages 38–50 explore and explain the authors' view of the seven key missionary relationships.
[8] Robert K. Yin, *Case Study Research: Design and Methods,* 5th edition (Thousand Oaks, CA: SAGE, 2014), 237.

studied, such as insights to a set of proposed research questions or problem statements.[9]
- Discipleship: Discipleship is teaching people to obey all that Jesus had commanded, such that the they are transformed toward a Christlikeness and a mature state of the Lordship of Christ, in their values, their worldviews, and their actions towards others in ways that reflect the attributes and character displayed by Jesus Christ.
- Relational Discipleship: Relational discipleship is the process of bringing others (people) to submit to the lordship (power and authority) of Jesus Christ primarily through vertical-relationship to the Triune God and secondarily through horizontal-relationship within the context of the Church/church in unity, mutuality, and reciprocity.[10]
- Mission: Mission is God's ultimate purpose for his creation and all that he is doing in the world to achieve that purpose. Also referred to as *missio Dei*.
- Mission Tasks: Mission tasks are a subset of mission and are the activities and specific work that God's people are called to do in mission participation.[11]
- Holistic mission: A frame for mission that does not subscribe to the dichotomy between evangelism and social action. It provides for ministering to both the spiritual and physical needs of the whole person and is described as Christians motivated by their love for God and neighbors (within or without one's socio-cultural context) mobilized to be engaged in multi-dimensional services to Him by serving others, inclusively caring for the spiritual, psychological, social, physical, etc. well beings of others with multi-facet services (religious & charity, public & private, etc.) and at multi-levels (personal and institutional, local and global), in the framework of reconciliation vertically with God, horizontally with humanity and hierarchically with the created order.[12]
- Missional Relationships: Missional relationships are the relationships that exist in the mundane, everyday activities of life where gospel truths can be presented using both words and deeds in creative ways that engage the culture yet are true to the Scriptures while holistically embracing spiritual formation, discipleship, and true community with others.[13]
- Partnership: Using founder of INTERDEV Phill Butler's definition, "A conscious decision on the part of two or more people or agencies to work together to realize an objective none of them could achieve alone."[14]
- Mission Partnership: Mission partnerships are relationships of two or more people or organizations, who possess complimentary resources and skills, who

---

[9] Robert E. Stake, *The Art of Case Study Research* (Thousand Oaks, CA: Sage, 1995), 3.
[10] Wan and Hedinger, 14.
[11] Some authors and scholars also refer to the concept of missions (plural) as the tasks of mission (singular). See the Chapter Two section "Holistic Mission – Description, Nature, and Scope" for further discussion of the concept of mission versus missions.
[12] Enoch Wan, "Mission Amid Global Crisis: Holistic Mission to Diaspora Groups." Paper presented to EMS at Tyndale University College and Seminary in Toronto, Canada, on March 8, 2019.
[13] John Jay Flinn, "Missional Community as Context for Disciple-Making: Theological and Theoretical Foundations," in *Missional Disciple-Making: Disciple-Making for the Purpose of Mission*, Ed. Michael J. Breen and David M. Gustafson (Pawleys Island, SC: 3DM Publishing, 2019), 171.
[14] Phill Butler, Well Connected: Releasing Power, Restoring Hope Through Kingdom Partnerships (Colorado Springs, CO: Authentic, 2006), 31.

have a common vision for Christian mission, and who, orchestrated by the Triune God, join forces to participate holistically in God's mission. The relationship of the partners to one another mimics that of the relationship of the Trinity through their unity with one another, their mutual love and respect for one another, and their mutual submission to one another.[15]
- Parachurch organization: The prefix *para* comes from a Greek word meaning "come alongside." Thus, parachurch means literally to come alongside the church in mission. A parachurch organization is an organization that operates alongside *(para)* the church. Parachurch organizations are groups of Christians, members of the universal church, who engage in specific areas of mission activities that serve or supplement the local churches in integration with the goals and activities of the local church.
- Total Health Partnership: For simplicity, the partnership studied in the case study and referenced in this book will often be referred to as "the Total Health partnership" or simply "the partnership." Definitionally, this term includes both the U.S. organization Total Health and the La Ceiba, Honduras GCLA church as organized in mission partnership.

The Organization of the Book

The book is organized into six chapters. Chapter 1 is introductory. Chapter 2 is foundational and reviews the historical aspects (past and present) of holistic mission and mission partnership including their description, nature, and scope. Chapter 3 examines several key partnership principles inherent in the Total Health partnership. Chapter 4 builds upon the previous chapters and connects partnership with holistic mission and explains the marks that provide for an effective mission partnership that facilitates holistic mission. Chapter 5 illustrates several missiological implications related to these types of partnerships. Chapter 6 is a conclusion, summarizing several of the book's key points and offering some concluding remarks

---

[15] This definition broadens the mechanical definition of partnership beyond the accomplishment of tasks by recognizing the spiritual and relational nature of the mission partnership union in the context of holistic mission. Chapter Three expands upon this concept of partnership relationality.

Chapter 2

Evangelical holistic mission and mission partnership: past and present

Introduction

The primary purpose of the case study on which this book is based was to gain missiological insights and understandings about achieving holistic mission through mission partnerships between churches and non-church organizations. This chapter begins to lay the foundation for each of these concepts, holistic mission and holistic mission partnership, by examining the historic and contemporary works of other scholars and authors. The chapter is organized into two primary sections, one for holistic mission and one for holistic mission partnership, followed by a summary. Section one begins by reviewing the historical perspectives of holistic mission and the various manner in which its definition has evolved over the years. This is followed by an examination of the nature and scope of holistic mission including definitions and descriptions of mission tasks and mission relationships. The second section begins by examining the practical nature of partnership including relationships, roles, and motivations. This is followed by a more specific review of cross-cultural partnerships and partnerships between churches and non-church organizations.

Holistic Mission – Description, Nature, and Scope

Holistic mission is one of those ideas and terms that can mean different things to different people. Likewise, the definition, nature, and objectives of holistic mission have been debated for many years. This debate is often answered by one's theology and/or by one's biblical view of the Great Commission (Matt. 28:18–20) and the Great Commandment (Mt 22:37–40). Holistic mission integrates the vertical and horizontal dimensions of Christian mission. Bryant L. Myers, professor of transformational development at Fuller Theological Seminary, describes it as a "frame for mission that refuses the dichotomy between material and spiritual, between evangelism and social action, between loving God and loving neighbor."[16] Often lost in the rhetoric of the debate is the realization that mission is not simply a definition; it is the actions that lay behind the definition. This section opens with a brief historical perspective of mission thought leading to the holistic view. It then moves to a more detailed description of holistic mission and the related tasks of mission.

---

[16] Bryant L. Myers, "Another Look at 'Holistic Mission': A Response." in *Evangelical Missions Quarterly* Vol. 35(3) (1999): 285–287. Accessed February 10, 2017. <https://www.emqonline.com/node/631>.

Historical Perspective of Evangelical Holistic Mission

Scholars and theologians define and describe mission and holistic mission in numerous ways. One of the primary tensions in the definition is the relationship between and priority of evangelism and social responsibility. David J. Bosch (1929–1992)[17] goes as far as to say that the "relationship between the evangelistic and the social dimensions of the Christian mission constitutes one of the thorniest areas in the theology and practice of mission."[18]

History indicates that this quest for definitive clarity in mission is a relatively recent development in church history. Edward L. Smither, Associate Professor of Intercultural Studies at Columbia International University, remarks that "unlike today, there was little debate [in the early church] over the relationship between proclamation and social action. Indeed, the bifurcation of the two areas and the response by way of the holism-prioritism debate are truly reflections of the late nineteenth- and early twentieth-century developments in the church in the West."[19] Bosch also notes that defining mission is of "recent vintage. The early Christian church undertook no such attempts—at least not consciously."[20]

The Book of Acts supports that there was no dichotomous view in the church of the first century. There is no doubt that proclamation was taking place in the first-century church. However, so too were acts of compassion. Acts, chapter six, provides the example of seven men chosen to serve and provide for widows in the community, and chapter eleven illustrates the church in Antioch providing relief funding for Judean famine victims.

Evidence exists that the early church cared for those outside the Christian faith as well. The apostate Emperor Julian is quoted as having noted, "Atheism [i.e. Christian faith] has been specially advanced through the loving service rendered to strangers… the godless Galileans care not only for their own poor but for ours as well."[21]

William Carey, a more recent example, is often described as a pioneer missionary and evangelist to India. Ruth and Vishal Mangalwadi studied and researched Carey's life and work and they point out that Carey's influence on culture and society in India far exceeded this description, calling him a "central character in the story of the modernization of India."[22] Carey advocated for many of India's societal issues, including the saving banks system, medical humanitarianism, agriculture, and indigenous industry, among others. Carey's missionary activities were holistic, not by some predetermined strategic design, rather by his desire to glorify God and, advance God's Kingdom to India. As a holistic minister, Carey was

---

[17] David J. Bosch was a noted missiologist and theologian, best known for his work *Transforming Mission* (1991), completed before his untimely death in an auto accident.
[18] David J. Bosch, *Transforming Mission: Paradigm Shifts in Theology of Mission*, 20th Anniversary Edition (Maryknoll, NY: Orbis Books, 2011), 410.
[19] Edward L. Smither, *Mission in the Early Church: Themes and Reflections* (Eugene, OR: Cascade, 2014), 146.
[20] Bosch, Transforming Mission, 523.
[21] As quoted in Stephen Neill, *A History of Christian Mission: The Penguin History of the Church 6* (New York: Penguin Books, 1990), 37.
[22] Vishal and Ruth Mangalwadi, The Legacy of William Carey: A Model for the Transformation of a Culture (Wheaton: Crossway, 1999), 25.

"an evangelist who used every available medium to illuminate the dark facets of India with the light of truth."[23]

Missionaries have always had some sort of social component to their evangelism and church planting ministries. Stan Guthrie, Editor of *Evangelical Missions Quarterly* and Associate News Editor of *Christianity Today,* points out that "down through the first two millennia, missionaries have built hospitals and schools. They have brought food and water. They have ministered not only to the spiritual needs, but to every wound common to humanity."[24]

There is both a vertical dimension and a horizontal dimension to the Christian faith, and church history reveals the dangerous results of drifting too far to either side. Paul G. Hiebert (1932-2007)[25] and Monte B. Cox, Dean of the College of Bible and Ministry at Harding University, suggest that the roots of the dichotomous view of mission go back to medieval Europe where "The Worldview of the Middle Ages… divided reality between the Creator and the creation," which led to a "distinction between religious and science, or between eternal and earthly needs." This separation, they suggest, has led to the view that evangelism and social responsibility are "two separate entities that need to be integrated."[26]

Significant changes in Western culture and thinking emerged from the enlightenment and the industrial revolution. The movement toward science, rationality, materialism, and individualism led to a changing view of the Bible. People were beginning to turn away from a belief in eternal damnation and to doubt the existence of a God who could predestine human beings to such damnation.[27] Mission for salvation was being replaced by missions of good works. "Sin became identified with ignorance and it was believed that knowledge and compassion would produce uplift as people rose to meet their potential."[28]

The social gospel was a reaction to the social and economic issues brought about by the societal changes. It was a call to expand the Christian mission beyond individual salvation into the work of reforming social injustices. Walter Rauschenbusch (1861-1918),[29] one of the champions of the social gospel, believed that the industrial revolution and the rise of capitalism had created a social crisis and were a "crushing demonstration that the moral forces in humanity failed to

---

[23] Mangalwadi and Mangalwadi, *The Legacy of William Carey,* 25.
[24] Stan Guthrie, Missions in the Third Millennium: 21 Key Trends for the 21st Century, revised & expanded edition (Milton Keynes, UK: Paternoster, 2014), 153.
[25] Paul G. Hiebert was an American missiological anthropologist. He taught at the Fuller Theological Seminary and was Distinguished Professor of Mission and Anthropology at Trinity Evangelical Divinity School.
[26] Paul G. Hiebert and Monte B. Cox, "Evangelism and Social Responsibility," *Evangelical Dictionary of World Missions*, Ed. A. Scott Moreau (Grand Rapids: Baker, 2000), 344–345.
[27] Bosch, *Transforming Mission,* devotes a lengthy chapter to the enlightenment and its impact on the Christian faith and Christian mission, 268 – 353.
[28] Bosch, Transforming Mission, 290.
[29] Walter Rauschenbusch was a New York pastor that served in a depressed area known as Hell's Kitchen and a faculty member of Rochester Theological Seminary. He was a champion of the Social Gospel, and his book *Christianity and the Social Crisis* was the primary thesis of the movement.

keep pace with its intellectual and economic development. Men learned to make wealth much faster than they learned to distribute it justly."[30]

On the surface, the social gospel was a movement to apply theology and Christianity to current social conditions and issues, a concept that would be theoretically embraced by all Christians. However, the social gospel leaders became known for liberalizing and modifying theology by interpreting the gospel to meet the reforms that they wanted to achieve. They were not simply using theology to apply to current social conditions. Willem Visser 't Hooft (1900–1985)[31] explains, "they were also constantly re-considering their theoretical positions on the basis of social experience that they gather in doing so."[32] Noted evangelist Billy Graham describes this as a period when,

Theological changes were subtly infiltrating Christian youth movements causing some to weaken their ties to orthodox faith. The authority of evangelism began to shift from the Scriptures to the organized church. They focused attention on the materialistic salvation of the *community* rather than the individual. This became known as the 'social gospel.' Emphasis turned to man 'in this world,' rather than 'in this *and* the next world.'[33]

Fundamental evangelicals resisted this change in what is known as "the Great Reversal" and responded by shifting away from outward displays of support for social action.[34] This position hardened as Christian social action became inextricably linked with theological liberalism, ultimately making it impossible to be evangelical and to support any tenets of the social gospel. Pointing to this as a "false dilemma," David O. Moberg, Professor Emeritus in the Department of Social and Cultural Sciences at Marquette University, observes that "Christians became either evangelistic or socially involved, not both."[35]

In the aftermath of two world wars and as technology began to bring the needs of the world into living rooms, Christians could no longer claim ignorance to the issues of the world. Evangelicals began questioning evangelism-only mission and began to reach back into the Scriptures for biblical support for social action and its relationship to evangelism.

In the 1940s and 1950s, fundamentalist Carl F. H. Henry (1913–2003)[36] is critical of the lack of social concern by evangelicals. He recognized the need to reject

---

[30] Walter Rauschenbusch, *Christianity and the Social Crisis* (London: The Macmillan Company, 1914), 218.
[31] Willem A. Visser 't Hooft was a Dutch theologian who became the first secretary general of the World Council of Churches in 1948.
[32] Willem Visser 't Hooft, *The Background of the Social Gospel in America* (St Louis, MO: Bethany, 1928), 16.
[33] Billy Graham. "Why Lausanne?" in *Let the Earth Hear His Voice*. Ed. J.D. Douglas (Minneapolis, MN: World Wide Publications, 1975), 26.
[34] David O. Moberg, *The Great Reversal: Reconciling Evangelism and Social Concern* (Eugene: OR: Wipf & Stock, 2006), 30. Moberg gives credit for the term "the Great Reversal" to noted evangelical historian Timothy L. Smith (1924–1997).
[35] Moberg, 34.
[36] Carl F. H. Henry is the founding editor of *Christianity Today* magazine. An American evangelical, Henry was critical of evangelicalism's rigid position against social action. His work *The Uneasy Conscience of Modern Fundamentalism* in which he rejects liberalism, affirms the Bible, and criticizes rigid fundamentalism established him as a leading evangelical scholar.

the non-evangelical liberalism, but he maintains that "the rejection of non-evangelical solutions does not involve—at least, logically—a loss of the social relevance of the Gospel."[37] Henry insists that it was the evangelicals' task to "explicitly sketch the social implications of its message for the non-Christian world." Instead, however, they had left the Christian social imperative "in the hands of those who understand it in sub-Christian terms."[38]

Injustices caused by faulty social structures were brought directly into view by post-colonialism and the civil rights movement in the 1960s and continued to encourage a rethinking of the role of evangelicals in society. By 1974, when the International Congress of World Evangelism met in Lausanne, many evangelicals, particularly those from less economically developed countries (the Third World), were ready for renewed approaches to social action.[39]

Contemporary Views of Evangelical Holistic Mission

The Lausanne Committee has actively addressed this matter on several occasions, reflecting the evolving evangelical position and continued evangelism prioritism.[40] John Stott (1921–2011)[41] was the primary facilitator at the Lausanne Congress and heavily influenced the drafting of the Lausanne Covenant. Stott had previously argued that the Great Commission mission was "exclusively a preaching, converting and teaching mission."[42] However, in his work leading up to Lausanne and a book follow-up to the conference, Stott confesses that he had changed his views on the holistic nature and the application of the Great Commission. He writes:

Today, however, I would express myself differently... I now see more clearly that not only the consequences of the commission but the actual commission itself must be understood to include social as well as evangelistic responsibility.[43]

The Lausanne Covenant addresses evangelism in Article Four, Christian social responsibility in Article Five, and the church and evangelism in Article Six. Reflecting a repentant attitude toward recognition of social responsibility, Article Five states, "we express penitence both for our neglect and for having sometimes regarded evangelism and social concern as mutually exclusive," while Article Six affirms the priority position of evangelism in the mission of the church stating, "In the church's mission of sacrificial service, evangelism is primary."

Continuing its work, in 1982, The Lausanne Movement held The International Consultation on the Relationship between Evangelism and Social Responsibility. In its subsequent report, the committee again reaffirms the priority of evangelism and suggests three ways social activities might relate to evangelism: first as a

---

[37] Carl F.H. Henry, *The Uneasy Conscience of Modern Fundamentalism* (1947, repr., Grand Rapids, MI: Eerdmans, 2003), 16.
[38] Henry, 39.
[39] Bosch, Transforming Mission, 414.
[40] See www.lausanne.org/content for all Lausanne documents subsequently referenced herein in their entirety.
[41] John Stott was an English Anglican priest with extensive influence in the worldwide evangelical movement. He was the principal framer of the Lausanne Congress in 1974 and has written extensively on a multitude of evangelical issues.
[42] John R. W. Stott, Christian Mission in the Modern World: What the Church Should Be Doing Now! (Downers Grove, IL: IVP, 2008), 25.
[43] Stott, Christian Mission in the Modern World, 25.

consequence of evangelism, second as a bridge to evangelism, and third as a partner to evangelism. In an earlier writing, Stott describes the same relationships, somewhat rejecting the first two, categorizing them to be "a means to an end," while affirming the third, social activity as a partner to evangelism, as the "truly Christian" relation.[44]

In 1983, the World Evangelical Fellowship convened a consultation in Wheaton, Illinois, and pressed forward even more toward a fully symbiotic relationship between proclamation and social action. Stemming from its conference track devoted to "The Church in Response to Human Need," paragraph 26 of the ensuing Wheaton '83 Statement states:

Evil is not only in the human heart but also in social structures… The mission of the church includes both the proclamation of the Gospel and its demonstration. We must therefore evangelize, respond to immediate human needs, and press for social transformation.[45]

As a result, Bosch asserts, "For the first time in an official statement emanating from an international evangelical conference the perennial dichotomy [between evangelism and social action] was overcome."[46]

The Manila Manifesto elaborated on the Lausanne Covenant in 1989. Article Four is entitled "The Gospel and Social Responsibility" and offers a further call for Christians to be committed to the Kingdom demands of justice and peace, and at the same time continues to affirm the priority of evangelism. More recently, The Lausanne Movement dealt with the social responsibility of the church by issuing the Lausanne Occasional Paper (LOP) No. 33 entitled "Holistic Mission." It acknowledges the church's failures in the past regarding social actions, seeks a more thorough understanding of holistic mission and a holistic Christian response to both evangelism and societal needs of the times.

Stott's work and the Lausanne Congress and its Covenant have been referred to as a watershed mark in the attempt to reconcile the dichotomous relationship between evangelism and social action within evangelical mission. It prescribes a two-mandate approach to mission, evangelism, and social action. The priority of evangelism was upheld, and social action was deemed a partner to evangelism. This was not without its drawbacks, however, as the debate then shifted to one of priority versus equality.

Bosch criticizes the two-mandate theology, noting the implication is that "it is possible to have evangelism without a social dimension and Christian social involvement without an evangelistic dimension." He goes on to write that "if one suggests that one component is primary and the other secondary, one implies that one is essential, the other part optional."[47]

C. René Padilla, South American theologian and former General Secretary of the Latin American Theological Fraternity, suggests that the years following Lausanne show that "far from settling the matter, the Lausanne Congress had done little more

---

[44] Stott, Christian Mission in the Modern World, 27.
[45] Lausanne Movement, "Transformation: The Church in Response to Human Need." 12 June 1983. *Lausanne Movement.* Accessed July 21, 2018.
<www.lausanne.org/content/statement/transformation-the-church-in-response-to-human-need>.
[46] Bosch, Transforming Mission, 417.
[47] Bosch, Transforming Mission, 415.

than point to the need to deal with the role of social involvement for the sake of the integrity of the church and its mission."[48] Padilla views these two mandates as not mutually exclusive; rather the biblical salvation mandate is a single mandate to save the whole person, spiritually and physically.

Padilla views holistic mission as biblically based in the theology of the Kingdom of God and affirms a more integrated approach to holistic mission with good works an integral part of reflecting Christ in the world and pointing to the Kingdom. Padilla writes that the mission of the Church is the "manifestation (though not yet complete) of the Kingdom of God, through proclamation as well as through social service and action."[49]

Ebbie Smith, former missionary to Indonesia and Professor of Missions at Southwestern Baptist Seminary, likewise states that the Great Commission includes humanitarian efforts, suggesting however that such efforts are secondary to evangelistic activities. These humanitarian efforts, he writes, "are to be part of the effort to make disciples and plant churches, not a substitution for evangelism. Missions must never lose the two main thrusts - evangelistic outreach and church planting."[50] Even so, Smith later asserts that "effective missionary strategy is holistic,"[51] defining holistic as an array of missionary activities, including evangelism, disciple making, church planting, humanitarian needs, and compassionate efforts. Smith also hints at partnership collaboration in the endeavor to create holistic mission by providing examples of specialized organizations that contribute to missionary effectiveness.

David J. Hesselgrave (1924–2018)[52] recognizes the tensions in the various positions and suggests that the tension between prioritism and holism is one of the ten key biblical paradigms that are in conflict. As shown in the chart below, he places holism theology as a midpoint on a scale between Prioritism Theology (evangelism only) and Liberation Theology (social justice only).[53]

A fervent critic of the holistic mission definitions, Hesselgrave espouses the traditional view of mission as solely evangelism, church planting, and training, concluding that "the primary concern of our Lord has to do with meeting spiritual needs, not with meeting physical, material, or social needs."[54] The Great Commandment he contends is just that, "a command to be obeyed along with all of

---

[48] C. René Padilla, "Integral Mission and its Historical Development." in *Justice, Mercy and Humility: Integral Mission and the Poor*. Ed. Tim Chester (Waynesboro, GA: Paternoster, 2002), 47.
[49] C. René Padilla, *Mission Between the Times: Essays on the Kingdom* (Grand Rapids, MI: William B. Eerdmans Publishing, 1985), 192.
[50] Ebbie Smith, "Introduction to the Strategy of Missions," *Missiology: An Introduction to the Foundations, History, and Strategies of World Missions*. Ed. John Mark Terry, Ebbie Smith and Justice Anderson (Nashville, TN: Broadman & Holman, 1998), 441.
[51] Smith, 442.
[52] David J. Hesselgrave was professor emeritus of missions at Trinity Evangelical Divinity School, served as a missionary in Japan for twelve years, and was executive director of the Evangelical Missiological Society.
[53] David J. Hesselgrave, Paradigms in Conflict: 10 Key Questions in Christian Missions Today (Grand Rapids, MI: Kregel, 2005), 122.
[54] Hesselgrave, Paradigms in Conflict, 136.

the other things Christ commanded," but it is secondary to the mission to evangelize the world.[55]

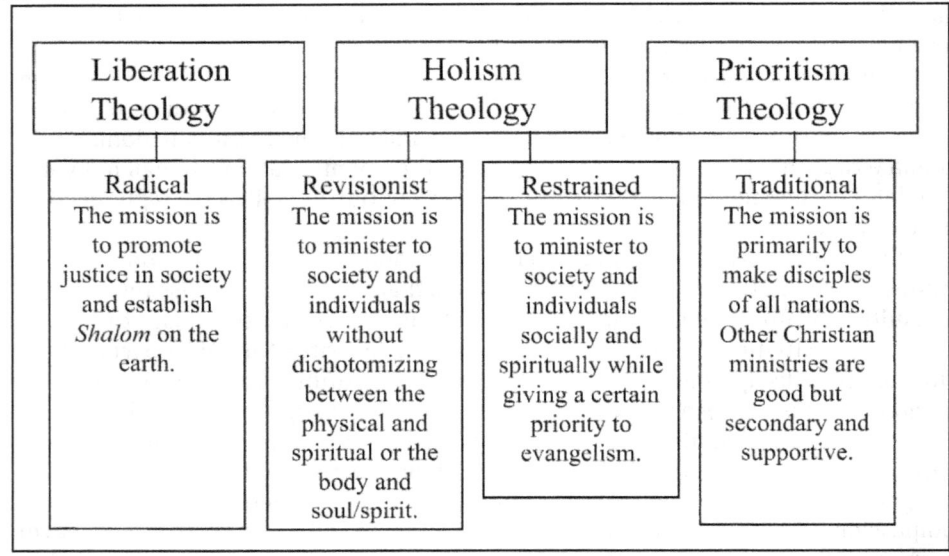

Figure 1. - Missiological Responses to the Plight of the "Poor"[56]

Each of the Holism Theology models illustrated in Hesselgrave's chart include ministering to both the physical and spiritual needs of individuals and society, with the "Restrained Holism" model maintaining a certain level of priority for evangelism.

Newbigin was more favorably disposed to social activity. He views Christian mission from a Trinitarian perspective "as proclaiming the kingdom of the Father, as sharing the life of the Son, and as bearing the witness of the Spirit."[57] Reacting to what he thinks was the secularization of mission and the misuse of the term *missio Dei*, Newbigin believes social activity to be a biblical mandate that had been secularized to the marginalization of the church.[58] Newbigin wants to show that evangelism would be ineffective unless those being evangelized could see the reflection of Christ in the words and deeds of the Christian. He maintains that church growth should come through evangelism and suggests that the church should also be involved in the struggle for justice in the world; it is acts of service and deeds that often allows one to get to gospel proclamation. For example, Newbigin points out that "almost all the great Christian preaching in Acts are made

---

[55] David J. Hesselgrave, "Redefining Holism." *Evangelical Missions Quarterly* Vol 35 (3) (1999): 278–84. Accessed February 10, 2017. <https://emqonline.com/node/632>.
[56] Hesselgrave, Paradigms in Conflict, 122.
[57] Lesslie Newbigin, *The Open Secret: An Introduction to the Theology of Mission*, Revised Edition (Grand Rapids, MI: William B. Eerdmanns Publishing, 1995), 29.
[58] Newbigin, *The Open Secret*, 18.

in a response to a question."[59] The questions arise because of a new reality, that being the new reality of the risen Christ. Newbigin suggests that it is not the church's business to answer all the world's questions. Rather, he maintains that answering the gospel question is "the church's first business. And the question is only asked if there is some evidence that a new reality is present."[60]

John Cheyne (1929–2016)[61] views the holistic principle as a major principle in the strategies of humanitarian missions. He points out that "humanity's spiritual nature cannot be dealt with in isolation from human circumstances."[62] Cheyne places the burden of holism on both the evangelist and the humanitarian servant. If holistic mission is to be successful, each must be sensitive to the needs of the whole person. He illustrates,

A mother holding her starving child may not be able to comprehend the message of the evangelist who proclaims, 'God loves you,' but then fails to provide for the starving child. On the other hand, a mother watching a caring and loving nurse ministering to her baby throughout the night may not understand the motivating power which impels the nurse to do so, unless someone takes the time to reveal the message of Christ inherent in the ministry.[63]

The evangelist must recognize and be sensitive to human physical needs, and the humanitarian servant must be aware of the human spiritual brokenness due to the nature of sin. Cheyne also warns against humanitarian effort becoming a "sort of spiritual bribery" used to elicit a conversion to Christ.[64]

Focusing on holistic ministry to the poor, Myers affirms a holistic approach to all ministries and cites the separation of the spiritual and physical realms during the enlightenment as the "great divorce."[65] He suggests that the "gospel message is an inseparable mix of life, deed, word, and sign. We are to be with Jesus (life) so that we can preach the good news (word), heal the sick (deed), and cast out demons (sign)."[66] From that basis, he offers practical applications and illustrates key principles and practices for successful holistic mission efforts.

Myers does not appear to subscribe to a priority model, rather a needs model, suggesting that the gospel should be shared in whatever way best speaks to those needs. He affirms also that all dimensions of the gospel (life, word, deed, sign) should be shared over time to provide a full understanding. Myers illustrates three types of indicators of a genuinely holistic ministry: people have a chance to respond to the good news of Jesus Christ, there is evidence of lasting value change or

---

[59] Lesslie Newbigin, *The Gospel in a Pluralist Society* (Grand Rapids, MI: William B. Erdmans Publishing Company, 1989), 132.
[60] Newbigin, The Gospel in a Pluralist Society, 133.
[61] John Cheyne served as a missionary to Africa for 24 years and as Director of Human Needs for the International Missions Board.
[62] John Cheyne, "Strategies for Humanitarian Ministries." *Missiology: An Introduction to the Foundations, History, and Strategies of World Missions,* Ed. John Mark Terry, Ebbie Smith, and Justice Anderson (Nashville, TN: Broadman & Holman, 1998), 518.
[63] Cheyne, 517.
[64] Cheyne, 517.
[65] Bryant L. Myers, *Walking with the Poor: Principles and Practices of Transformational Development*, Revised and Expanded Edition (Maryknoll, NY: Orbis Books, 2011), 5.
[66] Myers, Walking with the Poor, 201.

transformation, and there is transformation of social structures, institutions and processes.[67]

In a subsequent work, Myers and his coauthors examine holistic mission specifically as it relates to healing and healthcare, an area of specific interest to this study. This work continues Myers' position of inseparable witness through life, word, deed, and sign and grounds it in the theory of Christian witnessing with the concept that all Christians are called to witness, in all aspects of their lives, at all times.[68] Consistent with Newbigin's thought of deeds preceding and instigating questions that lead to proclamation, he suggests that deeds can serve as a means of proclamation. Related to medical mission work, he writes, "This framework suggests that we can also think of evangelism as the work that God does through us as long as we are acting in ways that provoke questions to which the good news of Jesus Christ is the answer."[69] He suggests that the whole person is an inseparable makeup of mind, body, and soul, thus to "save" the person holistically, each part must be ministered to appropriately in the same way Jesus addressed the heart, mind, body, and strength. Following Jesus' example would mean "demonstrating that 'Your sins are forgiven' and 'Take up your mat and walk' are interconnected."[70]

Amid all the theories and debates, various forms of holistic mission have been taking place around the world. To gain further practical insights into the dynamics of these missions, during the mid-1990s, Tetsunao Yamamori, President Emeritus of Food for the Hungry International, commissioned a series of case studies of specific holistic ministries with the poor that resulted in a related four-book series. This series is captioned "Cases in Holistic Ministry" and the four books are entitled based on the geographical area of the cases (Asia, Africa, Latin America, and the urban poor). The books were edited by Yamamori and others and include contributions by several prominent mission leaders such as Hiebert, Myers, and Padilla.

Yamamori wrote the introduction for each book, reflecting on the evolution of the definition of holistic mission and other key insights discovered from the work. The cases are summarized and critiqued for holistic insights and themes. Each book summarizes the key findings toward a goal of strengthening both the understanding and practice of holistic mission.

Consistent themes and contemporary views of holistic mission arise in the case studies. If the spiritual and physical realities of humanity are to be ministered to holistically, the local church must play a significant role in the community. Likewise, those ministering in deeds must do so with the proper witness to the gospel message, working in unison with the church to meet the spiritual needs of those in the community in which they serve.

Charles Ringma, Professor Emeritus, Missions and Evangelism at Regent College, suggests that the historic debate between evangelism and social action has been a disservice to holistic mission, observing that much of this debate has "focused on restoring what should never have been lost in the first place."[71]

---

[67] Myers, At the End of the Day, 200.
[68] Bryant L. Myers, Erin Dufault-Hunter, and Isaac B. Voss, *Health Healing and Shalom: Frontiers and Challenges for Christian Health Missions* (Pasadena, CA: William Carey Library, 2015), 42.
[69] Myers, Dufault-Hunter, and Voss, 51.
[70] Myers, Dufault-Hunter, and Voss, 277.
[71] Charles Ringma, "Holistic Ministry and Mission: A Call for Reconceptualization." In *Missiology: An International Review*, Vol. XXXII No. 4, 2004, 435.

Likewise, contemporarily, it appears that the "great reversal" is actually reversing as evangelicals embrace some forms of social action in mission or, at a minimum, recognizes some forms of social action as Christian responsibility.

Most proposed definitions of mission can be summarized into three primary positions related to the relationship of evangelism and social action in mission. One position retains the emphasis on evangelism and church planting with little regard to social action. A second position reflects evangelism as the primary purpose of Christian mission with Christian social action a secondary partner. The third position considers social action and evangelism as equal and integral to mission. While there are variants to these positions and different terms may be used to describe them, the variants are ultimately defined by the relative priority and relationship of evangelism and social action to one another.[72]

Nature and Scope of Holistic Mission

Meanwhile, many points of view surrounding the definition and purpose of mission remain and move beyond the common debate between evangelism and social activity. Mission priorities and definitions are debated using words such as *evangelism, witness, service, compassion, discipleship, reconciliation,* and *social actions.* There is a clamor for clarity, yet an inability to agree. The definition changes and evolves as does the world in which those who are trying to define it. Bosch asserts that his comprehensive work on the transformation of mission throughout history evolved "from the assumption that the definition of mission is a continual process of sifting, testing, reformulating, and discarding."[73]

As we progress into the twenty-first century, the lack of clarity continues. Ed Stetzer, Billy Graham Distinguished Chair for Church, Mission, and Evangelism at Wheaton, goes as far as questioning if any definition can provide a truly defining picture of what all evangelical churches are seeking to accomplish missionally in our day and suggests that perhaps "some agreed-upon description would provide what no definition can."[74] Stetzer does not advocate for an 'everything is mission' concept, but rather a meaningful way to provide people an understanding of mission that will entice them to become involved. He suggests,

It will help all of God's people to be involved in all of God's mission if we will do the work of both defining the mission and choosing an appropriate cultural articulation of the mission. As Stephen Neil said, "when everything is mission, nothing is mission." The mission of God cannot be the catch-all that includes everything from folding bulletins, to picking up trash on the highway, to coaching a ball team, to the gospel infiltrating a previously unreached people group... What can take place... is a local church can choose words that convey meaning in the context

---

[72] See A. Scott Moreau, "Mission and Missions," *Evangelical Dictionary of World Missions*, Ed. A. Scott Moreau (Grand Rapids, MI: Baker, 2000), 636–38 for further reading and discussion regarding the various positions.
[73] Bosch, Transforming Mission, 523.
[74] Ed Stetzer, "Responding to 'Mission' Defined and Described" and the Four Respondents," in *Missionshift: Global Issues in the Third Millenium*, Ed. David J. Hesselgrave and Ed Stetzer (Nashville, TN: B&H Publishing, 2010), 75.

of that body. In turn, those words can define the mission of God, the work of the church and the role of the members.[75]

Denny Spitters, Vice President of Church Partnerships for Pioneers USA, and Matthew Ellison, Missions Pastor and President and Church Missions Coach of Sixteen:Fifteen, argue against an everything-is-mission view and for a definitive definition of mission. They lament, "In our own generation, a strong embrace of the everything-is-mission paradigm has sometimes led us to a humanitarian mission devoid of the gospel."[76] They focus on a definition of missions based on their interpretation of the Great Commission, specifically making disciples of all nations. They write,

Modern history has shown us this: Whenever the primacy of disciple making and church planting have been replaced with efforts to eradicate the world's evil systems, diseases, and oppressions, the global disciple-making activities of the church have foundered…We do not oppose social transformation and holistic ministry but we do not believe they are the goal. Making disciples who birth the local church is the key to both evangelism and social transformation. Compassion ministry as missions—without the gospel as its primary vehicle for existence and expression—easily lapses into little more than humanistic accomplishment.[77]

Spitters and Ellison work through various examinations of biblical texts using their opinions and interpretations, along with those of other supporting authors, to develop a missions definition that centers on making disciples of all the nations. In doing so, they stress that this "is a mandate for every disciple of Christ… and every church… Every believer is to be living a lifestyle 'on mission' for the purpose of its [the Great Commission] completion."[78]

In the last century there has been a movement to recognize mission as God's mission, *missio Dei*.[79] This description provides that mission "has its origin neither in the official Church nor in the special groups within the Church. It has its origin with God."[80] The biblical story, or the "grand narrative," as Christopher J.H. Wright, International Ministries Director of the Langham Partnership International, calls it, is a holistic story that reveals God's heart for the entirety of his creation. [81] It is a story in which God invites us to participate in his mission through holistic missions of witness, service, and other related missional activities.[82]

Missio Dei is a comprehensive term that focuses on all that God has done and is doing in history to establish his kingdom. Bosch defines it as, "God's self-revelation

---

[75] Ed Stetzer, "Involving All of God's People in All of God's Mission, Part 2," *Christianity Today* (June 2010), <https://www.christianitytoday.com/edstatzer/2010/June/involving-all-of-gods-people-in-all-of-gods-mission-part-2.html>.
[76] Denny Spitters and Matthew Ellison, *When Everything is Missions* (Orlando, FL: BottomLine Media, 2017), 23.
[77] Spitters and Ellison, 45.
[78] Spitters and Ellison, 117.
[79] See Bosch, *Transforming Mission*, 398–402, for a brief history of the term *missio Dei* and what he deems the implications to the church and its definition and practice of mission.
[80] David J. Bosch, Witness to the World: The Christian Mission in Theological Perspective (1980, repr., Eugene, OR: Wipf&Stock, 2006), 239.
[81] Christopher J.H. Wright, *The Mission of God: Unlocking the Bible's Grand Narrative* (Downers Grove, IL: IVP Academic, 2006).
[82] Wright, *The Mission of God*, 22–23, Myers, *Walking with the Poor*, 98–100, and Ringma, 438.

as the One who loves the world; God's involvement in and with the world, the nature and activity of God, which embraces both the church and the world, and which the church is privileged to participate."[83] It is not limited to the activities of the church, rather all that God is doing in the world, both in and out of the church. Wright explains that it is not the case that "God has a mission for the church in the world, but that God has a church for his mission in the world. Mission was not made for the church; the church was made for mission—God's mission."[84]

The recognition that God's mission is broader than the activities of the church has led to a differentiation of terms and a changing narrative in the mission discussion. Previously, the terms mission (singular) and missions (plural) were used almost interchangeably. George W. Peters (1907–1988)[85] asserts that they are not synonyms, writing that mission, in contrast to missions, "is a comprehensive term including the upward, inward and outward ministries of the church. It is the church as 'sent' (a pilgrim, stranger, witness, prophet, servant, as salt, as light, etc.) in this world."[86]

In the same vein, Wright suggests that mission (singular) is "all that God is doing in his great purpose for the whole of creation and all that he calls us to do in cooperation with that purpose."[87] The term missions (plural) on the other hand, can be more narrowly used to describe the various activities and efforts of the church to carry out the task of mission in the world, or as Wright suggests, "the multitude of activities that God's people can engage in, by means of which they participate in God's mission."[88]

Wan concurs with this separation of mission from missions. He defines mission (singular) as "Christians (individuals) and the Church (institutional) continuing on and carrying out the *mission Dei* of the Triune God ('mission') at both individual and institutional levels spiritually (saving soul) and socially (ushering in shalom[89]) for redemption, reconciliation, and transformation ('missions')." He defines missions (plural as the "ways and means of accomplishing 'the mission' which has been entrusted by the Triune God to the Church and Christians."[90] Wan wraps these definitions into a comprehensive definition of holistic ministry/missions as follows:

Christians motivated by their love for God and neighbors (within or without one's socio-cultural context) mobilized to be engaged in multi-dimensional services to Him by serving others, inclusively caring for the spiritual, psychological, social, physical, etc. well beings of others with multi-facet services (religious & charity,

---

[83] Bosch, Transforming Mission, 10.
[84] Wright, The Mission of God, 62.
[85] George W. Peters was a Russian-born missiologist and former Professor of Missiology at Dallas Theological Seminary where he was also head of the missions department.
[86] George W. Peters, *A Biblical Theology of Missions*. 1972 New Edition (Chicago, IL: Moody Press, 1984), 11.
[87] Christopher J. H. Wright, The Mission of God's People: A Biblical Theology of the Church's Mission (Grand Rapids, MI: Zondervan, 2010), 25.
[88] Wright, The Mission of God's People, 25.
[89] Wan notes that "shalom" is the context of total wellness in which created humanity can reach his/her full potential and properly respond to God and his message relationally (Jer. 29:7; 1 Tim. 2:1–5).
[90] Enoch Wan "Diaspora Missiology and International Student Ministry (ISM)," *Diaspora Missions to International Students,* Ed., Enoch Wan (Portland, OR: Western Seminary Press, 2019), 11.

public & private, etc.) and at multi-levels (personal and institutional, local and global), in the framework of reconciliation vertically with God, horizontally with humanity and hierarchically with the created order.[91]

Thus, using this singular/plural definitional designation, mission is God's ultimate purpose and all that he is doing in the world to achieve that purpose. Missions are a subset of mission and are the activities and specific work that God's people are called to do in mission participation.[92]

Central Tasks of Mission

Another concept, and a systematic approach, is to classify a certain activity or activities as central tasks of mission rather than primary or secondary. Citing the debate between evangelism/proclamation and the social aspects of mission, Wright describes this as a hub-and-rim model where "evangelism is like the hub [central to mission], connected to the engine of the gospel power of God, with the living demonstration of the gospel by Christians (the rim) giving the hub connection to the context—the road."[93] Without both the hub and the rim, a wheel cannot function. In this example, proclamation (hub) and deeds (rim) are both integral for the full gospel message, with proclamation central to communicating the gospel and clarifying the meaning of the deeds. Proclamation is what ties Jesus to the acts of compassion.

For social action to be Christian witness it must point to God's missional response to human brokenness through the work of Christ, not to the individuals performing the acts or the acts themselves. Wright asserts, "Mission may not always *begin* with evangelism. But mission that does not ultimately *include* declaring the Word and the name of Christ, the call to repentance, and faith and obedience has not completed its task. It is defective mission, not holistic mission."[94] Moberg concurs, writing, "Without evangelism most efforts to restructure society will fail."[95]

Newbigin writes, "In the communication of the gospel, word and act belong together. The word is essential because the name of Jesus cannot be replaced by anything else… the deed is equally essential because the gospel is good news of the active presence of the reign of God."[96] The Bible often illustrates Jesus using acts of healing and mercy as a way of teaching and explaining God's power and kingdom (John 9). Holistic mission seeks to participate with God in mission, and mission practitioners must ensure that social actions point appropriately to that mission.

Proclamation, though essential and central to the message, need not be the first act of mission. Newbigin explains that proclamation in the New Testament, both from Jesus and in the Book of Acts, generally follows an act of healing, compassion,

---

[91] Wan, "Mission Amid Global Crisis: Holistic Mission to Diaspora Groups."
[92] See Moreau, "Mission and Missions," and Wright, *The Mission of God's People*, 25-26, for additional and more extended discussions on the terms mission and missions.
[93] Wright, The Mission of God's People, 278.
[94] Wright, The Mission of God's People, 319.
[95] Moberg, 147.
[96] Lesslie Newbigin, "Cross-Currents in Ecumenical and Evangelical Understandings of Mission," 148.

or power. Newbigin notes that these acts represent a "new reality" that elicits questions for which only the gospel is the answer.[97]

The story in John 9 of Jesus healing the man who had been born blind shows just how powerful a new reality can be at generating questions that require a gospel response. After being healed by Jesus, the man returned home. Upon his return, his new reality subjected him to questions from his neighbors, his family, and the religious leaders. Though he had not yet seen Jesus, he could testify to the Pharisees that it was Jesus who had healed him, saying, "Whether he is a sinner or not, I don't know. One thing I do know. I was blind but now I see" (John 9:25).

This is a powerful example of how the new reality of a transformed Christian life leads to questions only the gospel can answer. This pattern is replayed throughout Jesus' teachings. It must be understood as Newbigin points out, "The works by themselves did not communicate the new fact. That had to be stated in plain words: 'The kingdom of God has drawn near.'"[98]

This pattern of a new reality leading to questions that lead to proclamation is also seen in the major proclamations in the Book of Acts. Peter's speech at Pentecost is in response to the question, "What does this mean?" (Acts 2:12). Likewise, Stephen is responding to the false charges and the question of their truth (Acts 7:1). Those involved in Christian social actions must understand this framework and be ready with the Word when asked about the reason for the hope that they have (1 Pet. 3:15).

There are many terms used to describe Christian social activities, such as serving the poor, compassion ministry, mercy, and social justice. In its LOP 21 report, the Lausanne movement tried to create clarity by differentiating between types of social actions as shown in the following chart:

Table 1. - Social Service vs. Social Action[99]

Social Service	Social Action
Relieving human need	Removing the causes of human need
Philanthropic activity	Political and economic activity
Seeking to minister to individuals and families	Seeking to transform the structures of society
Works of mercy	Quest for justice

Social service is the act of addressing immediate needs of the poor, the homeless, etc. It is immediate relief. Social action is more in line with poverty alleviation and development, what Myers may refer to as "transformational

---

[97] See Newbigin, *The Gospel in a Pluralist Society,* pages 128–140, for biblical analysis and support for his assertions that gospel proclamations follow questions about acts generating a "new reality" observed by the crowds.
[98] Newbigin, The Gospel in a Pluralist Society, 132.
[99] Adapted from, John Stott, Ed. *Making Christ Known: Historic Mission Documents from the Lausanne Movement 1974–1989* (Grand Rapids, MI: William B. Eerdmans Publishing, 1996), 196.

development… seeking positive change in the whole of human life materially, socially, psychologically and spiritually."[100] Both are important acts of Christian witness and may be used interchangeably throughout this work.

God's concern for human needs, especially those of the poor and marginalized, is biblically documented in his actions throughout history, the life of Jesus, and in the writings of the early church. While the biblical mandate to helping those in need (social service) is voluminous and clear, there remains ambiguity with regards to Christian involvement in societal structures and related injustices (social action).[101] Leading Latin American theologian Samuel Escobar suggests, "Missionary action also needs to remember from its biblical standard and its historical development that the repentance to which Jesus calls us today may mean for some men the opening of their eyes to their condition as oppressors, and the change of their social practices."[102] This is not unlike a modern-day Zacchaeus (Luke 19:1–10). No further details of Zacchaeus' post-conversion story are provided though it appears that he repented of his part in the unjust social structure of his day while maintaining his tax collector profession.

The story of Zacchaeus is an example of a minor change in an unjust social structure through one individual's transformational exposure to Christ. Padilla writes that Christian missions focused on development and justice are "concerned with the development of the whole person and of all people. It includes, therefore, the shaping of a new lifestyle—based on new methods of production and new patterns of consumption."[103] Professor of Mission and Intercultural Studies at Trinity Evangelical Divinity School Craig Ott, and Stephen J. Straus (1955–2013), Dallas Theological Seminary, suggest "the question is not whether the church *should* be concerned about the poor and the economic systems that contribute to poverty and oppression; rather, the question is *how* such issues should be addressed and how such concerns relate to the overall task of mission."[104] It is the individuals transformed by God's mission, through God's instruments that will effect transformational changes to unjust social structures.

Holistic mission is not solely about the mission to the poor or the marginalized. It is also about contextualizing the gospel by making it visible to an unbelieving world. Myers points out, "The way we treat the poor can be a way of announcing that a different spirit is at work in us and in the community."[105] Gospel proclamation will never be seen as credible if its transforming power is not observable.[106] Christian holistic mission contextualizes the gospel message not only to the poor but also to those who perhaps may not need the material and physical aspects of

---

[100] Myers, Walking with the Poor, 3.
[101] For discussion of the differences between social service and social action, see John Stott, ed. *Making Christ Known*, 196.
[102] Samuel Escobar and John Driver, *Christian Mission and Social Justice*, (Scottdale, PA: Herald Press, 1978), 54.
[103] C. René Padilla, Mission Between the Times, 141.
[104] Craig Ott and Stephen J. Strauss, Encountering Theology of Mission: Biblical Foundations, Historical Developments, and Contemporary Issues (Grand Rapids, MI: Baker Academic, 2010), 132.
[105] Myers, Walking with the Poor, 322.
[106] John Stott. "Twenty Years After Lausanne: Some Personal Reflections," 1995, *International Bulletin of Missionary Research*, 53.

holistic mission but are just as much in need of the relational healing of Christ. Jesus understood that the non-poor often believe that they have no need for God, and he used his actions to contextualize and teach otherwise (see for example Matt. 9:12–13).

Al Tizon, Executive Minister of Serve Globally, the international ministries arm of the Evangelical Covenant Church in Chicago, Illinois, recognizes this aspect of mission beyond serving the needs of the poor and views the *missio Dei* through the lens of reconciliation. God's desire is to reconcile all things through Christ, and holistic mission is participation with God "in putting the world back together in Jesus Christ: reconciliation as mission."[107] Tizon goes on to explain that the church "engages in the ministry of reconciliation when it at once cares for and empowers the poor and exhorts the rich to denounce Mammon and to shift their gaze and resources toward the world's most vulnerable."[108]

Jesus taught his disciples to follow his holistic model of proclamation with acts of love and compassion for others. Jesus often followed an act of compassion with the proclamation or teaching that the kingdom of God was near. After teaching them, he sent them out to minister in word and deed, to proclaim the kingdom of God, and to heal the sick (Matt. 10:7–8; Luke 9:2), allowing them to put into practice the holistic ministry that they had learned.

Today's culture is a "show me" culture. Christian actions have become the barometer for the truth of the message. Citing the postmodern culture's desire for a message consistent with messenger actions, David F. Wells, Andrew Mutch Distinguished Professor of Historical and Systematic Theology at Gordon-Conwell Theological Seminary, writes:

Postmoderns want to see as well as hear, to find authenticity in relationship as the precursor to hearing what is said. This is a valid and biblical demand. Faith, after all, is dead without works, and few sins are dealt with as harshly by Jesus as hypocrisy. What postmoderns want to see, and are entitled to see, is believing and being, talking and doing, all joined together in a seamless whole. This is the great challenge of the moment for the evangelical Church. Can it rise to this occasion?[109]

North American communities today reflect the continuing signs of a dramatically changing context often described as post-Christian. Weekly church attendance is declining and the number of people professing no religious faith or non-Christian beliefs is on the rise. There is now an entire second generation of people who have never visited a church nor experienced the gospel presented in a meaningful way. People are looking not to Christ for significance but to "idols" of the world.

Three pervasive aspects observed in today's culture are individualism, consumerism, and materialism. These aspects of the culture's secular idolatry have also invaded many aspects of the North American church. Members are attending church to consume rather than to contribute. They are looking for the blessing rather than to be the blessing.

---

[107] Al Tizon, Whole and Reconciled: Gospel, Church, and Mission in a Fractured World (Grand Rapids, MI: Baker Academic, 2018), xii.
[108] Tizon, 15.
[109] David F. Wells, *Above All Eartly Pow'rs: Christ in a Postmodern World* (Grand Rapids, MI, Eerdmans, 2005), 314.

When "outsiders" view such secular behaviors within the church, it perpetuates disbelief among non-believers. They do not see the Christian life as any different or better than their own. In fact, many see Christians as worse. James Emery White, author and founding senior pastor of Mecklenburg Community Church in Charlotte, North Carolina, writes:

Many of those outside the Christian faith think Christians no longer represent what Jesus had in mind and that Christianity in our society is not what was meant to be. We're seen as hyperpolitical, out of touch, pushy in our beliefs, and arrogant. And the most dominant perceptions of all are that we are homophobic, hypercritical, and judgmental. Simply put, in the minds of many, modern-day Christianity no longer seems Christian.[110]

It is easy to see how it has become difficult to seek and save the lost. Not only do the lost not want to hear from Christians, but many Christians appear to be lost themselves. Christian words and actions must maintain that symbiotic holism if there is to be hope of reaching this post-modern culture. Anything less will be unacceptable. Newbigin explains that the "words explain the deeds and the deeds validate the words."[111] Jesus validated his authority to forgive sins with the act of healing the paralytic man (Mark 2:9–11) and his authority over the elements by calming the storm (Mark 4:35–41).

Discipleship and Spiritual Transformation as Mission Task

Historically, most discussions about holistic Christian mission have centered around proclamation/evangelism and service, noticeably void of references to discipleship or Christian spiritual formation. Hesselgrave highlights this issue in his proposal to redefine holism, calling discipleship "one of the most needed, and neglected, requirements of the Great Commission mission."[112] Tizon suggests that this de-emphasis on disciple making is related to "a rejection of narrow evangelical/fundamentalist definitions of discipleship that made evangelism the primary, if not sole, missionary task of the church."[113] Tizon recognizes that the task of evangelism is "indispensable" to mission, suggesting "without evangelism… the Great Commission would amount to international humanitarian aid and development work with a cross on top."[114] However, he describes evangelism as "essential, but not central."[115] It is discipleship, he maintains, that in its truest definition (not the narrow definition he cited above), is the "ultimate motivation" for a church's mission.[116] In other words, in his opinion, disciple making is the hub in the mission centrality model.

Peter Cotterell, formerly with the London School of Theology and founder of the Ethiopian Graduate School of Theology, points out that the Christian worldview is formed through three major components: existential awareness of the world (life

---

[110] James Emery White, The Rise of the Nones: Understanding and Reaching the Religiously Unaffiliated (Grand Rapids, MI: Baker Books, 2014), 39.
[111] Newbigin, The Gospel in a Pluralist Society, 137.
[112] Hesselgrave, "Redefining Holism."
[113] Tizon, 146.
[114] Tizon, 176.
[115] Tizon, 176
[116] Tizon, 146.

experiences), understanding of scripture, and self-interests.[117] However, the changing Western context is resulting in Christian worldviews that are being more heavily formed and influenced by life experiences and self-interests than by biblical truths.[118]

Unfortunately, this post-Christian formation has infiltrated the church to the extent that the Christian worldview often bears little visible difference to that of the overriding cultural worldview. Citing a lack of missional focus on discipleship, Myers observes, "In America, Christian behavior is indistinguishable from that of non-Christians."[119] James Davison Hunter, American sociologist and the LaBrosse-Levinson Distinguished Professor of Religion, Culture, and Social Theory at the University of Virginia, identifies the issue and suggests that the problem for Christians,

is not that their faith is weak or inadequate. In contemporary America, Christians have faith in God and... they believe and hold fast to the central truths of the Christian tradition. But while they have faith, *they have also been formed by the larger post-Christian culture,* a culture whose habits of life less and less resemble anything like the vision of human flourishing provided by the life of Christ and witness of scripture. The problem, in other words, is that Christians have not been formed "in all wisdom" that they might rise to the demands of faithfulness in a time such as ours, "bearing fruit in every good work."[120]

In the 1980s, Newbigin recognized this changing context and began to suggest that the Western culture was fast becoming a non-Christian society. He rejects the common view that the West was becoming a secular society without God; rather he viewed it as a pagan society filled with idols and false gods. He cites a need to missionally approach the local culture with the same kind of thought and effort put into international missions. Newbigin's insights are timely and prophetic when he writes:

What we have is... a pagan society whose public life is ruled by beliefs which are false. And because it is not a pre-Christian paganism, but a paganism born out of the rejection of Christianity, it is far tougher and more resistant to the Gospel than pre-Christian paganism... Here, without possibility of question, is the most challenging missionary frontier of our time.[121]

A missional theology has emerged with this changing Western context in mind. This theology calls for Christian engagement of and commitment to the world in which one is planted, becoming bearers of grace to one another, both inside and outside the community of believers. Christians should be known as those who use their gifts to work for the common good of all (1 Cor. 12:7).

---

[117] Peter Cotterell, Mission and Meaninglessness: The Good News in a World of Suffering and Disorder (London: SPCK, 1992), 25.
[118] Paul Borthwick, *Six Dangerous Questions to Transform Your View of the World* (Downers Grove, IL: InterVarsity, 1996), 11.
[119] Myers, "Another Look at 'Holistic Mission.'"
[120] James Davison Hunter, To Change the World: The Irony, Tragedy, & Possibility of Christianity in the Late Modern World (New York, NY: Oxford University Press, 2010), 227.
[121] Lesslie Newbigin, "Can the West Be Converted?" *The Princeton Seminary Bulletin,* Vol. 6 (1), (1985), 36.

A missional theology calls for Christians to be "missionaries" in the area in which God has placed them. Michael Horton, Professor of Systematic Theology and Apologetics at Westminster Seminary in California, explains:

the church must be missions minded, treating both its members and the unchurched... as sinners who need to hear and receive the gospel. And it also needs to be missional in the sense of living out its faith through its activity in the many callings that belong to every believer as employee, employer, parent, child, volunteer, citizen, and neighbor.[122]

This missional theology creates a missionary mindset within the local church that leads to key spiritual relationship opportunities. When disciples are on mission in their local community and spheres of influence, relationships are formed with other Christians as well as non-Christians. These relationships often become the beginning of new discipleship and formative relationships, allowing nonbelievers to see and experience Christlike behaviors and kingdom living. Missional church and incarnational ministry specialists Hugh Halter and Matt Smay refer to this aspect of discipleship as the "Discovery Zone," explaining:

The Discovery Zone is a sphere in which truth can be seen before it is spoken, where a new authority figure becomes trusted, and where people are able to weigh Christ's values over their own. In other words, where they can choose to "prefer" Christ's Kingdom ways over their own ways.[123]

The "discovery zone" is a place where Christian worldviews can be formed, and distorted cultural worldviews can be transformed into Christian worldviews.

Worldviews are not taught per se; they are formed over time through the internalizing and interpreting of one's influences and experiences through one's relationships. Robert N. Bellah (1927–2013)[124] relates a story of a medical director for a pharmaceutical company who had found himself as the final decision maker regarding a costly recall of a potentially contaminated production run of the company's product. Bellah indicates that the medical director "almost as instinct," made the decision to recall the product. To understand the director's decision "almost as instinct" Bellah suggests,

we have to assume that it [his decision] did not come simply from his having taken a course in medical ethics in medical school, or that he consulted a handbook of decision making prepared by a philosophical ethicist. Rather, it was his character, formed in family, church, and college, as well as in medical school, that he was drawing on, a character that had internalized the virtues, and, in particular, the virtue of justice and a concern for the common good.[125]

Bellah goes on to suggest that a "deep concern for justice and the common good as part of one's character is not an add-on that can be attained from a one-shot

---

[122] Michael Horton, The Christian Faith: A Systematic Theology for Pilgrims on the Way (Grand Rapids, MI: Zondervan, 2011), 898.
[123] Hugh Halter and Matt Smay, *The Tangible Kingdom: Creating Incarnational Community* (San Francisco, CA: Jossey-Bass, 2008), 65.
[124] Robert N. Bellah was an American sociologist and the Elliott Professor of Sociology at the University of California, Berkeley. He was internationally known for his work related to the sociology of religion.
[125] Robert N. Bellah and Steven M. Tipton ed, *The Robert Bellah Reader* (Durham, NC: Duke University Press, 2006), 438.

course in ethics. Rather it is a matter of what has been traditionally called formation… it really applies more generally to all of us as we learn what it is to become a responsible adult."[126] People with this commitment are "formed little by little, step by step, to become the kind of citizens they are… They had grown that way over the years."[127]

This type of formative learning is a lifelong process and takes place largely outside the structured classroom. Though humans learn in many ways, education is most often thought of as the structured transfer of information or knowledge from a teacher to a student. Schools in the United States are primarily designed in this passive learning format: the transfer of information to students via classroom methodologies using lectures, books, and memorization exercises. Yet much of what humans learn and retain is learned through active learning, when experience is gained through the act of participating and interpreting the results of their participations. Jesus' teaching methods exhibit a principle understanding that the observable demonstrations of his message by the transformed lives of his disciples carry more weight with the crowds than that of theological knowledge and education. The Apostle Paul too used "highly relational" ministry training methods by inviting others to learn through practicing ministry alongside him.[128]

Jack Mezirow (1923–2014)[129] defines learning as "the process of using a prior interpretation to construe a new or revised interpretation of the meaning of one's experience as a guide to future action."[130] Informational knowledge that has been passed on, or learned through previous experiences, is put into practice to see how it works. And throughout the process, additional learning occurs. Human learning comes from the life-long recursive cycle of integrating information and experiences, evaluating and interpreting feedback from experiences, and allowing the cycle to continually guide future actions. Each new action brings new experiences, and the learning cycle continues.[131]

This cyclical recursive learning process is the vehicle that drives the human transformation that is at the heart of holistic mission. The diagram that follows outlines the various stages of this recursive process of learning and formation, illustrating the continuous cycle of informational and experiential learning that motivates one to action, creating new experiences and new learnings. It is through

---

[126] Bellah and Tipton, 440.
[127] Laurent A. Parks Daloz, Cheryl H. Keen, James P. Keen, and Sharon Daloz Parks, *Common Fire: Leading Lives of Commitment in a Complex World* (Boston, MA: Beacon Press, 1996), 210.
[128] Wan and Hedinger, 80.
[129] Jack Mezirow was an American sociologist and Emeritus Professor of Adult and Continuing Education at Teachers College, Columbia University.
[130] Jack Mezirow, "Learning to Think Like an Adult," in Jack Mezirow & Associates, *Learning as Transformation: Critical Perspectives on a Theory in Progress* (San Francisco, CA: Jossey-Bass, 2000), 5.
[131] This learning style is inherent in the learning theory concept, introduced in 1978 by Jack Mezirow, coined "transformative learning." It involves the continual reinterpretation of experiences, which leads to challenging, and perhaps changing, one's attitudes, beliefs, and values.

this continual progressive cycle of learning that worldviews (attitudes, values, and beliefs) are continually formed, challenged, and transformed.[132]

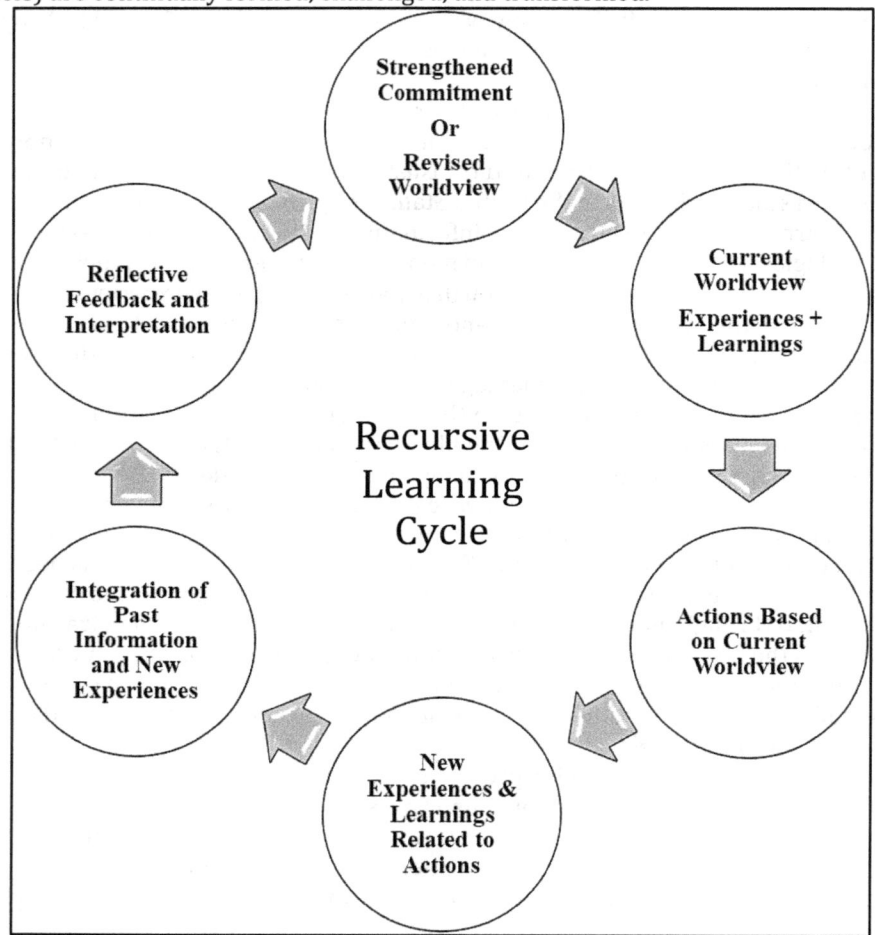

Figure 2. - Recursive Learning Cycle

Transformative learning is described as learning that "involves a fundamental questioning and reordering of how one thinks or acts... where the learner came to a new understanding of something that caused a fundamental reordering of the

---

[132] This diagram is meant to be a general depiction of the various stages of the cycle of human learning. Recognizably, learning does not take place in the same way and at the same pace for all individuals or all cultures. For example, some learn better in groups while others learn better individually; some require active verbal feedback and discourse while others desire quiet refelction. However, despite the differences, there is a cyclical learning process that occurs throughout the human life that is shaped by one's experiences and relationships. This diagram is meant to apply a general framework to this process regarding how one's experiences work themselves out into one's worldview.

paradigmatic assumptions she held about the idea or action concerned."[133] This is not a surface-level change of mind or opinion but a deep personal change related to experiences that challenge one's core attitudes, beliefs, and values. Christopher Beard, Program Director of the Master of Arts in Organizational Leadership program at Lincoln Christian University, writes:

Disciples are made [transformed] when information moves from a surface knowledge to affecting the believer from the inside out, in addition to behavior moving from something that is external in nature to activities and actions that spring forth from the very being of the believer.[134]

As referenced in the previous diagram, action is the visible result of the learning process. Cotterell suggests that "to know a truth is to act on that truth, and to fail to act is to demonstrate a failure of knowledge."[135] Those who profess a certain worldview but act otherwise demonstrate a lack of conviction and therefore a lack of transformation. True transformation results in the learning process translating into discernable actions. This deep transformation, perhaps, is what Paul expected when he wrote, "Do not conform to the pattern of this world but be transformed by the renewal of your mind" (Rom. 12:2). Christian mission that is holistic seeks to transform minds away from a self-absorbed worldview to a worldview that manifests a social responsibility, an internal desire to meet the needs of others, and a concern for the common good.

Transformation to a worldview committed to the common good is a never-ending process. Laurent A. Parks Daloz, Professor in Adult Education at Lesley College and Associate Director of the Whidbey Institute, suggests it is "understood not as a final state but rather as a stance of openness to necessary and ongoing dialog with those who differ or who may not yet be full participants on the commons."[136] It involves Mezirow's transformational learning concept, which refers to the process by which we transform our taken for granted frames of reference (meaning perspectives, habits of mind, mind-sets) to make them more inclusive, discriminating, open, emotionally capable of change, and reflective so that they may generate beliefs and opinions that will prove more true or justified to guide actions.[137]

Mezirow calls this incremental transformation, "involving a progressive series of transformations in related points of view that culminate in a transformation in habit of mind."[138] This process reflects the continual recursive learning cycle noted earlier, establishing that each cycle yields a progressive transformative mark on the learner.

---

[133] Stephan D. Brookfield, "Transformative Learning as Ideology Critique," in Jack Mezirow & Associates, *Learning as Transformation: Critical Perspectives on a Theory in Progress* (San Francisco, CA: Jossey-Bass, 2000), 139–140.
[134] Christopher Beard, "Missional Discipleship: Discerning Spiritual-Formation Practices and Goals with the Missional Movement," *Missiology: An International Review,* 43(2) (2015), 179.
[135] Cotterell, 248.
[136] Laurent A. Parks Daloz, "Transformative Learning for the Common Good." in Jack Mezirow & Associates, *Learning as Transformation: Critical Perspectives on a Theory in Progress* (San Francisco, CA: Jossey-Bass, 2000), 105.
[137] Mezirow, 7.
[138] Mezirow, 21.

Discipleship in holistic mission focuses on both the vertical (love of God) and horizontal (love of neighbor) relationships. Michael J. Wilkens, Dean of the Faculty at Talbot School of Theology, Biola University, suggests that discipleship should not be thought of solely in terms of personal spiritual growth when he writes, "growth is important, but the goal of growth is service [to others]."[139] Spiritual growth and service are integral components to holistic mission. Ronald J. Sider, President of Evangelicals for Social Action and Professor of Theology, Holistic Ministry, and Public Policy at Palmer Theological Seminary, *et al.*, explains:

Study and devotion should foster active obedience, and the experience of carrying out God's mission in the world deepens our desire to know God better. The more we know about who God is and what he is doing in the world, the more we act on our knowledge; the more we follow God's will, the more insights we gain into God's character and the closer we grow to Christ (Matt. 12:50).[140]

Jesus called his disciples to follow him not only as an invitation to experience eternal salvation but also as a call to serve others.[141]

Holistic Mission Relationships

Holistic mission is often misunderstood as solely humanitarian acts void of a salvific or divine component. Holistic mission is empowered by and requires the involvement of the Triune God. One's relationship with the Triune God is foundational to all other relationships, and it is the source of horizontal participation in Christian mission. In their relational model for training missionaries, Wan and Hedinger capture both the primacy of an upward relationship with God as well as the practical manifestations of the horizontal relationships:

This [transformation] process begins again with the active involvement of Triune God simultaneously in the life of the teacher, of the student, and of the faith community (church). These vertical relationships take place primarily between God and his people. His people act horizontally to bring the transformative Word into the non-Christian community. Some of that horizontal witness is through the gifted people within the church… Some of the horizontal witness is through Christian community as a whole, acting as salt and light within the realm of human society.[142]

Tizon maintains these relationships in his holistic mission as reconciliation theory and suggests three dimensions in the church's mission of reconciliation: vertical (God and people), horizontal (people and people), and circular (God, people, and creation).[143] He mirrors Wan and Hedinger in the primacy of the vertical relationship writing, "If reconciliation between people and people (horizontal) does not follow reconciliation between God and people, we have the biblical right to question the authenticity of the vertical… The horizontal verifies the vertical."[144]

---

[139] Michael J. Wilkins, *Following the Master: A Biblical Theology of Discipleship* (Grand Rapids, MI: Zondervan, 1992), 68.
[140] Ronald J. Sider, Philip N. Olson, and Heidi Rolland Unruh, *Churches That Make a Difference: Reaching Your Community with Good News and Good Works* (Grand Rapids, MI: Baker Books, 2002), 171.
[141] Wilkins, Following the Master, 186.
[142] Wan and Hedinger, 118.
[143] Tizon, 87.
[144] Tizon, 88.

This is illustrated by the narrowly defined Western view of poverty as a lack of material things. This view of poverty believes that if material wealth can be restored to the poor, the poor themselves will be restored. The true needs go much deeper than economic materiality. Poverty is the result of relationships that have been broken and marred by sin. Though the symptoms can be treated, the real need and the truthful answer to poverty is redeemed and restored relationships, the most important being a restored relationship to God. The figure below illustrates and describes the way sin has damaged our relationships with God, with others, with ourselves, and with creation.

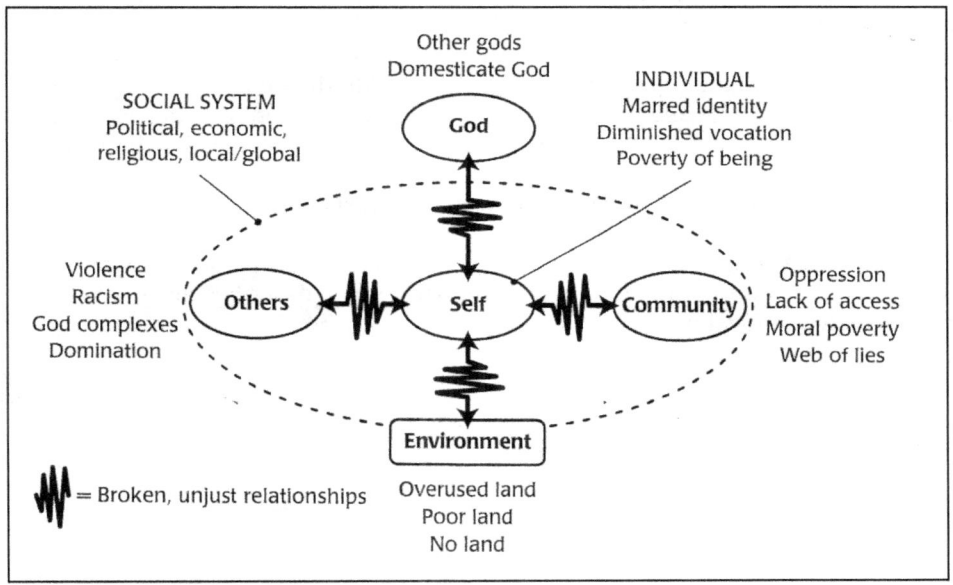

Figure 3. - A Relational Understanding of Poverty[145]

These broken relationships result in actions and activities that create poverty. This poverty is not only economic but extends into spiritual and personal relationships. Alva Couto, a social worker and Associate Director of the Instituto Polus in Belo Horizonte, Brazil, explains that holistic mission "demands vertical and horizontal relationships. Our actions as Christians and the church must be balanced between the vertical relationship with God and God's Word and the horizontal relationship with our neighbors and the world."[146] Accordingly, the goal of holistic mission is not solely focused on the materially poor, but the relationally broken and spiritually impoverished non-poor as well.

Is it possible to be economically full yet spiritually and relationally empty? Jim Wallis, American theologian and founder and editor of *Sojourners* magazine, tells of

---

[145] Myers, Walking with the Poor, 144.
[146] Alva Couto. "Latin American Social Contexts." *Serving With the Poor in Latin America: Cases in Holistic Ministry*. Ed. Tetsunao Yamamori, *et al.* (Monrovia, California: Marc Publications, 1997), 91.

a pastor's retreat at which a young Presbyterian pastor lamented about the spiritual poverty of his congregation, most of which were corporate executives, lawyers, and investment bankers. Their jobs required them to leave very early in the morning for a long commute, and they did not return until late in the evening. The pastor spoke of how they were forced to work constantly to support their lifestyles. There was no time for family, church, or anything besides work and consumer activities. He lamented about their broken marriages, addictions, and dead spiritual lives. He did not know how to serve them.

Wallis explains that after hearing this story, a pastor from South Africa, attending the same retreat, shared a similar story of having too many people who must get up very early in the morning, returning late in the evening. All they do is work, and it creates similar problems with alcoholism and family issues, along with problems in the community and the church. The South African pastor commented that it appeared that he and the U.S. pastor shared similar problems. In South Africa, they are called "slave labor" camps, and he remarked that it seemed like in the U.S. they are "corporate labor" camps.[147]

Wallis' story is a tale of drastically different contexts that result in very similar relational and spiritual depravity. Each person in the story needs the same thing: reconciled and restored relationships. Most importantly, each person's relationship to God must be restored. The figure below illustrates and describes the model of transformed relationships.

---

[147] Jim Wallis, Faith Works: Lessons from the Life of an Activist Preacher (New York, NY: Random House, 2000), 84–85.

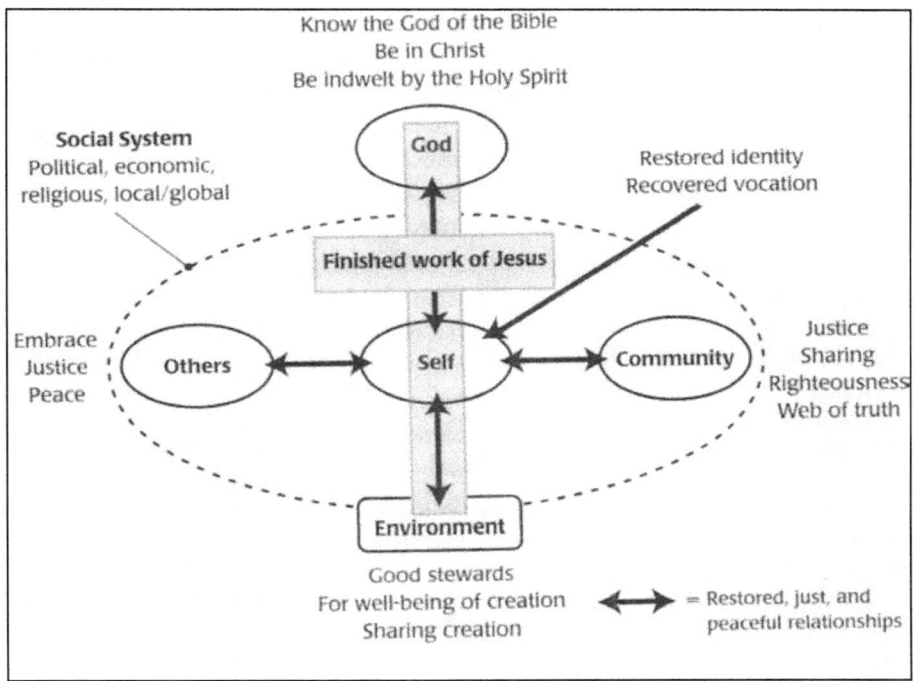

Figure 4. - Transformed Relationships[148]

At the essence of the gospel is a right relationship with God through Jesus Christ. The need is the same for both the poor and the non-poor. However, the related issues of a transformed self-identity are different. The poor suffer from feeling devalued and marginalized and need to understand that they are made in God's image and are his children. They also need to believe that they are valued and can contribute to God's creation.

The non-poor on the other hand have an overstated self-worth. They too need to understand that they are made in God's image, but they also need to understand that they are not God. Ridding themselves of their "god-complexes," the non-poor must understand and believe that the things they possess are meant to be shared, not used for control.[149] Jesus ministered to both of these contexts, and it is in these contexts that holistic mission seeks to serve all those in need, both the spiritually poor and the materially poor.

As illustrated in the diagrams above, these broken relationships exist in a set of social systems, society's structural makeup. One's identity is often expressed through one's relationships within these structures. Wallis suggests that we are "often involved in destructive social arrangements without being aware of it. We are barely conscious of the harm we inflict on others when it is done through social

---

[148] Myers, Walking with the Poor, 181.
[149] Myers, Walking with the Poor, 178.

institutions to which we belong."[150] He cites Zacchaeus as an example of someone that was involved in unjust social structures as an abusive tax collector. However, having his relationship to God rightfully restored through Jesus, Zacchaeus "recognized his social sin, turned from it, and sought to repair the damage he had done."[151]

Holistic Mission Summary

Often lost in the rhetoric of defining mission is the realization that mission is not simply a definition; it is the actions that lay behind the definition. Holistic mission must be more than a model for the symbiotic relationship of evangelism and social actions; it must integrate the vertical and horizontal dimensions of Christian mission with tasks that provide for "discipling the nations for spiritual and societal transformation—a gospel of life, deed, word, and sign."[152]

Holistic mission seeks to minister to the pressing need of the communities, and in the rapidly deteriorating post-Christian West, discipleship and worldview transformation are dire needs. Christians involved in holistic mission need to understand that they are not simply providers of services, evangelism, or compassion; they are participating in God's mission as agents of transformation. Kwame Bediako, Presbyterian minister and Director of Akrofi-Cristaller Center for Mission Research and Applied Theology in Akropong-Akuapem, Ghana, highlights the holistic nature of the Great Commission well:

The Great Commission, therefore, is about the discipline of the nations, the conversion of the things that make people into nations—the shared and common processes of thinking; attitudes; world views; perspectives; languages; and the cultural, social and economic habits of thought, behavior and practice. These things and the lives of the people in whom such things find expression—all of this in meant to be within the call of discipleship.[153]

Holistic mission should be the reflection of Jesus' words and deeds, the embodiment of faithful obedience to all that he commanded. Newbigin suggests that when the community of believers remain true to its calling, true to its mission, it becomes "the place where men and women and children find that the gospel gives them the framework of understanding the 'lenses' through which they are able to understand and cope with the world."[154] It is through the framework of holistic mission that secular worldviews are transformed to Christian worldviews that are at the core observable examples of loving God, loving one another, and loving our neighbors—worldviews that are committed to the common good. Such integration encompasses all of the tasks, elements, and dimensions of mission that God requests and requires.

---

[150] Jim Wallis, The Call to Conversion: Why Faith Is Always Personal but Never Private (San Francisco, CA: HarperCollins, 2005), 30.
[151] Wallis, The Call to Conversion, 33.
[152] Bryant L. Myers, Engaging Globalization: The Poor, Christian Mission, and Our Hyperconnected World (Grand Rapids: Baker Academic, 2017), 196.
[153] Kwame Bediako. "Theological Reflections." *Serving With the Poor in Africa: Cases in Holistic Ministry.* Ed. Tetsaunao Yamamori, Bryant L. Myers, Kwame Bediako, and Larry Reed (Monrovia, CA: MARC, 1996), 184.
[154] Newbigin, *The Gospel in a Pluralistic Society,* 227.

A growing number of people understand Christian missions to be holistic with the church, experiencing what Bosch describes as "a convergence of convictions."[155] This convergence is reflected by the Lausanne Movement in its Cape Town Commitment, which states in Part 1, Section 10, "We commit ourselves to the integral and dynamic exercise of all dimensions of mission to which God calls his Church." This statement is followed by two bullet points that add clarity:
- God commands us to make known to all nations the truth of God's revelation and the gospel of God's saving grace through Jesus Christ, calling all people to repentance, faith, baptism, and obedient discipleship.
- God commands us to reflect his own character through compassionate care for the needy, and to demonstrate the values and the power of the kingdom of God in striving for justice and peace and in caring for God's creation.[156]

Reflecting on the "seventy-five plus years" of the holistic mission debate, Tizon suggests "the call to bear witness to the gospel in both word and deed has, for the most part, come to define the church's essential mission across the conservative-liberal divide."[157]

Holistic Mission Partnership – Description, Nature, and Motivations

Mission is not only concerned with what things must be done; it is also concerned with how best to get things done. Escobar aligns with the holistic mission concept of "what" missions are to do and adds his insight as to "how" it should be done. He writes,

> Today mission should consist of service—service both of the spiritual in proclaiming the Word and of the physical in meeting human needs, according to Jesus' model and in his name. In this new era of globalization this means new patterns of cooperation and new forms of partnership for mission.[158]

Wayne L. Gordon, cofounder of Christian Community Development Association and lead pastor of Lawndale Community Church, indicates that "In Lawndale, partnership is one of the three Ps by which we practice holistic ministry."[159]

Still, these partnership arrangements remain elusive as much of the mission-related activity seems stuck in denominationalism, culturalism, or theological division, failing to understand that a combination of people and/or organizations with differing skills, talents, and abilities working together is needed to achieve fruitful holistic mission results. However, God's call for his people to be in

---

[155] Bosch, *Transforming Mission*, 417–18.
[156] Lausanne Movement, "The Cape Town Commitment: A Confession of Faith and a Call to Action." 2011. Lausanne Movement. Accessed April 22, 2019. <https://www.lausanne.org/content/ctc/ctccommitment#capetown>.
[157] Tizon, 157.
[158] Samuel Escobar, *The New Global Mission: The Gospel from Everywhere to Everywhere* (Downers Grove, IL: IVP Academic, 2003), 154.
[159] In Wayne L. Gordon's section of "Introduction: Personal Words from the Authors," in Sider, Perkins, Gordon, and Tizon. *Linking Arms, Linking Lives* (Grand Rapids, MI: Baker, 2008), 24. The three "Ps" he lists and describes are people, prayer, and partnership.

community aligned with his call to holistically participate in his mission is producing the call toward partnership relationships.[160]

A 2001 study found that churches in the U.S. are serving their communities "by weaving together a network of money, volunteers, and other supporters." The study found that the average congregation collaborates with six other community outreach organizations.[161] Recent trends in mission reveal a global "movement toward greater collaboration among agencies, churches, and other mission-minded organizations. This trend is the result of efforts to expand the impact of the gospel by building on the strengths of shared resources, ideally through the commitment to a common purpose."[162]

In addition, scholars are beginning to produce works that evaluate the merits of mission partnership and their practical application. Wan and Penman summarize a literature review, identifying specific works that deal with the "Why, how, and who" of Christian mission partnership.[163] This systematic categorization provides a pathway for reviewing mission partnership literature. Accordingly, this section will first examine literature related to the practical nature of partnership and its related principles, function, and form. This section will then look deeper into several crucial elements of partnership principles, including a deeper review of the relational aspects of partnership. The section will then review literature regarding the motivations to partner, including some specific motivations to partner in holistic mission. This section will finish with a review of the literature as it relates to partnership between constituents specifically related to this study, cross-cultural partnerships, and partnerships with non-church organizations.

Practical Nature of Mission Partnership

The focus of much of the literature related to mission partnership is on the practical aspects of establishing and sustaining a partnership. There are four contemporary authors whose works serve as the foundation of mission and ministry partnership principles.[164] Each offers practical insights into partnerships organizations and the authors' views regarding creating effective partnership relationships. These works are extensively cited by others as they begin to mold

---

[160] Ronald J. Sider, John M. Perkins, Wayne L. Gordon, and F. Albert Tizon, *Linking Arms, Linking Lives: How Urban-Suburban Partnerships Can Transform Communities* (Grand Rapids, MI: Baker, 2008), 42.

[161] Nancy T. Ammerman, "Doing Good in American Communities: Congregations and Service Organizations Working Together." An online research project from the Organizing Religious Work Project, *Hartford Institue for Religious Research,* Hartford, CT, 2001 http://hirr.hartsem.edu/orw/orw_cong-report.htm.

[162] Michael Pocock, Gailyn Van Rheenen, and Douglas McConnell, *The Changing Face of World Missions: Engaging Contemporary Issues and Trends* (Grand Rapids, MI: Baker Academic, 2005), 248.

[163] Enoch Wan and Kevin P. Penman, "The 'Why,' 'How' and 'Who' of Partnership in Christian Mission." April 1, 2010. *Global Missiology.* <http://ojs.globalmissiology.org/index.php/english/article/view/61> (October 1, 2015).

[164] Phill Butler, Louis Bush, Daniel Rickett, and Ernie Addicott are considered authorities in the area of mission and ministry partnership praxis. Their works are widely cited within the partnership and mission scholar domain, including this study. They who endeavor to implement partnership relationship in areas such as holistic mission rely heavily on the praxis principles presented by these authorities.

partnership principles into specific mission contexts. What follows is a brief summary of these four works. More specific and pertinent points from these authors will be illustrated as the literature review delves into more specific areas of mission partnership, such as cross-cultural partnership and the relational nature of partnerships.

Butler's book, *Well Connected,* serves as an extensive practical guide to establishing effective and fruitful partnerships with a goal of world evangelism. It illustrates how many of the organizational principles, such as communication, leadership, and strategy, rely on the biblical principles of unity and humility. Butler's goal is to show how to "bring God's people together in practical, working partnerships and networks for his glory."[165] He defines partnership as "a conscious decision on the part of two or more people or agencies to work together to realize an objective none of them could achieve alone."[166] Butler structures the book as a "how to" of partnering, addressing things from the motivation to partner, the principles of partnership, formation, and how to handle meetings. He summarizes his fifteen "critical principles of partnership," suggesting it as a "checklist" for evaluating partnership.[167] Butler provides a selected bibliography for his readers in the appendix in which he identifies specific themes of various works. In the theme labeled "Mission oriented 'how to' / thematic books on partnership", he lists six selections, five of which are cited throughout this research.[168]

Luis Bush and Lorry Lutz, Partners International executives and members of the "AD2000 and Beyond" movement, have worked extensively toward building methods and strategies for partnering in mission and ministry. Their coauthored book entitled *Partnership in Ministry* is known as a classic work that illustrates principles and strategies of ministry partnership. They define partnership as "an association of two or more autonomous bodies who have formed a trusting relationship and fulfill agreed-upon expectations by sharing complementary strengths and resources to reach their mutual goal."[169]

Bush uses the book of Philippians as an illustration of biblical partnership in action.[170] He asserts that "partnership is not an option" and illustrates the biblical basis for partnership by using the book of Philippians.[171] He suggests that "the theme of Philippians is joy in Christian Partnership" and that the book is "a manual

---

[165] Butler, Well Connected, xvii.
[166] Butler, Well Connected, 31.
[167] Butler, *Well Connected,* 16–18 and in the appendix 319–21.
[168] Butler, Well Connected, 322. The works listed in this theme and cited in this research include Addicott, Body Matters; Bush and Lutz, Partnering in Ministry; Rickett, Making Your Partnership Work; Taylor, Kingdom Partnerships for Synergy in Mission; and Rickett, Building Strategic Relationships.
[169] Luis Bush and Lorry Lutz, *Partnering in Ministry: The Direction of World Evangelism* (Downers Grove, IL: InterVarsity Press, 1990), 46.
[170] Luis Bush, "In Pursuit of True Christian Partnership: A Biblical Basis from Philippians." in *Partners in the Gospel: The Strategic Role of Partnership in World Evangelism.* Ed. James H. Kraakevik and Dotsey Welliver (Wheaton, IL: Billy Graham Center, 1992), 3–14. Bush and Lutz, *Partnering in Ministry*, 22–32.
[171] Bush, "In Pursuit of True Christian Partnership," 3–5.

on genuine Christian partnership" because it illustrates the "essential ingredients of genuine Christian partnership."[172]

Daniel Rickett, recognized authority in cross-cultural ministry partnerships, defines partnership in a ministry context as "a relationship between ministries and people who share common aspirations, strive to achieve them together, and do so in the spirit of brotherly love" and identifies vision, relationship, and results as "the imperatives of partnership."[173] Rickett expands on these imperatives through practical guidelines for the organizational inner workings of partnerships. His book, *Making Your Partnership Work*, is a self-proclaimed "practical guide for church and mission partnerships."[174]

Ernie Addicott, noted cross-cultural mission partnership specialist, writes that partnership "is when two or more individuals or organizations, having different assets to bring to the table, agree to share resources, plan, pray and work together to fulfill a common purpose."[175] He suggests that there are four foundations to mission partnership, "sharing, agreed plans, common purpose, and good personal relationships (the ultimate foundation), which all sit upon the bedrock of the will, the word, and the work of God."[176] Addicott uses the biblical body metaphor to work through his mission partnership principles and to demonstrate the need for partnership in mission.

Sider, John M. Perkins, cofounder of the Christian Community Development Association, Gordon, and Tizon coauthor a book that illustrates the fullness of holistic mission done in partnership.[177] This book offers the authors' opinions on partnership principles and practicalities while doing so in a most complete picture of holistic mission. Its completeness comes from the nature of partnership the authors are presenting. They present partnership with a holistic mission to transform people both spiritually and physically and to transform communities in which these people live. The nature of the partnerships they present cross the urban-suburban cultural divide allowing them to illustrate practical "dos and don'ts" for cross-cultural partnerships. They include practical steps to partnering as well as a detailed chapter of suggested resources for "Kingdom Partnership."[178]

Sider *et al.* also include a chapter on the fruits of partnership, breaking it into four categories—theological, sociological, cultural, and practical—as summarized:

- Theological – effectively fulfills the call to model and to proclaim the kingdom of God.
- Sociological – significantly contribute to community building.
- Cultural – contribute to development of intercultural perspectives.
- Practical – transformation on both personal and social levels, evangelism and social action.[179]

---

[172] Bush, "In Pursuit of True Christian Partnership," 5.
[173] Daniel Rickett, *Making Your Partnership Work, Third Edition* (Roswell, GA: Daniel Rickett, 2014), 23.
[174] Rickett, *Making Your Partnership Work*, back cover of the book.
[175] Ernie Addicott, *Body Matters: A Guide to Partnership in Christian Mission* (Edmonds, WA: Interdev Partnership Associates, 2005), 20.
[176] Addicott, 32.
[177] Sider et al., Linking Arms, Linking Lives.
[178] Sider et al., Linking Arms, Linking Lives, 201–15.
[179] Sider et al., Linking Arms, Linking Lives, 111–21.

In addition to these four "fruits," the authors cite the personal spiritual growth and transformation of the individual partners as another type of fruit when they write, "In other words, part of the very core of what grows from an urban-suburban partnership includes the personal development of the partners themselves."[180]

Embedded within the informational aspects of the book are examples of mission partnerships occurring in today's context that are achieving holistic mission. In their concluding chapter, the authors reflect the results of the current work being done with a plea for more while also capturing the essence of mission partnership:

We know what to do. This book demonstrates that some urban-suburban partnerships are already transforming countless numbers of broken people and renewing devastated neighborhoods throughout the land. The right kind of urban-suburban partnership is crucial to this wonderful transformation. Suburban churches are working with urban ministries. Business leaders, national organizations, and faithful individuals are linking arms with holistic urban ministries. Broken, despairing persons are both coming to personal faith in Jesus and experiencing life-changing transformation in all aspects of their lives.[181]

The various partnership definitions found in the literature illustrate that partnering involves joining forces with others to accomplish specific goals or sets of objectives. This can be a formal arrangement, such as corporations coming together to form strategic partnerships and alliances, or it can be more of an informal type of arrangement or collaboration. Regardless of the formality, a partnership requires two or more individual participants focused on accomplishing a mutually agreed-upon task or set of tasks. Ultimately, the form of the collaborative structure is dictated by the objectives that the partnership seeks to achieve. Butler suggests, " to be effective, form must follow function. First, there has to be agreement on the vision and what success will look like. Only then do the other questions follow. In short, *what* you do should always precede *how* you do it."[182]

A partnership organization has some distinct characteristics that differ from other types of collaborative combinations. One primary characteristic that sets partnerships apart is the continuity of the partner identity outside the partnership. As the definitions describe, the partners come together with differing but complementary assets to be used to accomplish a common goal or set of objectives. The partners do not lose their individual identity outside the partnership, nor do they lose their individual purposes. These individual purposes combine to complement one another in achieving the common goal of the partnership.

Max Warren (1904–1977)[183] suggests that the continuity of the partners' separate identity requires that the partnerships must include three factors regarding the partners' participation: a "genuine involvement" of the partners, an "acceptance of responsibility" defined as a readiness to serve the purpose of the common enterprise, and a readiness to "accept all of the liabilities and limitation" that arise in the partnership. He goes on to write that "involvement, responsibility

---

[180] Sider et al., Linking Arms, Linking Lives, 111.
[181] Sider *et al., Linking Arms, Linking Lives,* 195.
[182] Butler, Well Connected, 240.
[183] Max Warren was former General Secretary of the Church Missionary Society.

and liability are meaningless unless the conscious identity of each partner survives."[184]

An effective manner to describe what a partnership form entails is to describe what it is not. From a relational perspective, partnership is often viewed as being "like" a marriage. However, this perspective represents a faulty view of mission partnering and can lead to misconceptions, faulty assumptions, and misguided expectations. Describing this misconception and its flaws provides a meaningful description of the unique features of the partnership form. The marriage concept (from a North American Christian perspective) maintains three key principles that are not consistent with a partnership model. Marriage is meant to be permanent, but a mission partnership should include (unlike a marriage) a "de-partnering" process for when the set of mutual objectives are completed.[185] Marriage is meant to be exclusive, but partnerships may add or delete members as differing resources are required. And marriage is meant to be a total commitment. The two become one. In a partnership, each of the partners maintain its own identify outside the partnership and may also partner with others. A partnership relationship can become very complex and very deep, but it is not a relationship in which two become one. It is more like partial overlap of two in areas of complementary resources.[186] Though there are some similarities in relationship, to avoid a faulty perspective, partnership should be viewed more as collaboration than as a marriage.[187]

Role of Relationship

The concept of partnership does not exist without relationships, and the strength of these relationships can dictate success or failure. Most partnership leaders list relationships as a key ingredient to successful and effective partnering. Addicott calls good, strong, healthy, personal relationships the "Ultimate Foundation" of partnership and suggests,

This Ultimate Foundation is the place that more partnerships come unstuck than any other. You can write water-tight agreements, do risk-analysis till you're fire-proof, develop a strategic plan that will evangelise the world by a week next Friday, but if the personal relationships are rotten, or even just a little bit off-colour, your partnership will struggle to get off the ground and may never fly at all.[188]

Warren writes, "The essence of partnership is that it is a relationship entered upon in freedom by free persons who remain free. Their relationship is a dynamic one. It cannot be stereotyped. For only in such a dynamic relation to one another can each do justice to the other so that together they can do justice to the object of their partnership."[189] He expands on the relationship theme, suggesting three

---

[184] Max Warren, *Partnership: The Study of an Idea* (London: SCM Press LTD, 1956), 12–13.
[185] Bush and Lutz, Partnering in Ministry, 66.
[186] This viewpoint comes from a Western Christian perspective of marriage. To the extent that potential partners from other cultures view marriage in a differing perspective than the three tenets of permanence, exclusivity, and commitment mentioned above, that potential partner might perceive the partnership model versus the marriage model differently than presented here.
[187] Much of this section comparing partnership to marriage was taken from Addicott, *Body Matters*, 15–16.
[188] Addicott, 30.
[189] Warren, 13.

categories of relationships in partnership understanding: "First, that partnership is an idea congenial to the very nature of God; second, that partnership speaks of God's relationship with man; third, that partnership indicates the true relationship between man and his fellow-men."[190] Holistic mission and its related tasks are performed by human beings in relation with one another and, more importantly, in relation with the Triune God. Any view of partnership principles must begin with relationality.

Vertical Relationship

Partnership relationships are typically viewed as the horizontal relation of the member partners to one another and those they strive to serve. However, while the trusting, interdependent relationship of the members to one another is obviously of great significance, the members' vertical relationship with God as the empowering point is even more important to the effectiveness of a mission partnership. Rickett observes that "unless you are attending to partnership with God, no amount of effort will produce the fruit of the gospel (John 15:1–17)."[191]

Wan emphasizes a dynamic vertical relationship theme in a paradigm he calls "relational realism." He writes that "reality is primarily based on the vertical relationship between God and the created order and secondarily horizontal relationship within the created order."[192] Wan suggests that this relationship paradigm emphasizes a relational network that transcends culture, "trans-culturally relevant," making it an essential element to cross-cultural partnership relationships.[193] Partners experience the complexities of doing mission in the world and strive to overcome them with sound strategies and operational plans. God understands and transcends these complexities. He is working in all cultures.

Much of what leaders are taught today are systematic methods to evaluate issues, to develop solutions, and to create a vision and strategy for implementation. In mission leadership, these methods promote the creation of missional strategies that can be broken down into operational tasks. These methods provide meaningful and programmatic ways to manage progress and to stay on task, but they can also lead to the temptation to reduce mission to a rational set of manageable tasks, a "manageable enterprise."[194] If partners have a weak relationship with God, they can become immersed in the visible problems of the day, often arrogantly placing great value on their own abilities to solve these problems. However, what they may not realize is that the problems they strive so diligently to solve may not be the problems that God has called them to solve. Partners having a strong relationship with God recognize that vision is the result of the work that God is doing through his relationship with the partners.

Carson Pue, President of Arrow Leadership Ministries, suggests that ministry leaders must understand their limited role in the vision-setting process as it intersects with their relationship with God:

---

[190] Warren, 35.
[191] Rickett, Making Your Partnership Work, 69.
[192] Wan, "The Paradigm of 'Relational Realism,'" 1.
[193] Wan, "The Paradigm of 'Relational Realism,'" 2.
[194] James F. Engel and William A. Dyrness, *Changing the Mind of Missions: Where Have We Gone Wrong?* (Downers Grove, IL: InterVarsity, 2000), 69.

Much that is written about vision gives the dangerous impression that we can somehow have a much more important role in developing of vision than we ought. Followers of Jesus who are called to lead are not self-made people on some personally concocted journey. Vision is God's taking you from one place to another for his purpose – not our own. Vision is more about being "taken".[195]

God is creating the vision for the partners to receive it and to act on it.[196] Partnership efforts may be honorable, but without God's leadership, they are rendered ineffective. James F. Engel, founder and president of Development Associates International, and William A. Dyrness, American theologian and Professor of Theology and Culture at Fuller Theological Seminary, capture and summarize this principle well:

In short, *we are not expected to be autonomous problem solvers;* human reasoning in and of itself will not reveal God's perspective. And in sharp contrast to business entrepreneurs who assume total responsibility for long-term, sustained profitability, God and God alone is responsible for the outcome of those who labor in his vineyard, not the leaders and workers themselves.[197]

Horizontal Relationship

A discussion of horizontal partnership relationships must begin with a view of the greatest example of a functioning interdependent partnership relationship, the Trinity. Bosch reminds us that the conviction of the *missio Dei* is that "mission is, primarily and ultimately, the work of the Triune God, Creator, Redeemer, and Sanctifier, for the sake of the world."[198] Rev. J. Andrew Kirk, retired former Dean and Head of the School of Mission and World Christianity at Selly Oak Collages, Birmingham, England, suggests that when Christian communities speak about God, "by definition they have to speak about Father, Son and Holy Spirit. There is no other God. Therefore to speak about the *missio Dei* is to indicate, without qualification, the *missio Trinitatis*."[199] Wan and Penman point out, "The interdependence of the Godhead is shown in how the different Persons contribute to different aspects of the overall purpose of God" and how the totality of the biblical story testifies to the involvement of each Person of the Trinity in God's historical actions toward completion of his mission.[200] Wan and Penman explain that seven Trinitarian principles (love, diversity, unity, humility, interdependence, relationships, and peace and joy) are key for partnership in mission.[201] Bush and Lutz also reference the Trinity as a model of partnership, stating, "When God said,

---

[195] Carson Pue, Mentoring Leaders: Wisdom for Developing Character, Calling, and Competency (Grand Rapids, MI: Baker Books, 2005), 80.
[196] Pue, 93.
[197] Engel and Dyrness, 86.
[198] Bosch, Transforming Mission, 402.
[199] J. Andrew Kirk, *What Is Mission? Theological Explorations* (1999 repr., Minneapoliss, MN: Fortress Press, 2000), 27.
[200] Enoch Wan and Kevin P. Penman, "The Trinity: A Model for Partnership in Christian Missions." April 1, 2010. *Global Missiology.* <http://ojs.globalmissiology.org/index.php/english/article/view/138>. October 1, 2015. Wan and Penman cite the respective involvement of the Persons of the Trinity in specific examples of major biblical actions, such as creation and redemption.
[201] Wan and Penman, "The Trinity: A Model for Partnership in Christian Missions."

'Let us make man in our image,' he gave us a glimpse of the divine cooperative purposes of the Trinity right from the time of creation."[202]

Christian mission is empowered by and requires the involvement of the Triune God. One's relationship with the Triune God is foundational to all other relationships, and it is the source of horizontal participation in mission. For successful mission partnerships, William D. Taylor, first Executive Director of the World Evangelical Alliance Mission Committee, suggests,

> We must see partnerships as God sees them. He [God] is modeling it within the Trinity and by delegating the major mandates to his people, partners with us in history, both with Israel and the church. Partnerships are rooted in the nature of God and therefore are crucial elements to our life and ministry…[203]

Successful partnerships recognize the interdependent nature of the horizontal relationship that is required to accomplish the shared vision and objectives of mission. There is no greater model of such a functioning interdependent relationship than the Trinity.

Mission partnerships are, however, made of human beings, and successful partnering depends on the abilities of these humans to communicate and to work together. A relationship between the partner members is implied in any definition of partnership.

Relationships at creation were complete and made in God's image. All elements of created order were made to complement one another and to exist for each other's benefit. The fall changed all of that and left relationships broken. Butler suggests that "restored open relationships are critical to lasting, effective partnerships,"[204] and "people and ministries simply cannot work together effectively over any length of time without dealing with the relational brokenness."[205] Rickett suggests that the partners may "have a compelling strategy, state-of-the art technology, and a proven promotional plan, but you won't achieve real partnership if you don't have the right people involved and committed to the relationship."[206]

The unique nature of an organization's form or function does not drive this relationship; rather it is dependent on the commitment of the partners. However, success of the partnership's form and function is highly dependent on the quality of these relationships. If the relationships are effective, the success of the form and function will follow.

When partnerships are created, the focus is often on the formal organizational structures that are needed to accomplish a specific function or set of goals. In the business world, this function or goal might be to capitalize on a market opportunity or to exploit a specific situation in order to realize a financial gain for the partners. In mission, this shared vision might be evangelizing a specific region or caring for a certain group of people.

---

[202] Bush and Lutz, 21.
[203] William D. Taylor, ed. *Kingdom Partnerships for Synergy in Missions,* (Pasadena, CA: William Carey Library,1994), 237.
[204] Butler, *Well Connected*, 49.
[205] Butler, Well Connected, 51.
[206] Daniel Rickett, Making Your Partnership Work, 63.

Partnership leaders can spend considerable time and energy on the form and function of the partnership, going to great lengths to analyze the potential benefits of forming the most advantageous structure. They begin to believe that having the correct organizational form is the key to successful mission. Sherwood G. Lingenfelter, Provost Emeritus and Senor Professor of Anthropology at Fuller Seminary, calls trusting the form of ministry (in this case, partnership) the "illusion that seduces all leaders and followers" by thinking they have the "right form" for God's work and trusting the form and the system rather than God. He suggests that leaders "become power seekers, rather than servants in the work of the Master, the mission of God."[207] When partners place their trust in the form of the organization, they neglect the importance of the trusting, interdependent relationships of and between the various constituents that are required for effective and successful mission partnership. With a view solely toward achieving the benefits, partners often assume that effective partnership and leadership principles will allow them to manage through and withstand relationship incongruities. They fail to understand that collaboration requires trusting, interdependent relationships to succeed.

Individualism is a prevalent characteristic found in Western cultures. Individualistic leaders analyze opportunities and make decisions through the lens of self. These same leaders then fail to understand when those they seek to partner with do the same. Successful partnership leaders can move beyond self-seeking and recognize the interdependent nature of the relationship that is required to accomplish their shared vision and objectives.

The Trinity again points to an effective model for bridging the tension between individualism and collaboration. Charles A. Davis, former Executive International Director of TEAM (The Evangelical Alliance Mission), writes:

The Trinity beautifully demonstrates relational interdependence, where individual and community are held in perfect tension. Each member of the Trinity is a whole person with individual responsibilities, but they function as a collective unity to such a degree that they are one God.[208]

Partners working together on a truly aligned vision and set of goals will mirror a Trinity-like interdependency relationship. God has invited his people to participate in his mission. It is only fitting that holistic mission is modeled after his example with appropriate horizontal partnerships among those many others whom he has invited. Butler explains, "To realize the full potential of what God can do, we need a new respect for the importance of the roles of others. Realizing that meaningful change may take time and that participation by others has value can bring us balance and new hope while *never diminishing the urgency of the vision.*"[209]

Interdependence requires mutuality in the relationship, yet James E. Plueddemann, retired Professor of Missions at Trinity Evangelical Divinity School, suggests, "The idea of equal partners is foreign to most of the world. Most of the world assumes a junior and senior member."[210] Such a model creates

---

[207] Sherwood G. Lingenfelter, Leading Cross-Culturally: Covenant Relationships for Effective Christian Leadership (Grand Rapids, MI: Baker, 2008), 101.
[208] Charles A. Davis, Making Disciples Across Cultures: Missional Principles for a Diverse World (Downers Grove: InterVarsity, 2015), 78.
[209] Butler, Well Connected, 61.
[210] James E. Plueddemann, Leading Across Cultures: Effective Ministry and Mission in the Global Church (Downers Grove, IL: InterVarsity, 2009), 26.

unbalanced relationships with one partner operating from a position of power. This lack of mutuality can be heightened when a disparity of affluence exists between the partners or one partner brings more economical resources to the relationship.[211] Without a foundational interdependent leadership philosophy, partners may begin to view the monetary resources as the primary missional tool and those that supply the monetary resources as the primary leaders and decision makers.

Mary T. Lederleitner, Founder and Executive Director of Missional Intelligence, provides practical guidance specifically related to monetary matters and funding relationships for those entertaining a cross-cultural partnership.[212] Her work focuses on the cultural differences and related issues that can arise in funding relationships due to these differences. Reflecting on unintended consequences of foreign funding, she writes that "it's often not the money, but how the money factors into who leads" that has an impact on the local partner and its actions.[213]

Partnership leaders must recognize and value the entirety of resources that God has provided, including the provision of non-monetary gifts and talents. Rickett explains that if the "accent is on the exchange of money or personnel and not on the complementary contributions each partner makes, reciprocity is easily overlooked."[214] It is relatively easy to recognize the monetary contribution of the funding partner, but reciprocal resources can be far more ambiguous. The Western funding partner may provide financial and other technological resources that are somewhat easily quantifiable. However, these Western funding partners must "depend on the human resources, linguistic skills, cultural insights, and relevant lifestyle of its non-Western partners," which are much more difficult to value.[215] Effective partnerships recognize the reciprocity of the partner relationship.

Such a partnership creates the environment in which each member understands that what he or she provides is vital to God's mission. Davis summarizes the beauty of interdependent mission partnerships when he writes:

When disciples develop relational interdependence, real community flourishes, teamwork emerges, mutual trust and commitment build. We develop a collective vision both for the church and for the mission, within each individual has a specific and meaningful role. My individual work has value, because it contributes to our collective work.[216]

The horizontal relationships include not only the partners themselves but extend to those that the partnership serves as well as those that may work with the partnership to serve others. For example, a healthcare agency and a church partnering to holistically serve the church's community will have relationships with the patients in the community, with any missionary medical professionals that may serve from time to time, and many others that could be involved in serving the community alongside the partnership members.

---

[211] Mary T. Lederleitner, Cross-Cultural Partnerships: Navigating the Complexities of Money and Mission (Downers Grove, IL: InterVarsity, 2010), 123.
[212] Lederleitner, Cross-Cultural Partnerships: Navigating the Complexities of Money and Mission.
[213] Lederleitner, 91.
[214] Daniel Rickett, Building Strategic Relationships: A Practical Guide to Partnering with Non-Western Missions, 3rd edition (Minneapolis, MN: Stem Pres, 2008), 32.
[215] Rickett, Building Strategic Relationships, 35.
[216] Davis, 77.

The *Common Fire* research studied people that have demonstrated a commitment to the "common good" of society seeking to understand commonalities regarding how this commitment was developed within the research subjects. Specifically, the researchers sought to "achieve a richer understanding of how lives of commitment to the common good are formed and sustained."[217] One might paraphrase the objective as "how have these subjects been discipled" into forming a world view committed to the common good?

In the epilog chapter of the study, the authors focus on twelve specific "sectors" of society that they suggest are "primary institutional forms that can foster the learning now needed [to foster this commitment to the common good], and they have the power to encourage ways of living that directly serve the well-being of the commons."[218] Nonprofits, they suggest, "are key settings in which commitments to the common good can ferment and mature," and the authors challenge nonprofits to build commitment to the larger common good as part of the organization's mission and to pave the way for this commitment among the organization's relationships.[219] These relationships are illustrated to include internal relationships (staff and board members) as well as those the organization serves. The authors summarize the collaborative and partnership foundational aspects of the relationship philosophy:

As the commitment builds, staff and trustees can together examine how programs might extend the positive participation of clients in the wider life of the commons. By examining the *relationships* among the organization, clients, and the public, it may be possible to include clientele as *partners* in the larger work and to expand their participation in the public life (emphasis added).[220]

Wan and Hedinger use a relational realism paradigm to construct a framework for relationally training intercultural missionaries. Using this framework, they identify and examine the key relationships, both vertical and horizontal, that are important in training intercultural workers.[221] Though their relational framework is focused primarily on training intercultural workers, the conceptual framework fits nicely into a relational partnership framework model that can be used to evaluate a partnership's relationships for missional engagement.

Motivations to Partner

Partnerships, whether in the secular world or in mission, are driven by several foundational but practical motivations. First and foremost, the spiritual and physical needs of a rapidly changing world continue to grow in number and complexity. Holistic mission is a huge endeavor and "the concept of a single group, company, or mission society possessing the needed human financial, physical, and spiritual resources may be immediately dismissed as a hollow claim."[222] Butler concurs,

---

[217] Daloz, et al., Common Fire, 5.
[218] Daloz, *et al.*, Common Fire, 213. The twelve sectors cited are households (children, youth and family); schools; higher education; the professions and professional education; religion; arts and media; public policy; business; nonprofit organizations; the health and therapeutic community; foundations and philanthropy; and the readers of the book.
[219] Daloz, et al., Common Fire, 235–237.
[220] Daloz, et al., Common Fire, 237.
[221] Wan and Hedinger, 40. Pages 38–50 explore and explain the authors' view of key missionary relationships.
[222] Pocock, Van Rheenen and McConnell, 255.

suggesting that current global realities "make partnership an imperative, not an option."[223]

Accordingly, partners are motivated to work together to accomplish a shared vision or set of common goals that limited resources may prohibit them from achieving on their own. Corporate profits and holistic mission, while fundamentally different, are examples of mutually agreed-upon visions that might exist within a partnership, and there are fundamental practical benefits to be gained by working together. Butler writes, "In the practice of partnerships, it should not be surprising that businesses and ministries often find *parallel* motivations or benefits [to partnering]."[224] He goes on to summarize several practical examples that motivate organizations to partnership: efficiency, an ability to focus on strengths, increased effectiveness, greater flexibility, expanded resources, reduced risk, and expanded options for action.[225] Sider *et al.* note that churches involved in holistic mission identify collaboration as one of the keys to concentrating on a specific area of ministry while maintaining the ability to address multifaceted community needs. They suggest that "your church does not have to develop expertise or programming on every social issue—you just have to find out who has. By pooling resources and ideas with a cluster of churches or organizations, each contributing a different facet of ministry, you can increase your effectiveness."[226]

Mission partners having a diversity of gifts can join forces to maximize resources, to reduce risks, to enhance strengths, and to build efficiencies, thereby sharing in the responsibility of holistic mission and allowing them effectiveness that they otherwise could not achieve on their own. Michael Griffiths, former professor of Mission Studies at Regent College in Vancouver, maintains, "The idea is simple: we should never struggle to do something alone, that we can do better if we cooperate with others in 'partnership.'"[227]

Each Christian has been gifted as determined by the Holy Spirit and these gifts are to be used in unity (the one-body, several-parts metaphor) for the common good (1 Cor. 12:7). Jerry A. Rankin, President Emeritus of the Southern Baptist International Mission Board, writes, "As individuals within the body of Christ have different gifts to serve the needs of the church, different mission organizations have unique callings and gifts to offer the larger body of Christ to complete the Great Commission." He continues, "Through partnerships, the larger Christian community can make an impact, utilizing multiple channels and strategies, far beyond what a token representative of one organization could do."[228]

Bush and Lutz add further to the concept of combining gifts and resources as a motivation to partner when they suggest partnership to be the "Cords of Victory," writing:

---

[223] Butler, Well Connected, 26.
[224] Butler, *Well Connected*, 27.
[225] Butler, *Well Connected*, 27–28.
[226] Sider, Olson, and Unruh, Churches That Make a Difference, 89.
[227] Michael Griffiths, "Preface." *Kingdom Partnerships for Synergy in Missions*, ed. William D Taylor (Pasadena, CA: William Carey Library, 1994), ix.
[228] Jerry A. Rankin, "The Present Situation in Missions." *Missiology: An Introduction to the Foundations, History, and Strategies of World Missions*, Ed. John Mark Terry, Ebbie Smith and Justice Anderson (Nashville, TN: Broadman & Holman, 1998), 47.

By now everyone involved in missions will have realized that partnership is a major issue. The task of world evangelism will most likely be fulfilled when we join our resources and personnel, eliminate duplication and competition, and let God's holy synergism work through partnership. It is not only the mission agencies and national ministries around the world who need to understand partnership, but those interested in serving cross culturally, mission committees, church leaders and donors.[229]

Mission partnerships striving to serve holistically exist to serve and minister to the needs of a broken and fallen world. These needs can be many, often including immediate needs such as families needing food or shelter, victims of abuse, victims of fire, etc. These immediate needs call for immediate efforts of compassion relief. Like the story of the Good Samaritan, mission leaders move to action, garnering resources to participate in the relief efforts to the extent practical. However, the deeper need is moving the community toward long-term positive transformation, both spiritually and physically. Myers uses the term "transformational development" to express his "concern for seeking positive change in the whole of human life materially, socially, psychologically, and spiritually."[230] These needs can often go beyond personal transformation of individuals, reaching toward social and economic transformation of communities. Mission partnerships may target many of these community and structural needs such as healthcare or affordable housing as examples. Sider, Olson, and Unruh point out:

> Just because community development achieves 'secular' results does not mean it has no spiritual roots or fruits! Community development... serves as a tangible expression of the Good News the church proclaims... It nurtures an environment that affirms the church's message of God's love and human dignity. By identifying the church with the good things happening in the community, it points people to the reign of Christ.[231]

In other words, mission leaders desiring transformational development within their sphere of influence seek to holistically minister to their community. They must identify the needs of the community, both physical and spiritual, and determine the means to best minister to those needs with a motivation to move past immediate relief efforts toward long-term sustainable transformative growth that empowers the community and moves people to a renewed relationship with the Creator.

Long-term development, whether spiritual or physical, by definition, takes time. Working toward development, whether personal development or community development, is a process and not an event. Lederleitner and Rickett call this the process of "building capacity."[232] Lederleitner considers the question of capacity as one of her top four foundational principles of leadership in a partnership relationship.[233] The term *capacity* reflects the abilities or resources available to the

---

[229] Bush and Lutz, Partnering in Ministry, 173.
[230] Myers, Walking with the Poor, 3.
[231] Sider, Olson, Unruh, 41.
[232] Lederleitner, 135, and Rickett, *Building Strategic Relationships*, 63.
[233] Mary T. Lederleitner. Interview about Foundational Leadership Principles of Cross-Cultural Partnerships. Interviewed by author, November 20, 2017. Lederleitner lists four foundational

partnership members for attending to the existing needs of the community. The capacity concept asks how much capacity the partnership currently has and how much capacity can be envisioned in the future. A goal of the partnership becomes the realization of incremental capacity development to be used to further the vision. Successful leadership requires a determination of the partners' true capacity level, what the partners can reasonably expect to do. A false motivation to do more can effectively create a shortage of capacity and weaken the ability to meet the demands of the primary mission vision. Myers' definitional use of the term transformational adds additional caution to this capacity concept:

The term transformational is used to remind us that human progress is not inevitable; it takes hard work... True human development involves making choices, setting aside that which is not for life in us and in our community, while actively seeking and supporting all that is for life. This requires that we say no to some things in order to say yes [to have the capacity to say yes] to what really matters.[234]

Creating capacity requires making those choices about what really matters and being honest about the available capacity to take on more mission activity. It also requires mission partners to have a strong self-awareness of their motivations. Lederleitner suggests that "innate in all of us is a desire to be needed. However, if we work from that motivation or ethos, any short-term gains... will likely be overshadowed by long-term dependency."[235] Rickett suggests, "The key to building capacity is not developing programs. The key is enabling people—the leaders and members of the partner ministry. Helping people learn and effect changes in their own ministry is the most essential—and most difficult—part of developmental partnering."[236]

Reasons to partner in holistic mission extend beyond the practical resource-related issues. Writing from a holistic mission perspective, Sider, Olson, and Unruh suggest eleven reasons (seven practical and four theological) that churches should work through partnerships for effective holistic mission.[237] While several of the practical reasons they note fall into the category of resource sharing and the related practical benefits, other reasons offer unique outcomes that churches can realize through mission partnerships. For example, consistent with the relationality benefits noted in the previous section, Sider, Olson, and Unruh suggest that "partnerships expand a church's opportunity to form evangelistic relationships beyond those being served, offering "a unique avenue of reaching co-laborers in social action with the gospel."[238] This is coupled with one of their theological reasons when they reference a strengthening of evangelistic witness through partnership. They suggest that "When Christians of different denominations, races, and socioeconomic backgrounds come together around the banner of holistic

---

principles: partnership capacity, listening for understanding, clarity in the relationships, and the need for a partner champion to advocate for the agenda and goals.
[234] Myers, 3.
[235] Lederleitner, 137.
[236] Rickett, Building Strategic Relationships, 65.
[237] Sider, Olson, and Unruh. See pages 224–229 for a complete list and description of the authors' suggested reasons to partnership in holistic ministry.
[238] Sider, Olson, and Unruh, 225.

ministry, people take notice. Such ministry partnerships are a living testimony to the reconciling power of the gospel."[239]

In the Christian faith, mission actions and the outcomes are important. However, even more important are the motives behind the actions. Christians understand that they are to love their neighbor, but motivation for that love comes from the love for Christ. Jesus said, "If you love me, keep my commands" (John 14:15), and again, "Anyone who loves me will obey my teaching" (John 14:23). The Apostle Paul adds that no matter how great our actions, if not properly motivated in love we are "only a resounding gong or a clanging cymbal" (1 Cor. 13:1); essentially, we are nothing. Partnerships in mission should be strongly motivated by these biblical principles, looking not toward worldly achievements per se but motivated by the fruits of joining together to participate in God's mission.

However, mission partnership leaders often elevate the mission tasks to a greater level of importance than the actual mission purpose. Pue observes, "We are tempted to seek what God wants us to do rather than what he wants us to be."[240] Mission leaders must be motivated by and motivated to the ultimate purpose of the *missio Dei*. Plueddemann suggests, "The ultimate purpose of leadership is to bring people into full relationship with their Creator." He goes on to explain that this ties to the biblical "assumptions" about the "ultimate" purpose of life, which he describes as knowing God, glorifying God, loving God, and fearing God.[241] It is this same purpose that must motivate mission leaders to work together in collaborative relationships. Mission partners must look beyond a view of their own desires for mission and ask how their gifts might be used to facilitate even greater spiritual gains when used in partnership with others in mutually shared mission.

These principles are manifested in the mission leaders' motivation to partner together out of love for the communities they serve. They recognize that differing situations result in a diversity of needs throughout the community. Holistic ministering to this diversity of needs requires the diversity of gifts and talents that only a mission collaboration can provide. As Davis puts it, "Love desires the deepest good for the whole person,"[242] and to love and serve these communities to the fullest requires a tangible action of partnership by the leaders. James M. Kouzes, Dean's Executive Fellow of Leadership, Leavey School of Business at Santa Clara University, and Barry Z. Posner, Accolti Professor of Leadership and Former Dean of the Leavey School of Business, Santa Clara University, suggest that love is the "leader's secret to success in life," and dedicate the closing of their book to this concept:

Of all things that sustain a leader over time, love is the most lasting. It's hard to imagine leaders getting up day after day, putting in the long hard work it takes to make extraordinary things happen, without having their hearts in it. The best-kept secret of successful leaders is love: staying in love with leading, with the people who

---

[239] Sider, Olson, and Unruh, 228.
[240] Pue, 97.
[241] Plueddemann, 159–61.
[242] Davis, 97.

do the work, with what their organizations provide, and with those who honor the organization by using its products and services.[243]

Despite the theoretical benefits and the rhetorical support, Christian partnership relationships in missions remain elusive. Jonathan S. Barnes, Executive of Mission Interpretation for Global Ministries, begins the abstract of his article writing, "Despite the fact that *partnership* has been a pronounced goal in ecumenical relationships for over eighty years, the realization of mutuality, solidarity, and *koinonia* has, even until present times, proven to be elusive."[244] Barnes examines the history of partnership through the various chronological stages of the Protestant mission movement. He specifically examines this history in terms of "churches of Global Christianity churches (churches in the North or Western world, also formerly known as 'sending' or 'older' churches) and churches of World Christianity (the churches of the South and East, formerly known as 'receiving' or 'younger' churches)."[245]

Barnes' historical analysis reveals four themes that he suggests are recurring problems to the effective practice of partnership. These themes are "issues involving power which have allowed colonial and neocolonial interpretations of partnership to persist."[246] His list and descriptions are paraphrased below:[247]

- The Home Base – Described as the constituencies of the Global churches and their inability to adjust from traditional understandings of mission. Barnes suggests that this is "clearly the most important to address."
- Humanitarianism and Development – An inability of Global churches to move past paternalistic motives of superiority have hindered mutuality in relationships.
- Authority – Historical colonial issues related to Global church power, paternalism, and control, especially in the area of finances, continue to be lived out in present relationships.
- Rhetoric and Reality – Many historic resolutions have been made and policies passed seeking changed partnership relationships, however, these resolutions and policies have rarely been followed up with actions.

Barnes concludes that Global church attitudes regarding mission have remained unchanged for over eighty years. Accordingly, he suggests,

Given this long history of paternalism, it seems clear that partnership between Global and World churches will continue to be unattainable, for Global Christianity's worldview, how it sees itself and others, is linked to the idea of 'Christendom,' power and control. And while during colonial times issues of power and control are

---

[243] James M. Kouzes and Barry Z. Posner, The Leadership Challenge: How to Make Extraordinary Things Happen in Organizations, 6th edition (Hoboken, NJ: Wiley, 2017), 311.
[244] Jonathon S. Barnes, "Whither Partnership? Reflections on the History of Mutuality in Mission." *Review and Expositor,* Vol. 113 (1) (2016), 32.
[245] Jonathon S. Barnes, *Power and Partnership: A History of the Protestant Mission Movement,* (Eugene, OR: Pickwick Publications, 2013), 1. He credits these terms to Lamin Sanneh, (1942-2019), formerly D. Willis James Professor of Missions and World Christianity at Yale Divinity School and Professor of History at Yale.
[246] Barnes, Power and Partnership, 410.
[247] Barnes, Power and Partnership, 412–18.

readily apparent, in our postcolonial and neocolonial setting today issues of power are much more subtle.[248]

Human participation in mission is subject to the same human character flaws that obstruct a willingness to partner. Butler identifies sin as the primary reason that God's people fail to effectively work together. He writes that sin "shows in our fear, selfishness, ego, individualism and protection of 'turf.'"[249] Effectiveness begins when those in leadership are motivated beyond their selfish ambitions or vain conceit, looking not only to their own ministry interests but also to the interests of others (Phil. 3:3-4). However, Sider, Olson, and Unruh remind us that mission is God's and the importance of recognizing the outcome is his. They suggest:

> Our physical limitations, fallibility, and sinfulness will invariably bring us up short of hoped-for outcomes. Accepting that we can't meet every need, we must trust that God is sufficient—not as an excuse for inaction but as the foundation for peace and hope in the midst of action. If we expect our church's ministry [or partnership's ministry] to wipe out the problems of our community, we will be disappointed and so will the community. The church [partnership] is not the hope of the world; Christ is.[250]

Cross-Cultural Partnerships

The Total Health partnership is cross-cultural, and cross-cultural mission is a subject of vast importance in the efforts to effectively minister to and serve this rapidly changing world. Butler suggests:

> The heartbeat of every effective, lasting partnership is that it focuses the power of Kingdom diversity in a unified process and vision. Partnerships celebrate the diversity and empower the focused integration of the whole range of available Kingdom resources. All gifts, personalities, individuals, and ministries have potentially valuable roles in a coordinated strategy that is well beyond the potential of any single individual or ministry. The great power of the God design of unity and diversity can be experienced through an effective partnership in ways that are rarely experienced in other forms of witness.[251]

Myers asserts that due to globalization and expansion, "Christianity is now a non-Western religion" and the "center of gravity" of the Christian church has shifted from the West to the Global South.[252] Engel and Dyrness likewise suggest a shift of mission leadership and momentum to the Two-Thirds world church.[253] At the same time, the majority of global wealth remains in the West, exacerbating an increasing imbalance of resources and a need to share.

Citing the globalization of Christianity, Guthrie suggests that, "While the day of Western missionary dominance is probably over, both raw need around the world and the biblical mandate to all Christians to spread the gospel ensure that

---

[248] Barnes, Power and Partnership, 419.
[249] Butler, Well Connected, 204.
[250] Sider, Olson, and Unruh, 141.
[251] Butler, *Well Connected*, 55.
[252] Myers, Engaging Globalization, 197–98.
[253] Engel and Dyrness, 21.

Westerners will continue to have a job to do in world evangelization in the future. But perhaps it will be more as partners, and encouragers, and less as leaders."[254]

This shift creates some unique dynamics in mission partnership between the West and the Global South. The financial needs remain significant in the Global South, yet, partnerships with the West are beneficial only when the West comes prepared to supply what is needed, led by the Global South partner. The needs of the two can be significantly different as evidenced by the differing theological questions Myers points out:

In the modern and largely secular West, the critical theological issues focus on gender and sexuality, the dangers of consumption and materialism, and the challenges of multiculturalism and pluralism. In the Global South, the pressing theological questions are different: morality and holiness, poverty and justice, political violence, the rule of the law, corruption, and coexistence with primal or traditional religion.[255]

The Global South needs expertise in areas that help them address their specific local issues and has no need for ideas and programs that the West may bring to "fix" problems that the West is experiencing. The Global South still needs help from the West, but not help patterned after the specific problems of the affluent West. Engel and Dyrness recognize this issue and cite the need for North American churches to "come alongside in a spirit of partnership and submission, participating where we can in an enabling and facilitating manner to help increase the impact of all that God is doing in this era."[256] They add,

> In short, the West is welcome on the pilgrimage only if there is a willingness to join as fellow Galileans in humility with strugglers who learn as they go and are willing to sacrifice a Western urgency to achieve kingdom-oriented outputs. A very different kind of missionary is required today—one who is willing to come in submission as an *enabler,* who serves by empowering others through an offering of much-needed gifts and skills that others do not possess.[257]

Duane Elmer, G.W. Alden Professor of International Studies at Trinity Evangelical Divinity School, writes about managing cross-cultural conflicts primarily from a Western perspective. His stated purpose is to clarify issues in intercultural and interracial conflict, to provide insights on the different ways people of various cultures handle conflict, to evaluate these according to Scripture, and to provide practical guidelines for (1) helping us to live more harmoniously with our cultural differences, (2) developing a positive strategy for dealing with conflict, and (3) communicating the gospel of Jesus Christ more effectively and ministering the nurturing grace of God.[258]

Elmer lists and explains five conflict resolution strategies that he suggests are "the American Way" of resolving conflict: "Win/Lose Strategy, Conflict Avoidance,

---

[254] Guthrie, 164.
[255] Myers, Engaging Globalization, 202.
[256] Engel and Dyrness, 21.
[257] Engel and Dyrness, 167.
[258] Duane Elmer, *Cross-Cultural Conflict: Building Relationships for Effective Ministry* (Downers Grove, IL: InterVarsity Press Academic, 1993), 22.

Giving In, Compromise, and Carefronting."[259] He defines "carefronting" as directly approaching the other person in a caring way so that achieving a win/win solution is most likely."[260]

In his Doctor of Philosophy thesis, Joshua Stephen Bowman acknowledges the inherent tension in cross-cultural relationships and posits that "healthy partnership between culturally diverse groups of believers mediates relational, cultural, and hermeneutical tensions, thereby contributing to mutual faithful engagement in the mission of God."[261] He enhances the definitions of partnership by defining cross-cultural mission partnership as "a kingdom-oriented relationship of culturally diverse groups of believers who share common values and goals, who possess complementary spiritual gifts, skills, and resources, and who mutually engage in the mission of God."[262] Bowman suggests three main tensions in cross-cultural relationships, cultural, relational, and hermeneutical, and describes them:

Cultural tensions explain the desire to be faithful to Scripture while simultaneously being relevant to culture. Relational tensions describe the problems of misunderstanding and miscommunication that come when people from different cultures interact with one another. Hermeneutical tensions are those tensions related to the application of diverse perspectives and cultural backgrounds as [different local groups] interpret Scripture, their own culture, and the culture of others.[263]

Bowman suggests that healthy partnerships between believers of other cultures will provide a means of mediating these tensions. He uses the following table to summarize mediating factors and the relationship to partnership.

Table 2. - Mediating Factors in Cross-Cultural Mission Partnerships[264]

Tension	Mediating Factor	Relationship to	Mark of Church	Description	Relation to Partnership
Hermeneutical	Common Values	Revelation - Scripture	Apostolic	*Kerygma* - Message	Share Values
Relational	Mutual Submission	Body of Christ - Church	One	*Koinonia* - Fellowship	Kingdom Orientation
Cultural	Complementary Service	Cultural Context - World	Holy	*Diakonia* - Service	Possess Gifts
Cultural, Relational	Common Goals	Unbelieving World	Catholic	*Martyria* - Witness	Engage in Mission

Cross-cultural need not be restricted to nationality. Sider, along with his coauthors, writes about partnerships between urban and suburban churches in the U.S. Coauthor Tizon comments on the cross-cultural nature of these partnerships, noting "the considerable overlap that exists between the urban-suburban encounter

---

[259] Elmer, Cross-Cultural Conflict, 33–44.
[260] Elmer, Cross-Cultural Conflict, 42.
[261] Joshua Stephen Bowman, Cross-Cultural Mission Partnership: Mediating Relational, Cultural, and Hermeneutical Tensions for Mutual, Faithful Missional Engagement (PhD Thesis, Southeastern Baptist Theological Seminary, 2019), 2.
[262] Bowman, 15.
[263] Bowman, 55. See also Bowman 67.
[264] Bowman, 200.

and the Western-non-Western encounter."[265] The nature of the cultural differences are remarkably similar, with the more wealthy suburban churches taking on the motif of the more wealthy West and the urban churches the non-West. Tizon further explains,

Just like in the Western-non-Western relationships, Christians involved or who desire to get involved in the urban-suburban ministry partnership must strive toward equality, mutual respect, an affirmation of diversity, a biblical understanding of the rich and poor in God's economy, and a shared sense of mission.[266]

Dependency and paternalism are the antithesis of creating long-term capacity, and these types of partnerships can be prone to creating dependent relationships. Partnership leaders must be aware of this potential and protect themselves and their organizations from sliding into paternalistic habits that can create dependency. Rickett suggests that the best way for leaders to protect against this is with a continued focus toward development. Focusing on development, he writes, *"it forces us to ask whether our involvement makes each other better able to serve God with our gifts and calling.* Are we helping to build one another's capacity or are we simply relieving needs?"[267]

Rickett defines dependency as "the state of relying on someone or something." He argues for an "acceptable" kind of dependency based on the dependent's "willingness to do his or her part—that is, to take responsibility to give something back." He suggests that the biblical metaphor of the body implies a "complementary and reciprocal" dependency. All parts of the body have something to contribute and each has some need. In a healthy partnership relationship, he suggests, "partners recognize their responsibilities and work to fulfill them."[268]

Its relative wealth causes Western culture to often try to solve problems with money. Lederleitner suggests, "We often do this instinctively because we internally feel such great disequilibrium and heartache at the disparity of resources. We give quickly out of instinct, because we want that uncomfortable and unpleasant feeling to go away," and by giving in to these self-centered motivations "we short-circuit God's process for lasting transformation."[269] Bush and Lutz caution against a "donor mentality" related to the vast resources of the West, indicating that "Western churches have been guilty of showering money and personnel on the national churches without thinking through the potentially negative results."[270] If not managed properly, funding partnerships can become unhealthy dependent relationships.

Conversely, Lederleitner suggests that the "fear of creating unhealthy dependency" can result in the potential funding partners simply choosing not to give.[271] She adds, "It is often not the money, but how the money factors into who leads, who makes decisions and who sets priorities for ministry. If these other

---

[265] Sider et al., Linking Arms, Linking Lives, 25.
[266] Sider et al., Linking Arms, Linking Lives, 26.
[267] Rickett, Building Strategic Relationships, 15.
[268] Rickett, Building Strategic Relationships, 29–32.
[269] Lederleitner, 89.
[270] Bush and Lutz, 38.
[271] Lederleitner, 92.

factors are set up well, foreign funding is able to be a true blessing and not a disincentive for action."[272]

Cultural backgrounds factor into these increased complexities of intercultural partnerships. Behaviors, motivations, and expectations have been molded by this phenomenon labeled as culture. A cross-cultural partnership relationship brings with it the additional complexities of nationality identity and cultural differences. Hiebert writes, "All people see the same world, but they perceive it through different cultural glasses. And they are often unaware of their culture and how it colors what they see."[273] Bush and Lutz also recognize this cultural issue as an obstacle to partnership. Commenting on the need for those working in Western missions to work through ethnocentricity, they write, "The belief that 'west is best' blinded us to the values found in other cultures and to the realization that the truth of Scripture can be adapted to each culture, allowing each people to develop its own forms of worship and lifestyle."[274]

Mission leaders see the same issues, but their cultural biases can lead to different interpretations of the causes and potential solutions. As an example, one's cultural foundations shape one's perspectives related to poverty and opportunity. Are the materially poor simply lazy and not willing to put in the effort to break the cycle, or is poverty the result of other systemic factors? The answer to that question might have much to do with one's cultural experiences and perspectives on equality and opportunity.

In addition, one's view of the causes of poverty also serves to provide the backdrop for one's development of poverty alleviation methods. In other words, the perception of the cause drives the methodology of the cures as illustrated in the following chart taken from Myers:

Table 3. - How Cause Shapes Response[275]

View of cause	Proposed response
The poor are sinners	Evangelism and uplift
The poor are sinned against	Social action; working for justice
The poor lack knowledge	Education
The poor lack things	Relief/social welfare
The culture of the poor is flawed	Become like us; ours is better
The social system makes them poor	Change the system

As Hiebert also points out, people are often unaware of cultural biases and the impact these biases can have on their personal behaviors. Partnership by definition means working with others and working with others has a way of revealing

---

[272] Lederleitner, 91.
[273] Paul G. Hiebert, *Anthropological Insights for Missionaries* (Grand Rapids, MI: Baker Academic, 1985), 62.
[274] Bush and Lutz, 37.
[275] Myers, Walking with the Poor, 133.

character blind spots that may hinder effective relationships. Butler observes that "When forced into a relational situation, particularly when stress is involved, our true character emerges with remarkable clarity."[276] When forced to deal with cultural differences in partnership, no matter the magnitude, partners may discover within themselves hidden character flaws such as trust or control issues. Vanier writes about living in community with others, but his words ring true regarding partnering with others when he writes:

> Community is the place where our limitations, our fears, and our egoisms are revealed to us. We discover our poverty and our weaknesses, our inability to get on with some people, our mental and emotional blocks, our affective sexual disturbances, our seemingly insatiable desires, our frustrations and jealousies, our hatred and our wish to destroy.[277]

Using what he calls "bicultural communities," Hiebert writes about the blending of cultures in the realm of mission work.[278] This concept of bicultural communities has direct application to mission partnership. Each member comes to the partnership with the behaviors driven from their respective cultural experiences. The partnership relationship becomes by definition a form of Hiebert's bicultural community where "the two worlds meet... made up of people who retain ties to their original cultures, but who meet and exchange ideas."[279]

These behavioral differences can be significantly magnified when the partnership relationship is cross-cultural. The enculturation of people groups into societies across the globe has created worldviews that differ considerably from one culture to another. The cultural experiences over time have shaped the different principles and attitudes that have cultivated these different worldviews. As a result, when people from differing cultures attempt to work together and get to know one another, certain traits and characteristics are exposed and become associated with those specific cultures. Bush and Lutz observe, for example, "Experience has taught the Two-Thirds World mission leaders that Western missionaries tend to take control and that non-Westerners may too easily accept structures and teaching that are foreign to their society because of their poor self-image and/or lack of training."[280] A prospective group of partners must understand the differences between themselves in order to fully understand how to work together effectively and efficiently.

Melba Padilla Maggay, Executive Director of the Institute for Studies in Asian Church and Culture, reminds us:

> Studies show that increased cross-cultural contact does not necessarily lead to cross-cultural understanding... It is one thing to see other cultures on TV, with their exotic habits and colorful costumes; it is another thing to see them invading our living space and smell their cooking. Once contact becomes real rather than virtual; once it engages that part of us which has to do with perceptions, values, beliefs and world views, coming together becomes awkward, tense, messy, and

---

[276] Butler, Well Connected, 51.
[277] Jean Vanier. *Community and Growth*. Revised edition (Mahwah, NJ: Pualist Press, 1989), 26.
[278] Hiebert, 228.
[279] Hiebert, 229.
[280] Bush and Lutz, Partnering in Ministry, 14.

often painful. This is the kind of discomfort we all go through once we truly cross cultures.[281]

Butler suggests that even before understanding the differences, one must acknowledge the existence of these differences and their potential impact on the partnership. He lists acknowledgment of these differences as the first step toward mitigating them and he accusingly points out:

> We may acknowledge that we are involved in cross-cultural ministry. However, it is remarkable how frequently Christian leadership can and do gloss over the deep differences in worldviews, assumptions, social dynamics, decision-making processes, and expectations between cultures. And in so doing, we set ourselves up for, at best, great difficulty; at worst, failure.[282]

Mission partners must resist the "my culture is best" perspective, acknowledging that culture is important and that cultural differences exist.

Partnering between those coming from a culture of individualism such as in the West with those from a collectivism culture such as Latin America is but one example of cultural complexity. Generally, Western individualism reflects independence and self-sufficiency. However, those from a more collective culture participate more easily in groups. Working together is not intuitive to the Western culture, resulting in duplicate organizations working to serve the same people and to solve the same problems. This leads Griffiths to suggest, "Western individualism multiplies organizations as a carcinoma multiplies cells—and with not altogether dissimilar pathological effect upon the Christian body."[283]

Adapting to these differences in order to successfully work together is not a concept of one culture changing to accommodate the other. Rickett suggests that a great deal of cultural accommodation does indeed occur and is most often one-directional, with non-Western ministries routinely accommodating their Western partners.[284] However, culture accommodation is not a healthy partnership. It is important, rather, to understand that because culture is man-made there is good and bad in all of it. Paragraph 10 of The Lausanne Covenant states, "Because man is God's creature, some of his culture is rich in beauty and goodness. Because he is fallen, all of it is tainted with sin and some of it is demonic."[285] Partners are wise to understand this concept and work diligently to learn and understand which of the other partner's cultural practices are "bad" and which are simply different. Likewise, one might find that some of the practices of one's own culture can appear very bad to another, but again are simply different. Elmer defines different as "all those things, which Scripture does not directly or in principle identify as sinful, wrong, or destructive," referencing Paul's handling of differences in Romans 14 and

---

[281] Melba Padilla Maggay. "Engaging Culture: Lessons from the Underside of History." *Missiology: An International Review,* Vol. 33 no. 1, January 2005, 62.
[282] Phillip Butler, "Kingdom Partnerships in the '90s: Is There a New Way Forward?" *Kingdom Partnerships for Synergy in Missions.* Ed. William D. Taylor (Pasadena, CA: William Carey Library, 1994), 20–21.
[283] Griffiths, vii.
[284] Rickett, Making Your Partnership Work, 78.
[285] Stott, Making Christ Known, 39.

1 Corinthians 8.[286] The partners must endeavor to recognize and acknowledge the differences while finding ways to coexist and work together in Christian humility.

An effective partnership relationship requires at least some understanding of one another's culture. Human nature is to be drawn to those that are similar. It is where humans feel safe and comfortable. Bush and Lutz observe, "Western and non-Western churches have been slow to understand each other's heartbeat and reluctant to speak openly and candidly."[287]

Trying to interpret meanings that others find in similar experiences can be difficult. Other cultures can seem to be at extremes, yet the meanings of these extremes when understood can reveal very similar aspects of each culture. For example, Richard H. Robbins, SUNY University Distinguished Teaching Professor of Anthropology at the State University of New York, College at Plattsburg, and Rachel Dowty, Visiting Assistant Professor in Emergency Management at the University of New Haven, Connecticut, write about the comparisons and similarities of a Balinese cockfight to the sport of football in North America. On the surface they are very different spectator sports, yet they reveal several similarities between the two cultures related to manhood, competition, and status.[288]

To successfully begin to understand other cultures, Robbins and Dowty, suggest that our task is to "take the abilities that have enabled us to dwell in our own culture and use them to understand the culture of others."[289] A starting point is the recognition and understanding that all members of human societies experience many of the same life events and face many of the same life challenges. While each culture may interpret these events and challenges differently, humanistically, they are basically the same. Hiebert reflects:

Without such universals, it would be impossible for people in one culture to communicate with people in another. In fact, recognizing our common humanity with other people is the first step in building the relationship of love and trust that can bridge the deep differences that separate "us" from "them."[290]

Sometimes, however, members maintain an unhealthy affinity for their own culture. It is the one with which they are the most familiar, and it is often the one they believe is "right." Robbins and Dowty call this belief in one's own culture the "ethnocentric fallacy - the idea that our beliefs and behaviors are right and true, whereas those of other peoples are wrong or misguided."[291] The U.S. provides a somewhat tragic example of ethnocentric fallacy. The nation has grown rapidly in wealth, power, and influence. This growth has led to an outward attitude of superiority when dealing with other cultures. Bush and Lutz recognize this as a cultural obstacle to mission partnership writing that "The belief that 'West is best' blinded us to the values found in other cultures..."[292] As a result, U.S. constituents

---

[286] Duane Elmer, *Cross-Cultural Connections: Stepping Out and Fitting in Around the World*, (Downers Grove, IL: InterVarsity Press Academic, 2002), 23.
[287] Bush and Lutz, 42.
[288] Richard H. Robbins and Rachel Dowty, *Cultural Anthropology: A Problem-Based Approach*. 7th Edition (Boston, MA: Cengage Learning, 2016), 23–28.
[289] Robbins and Dowty, 23.
[290] Hiebert, 23.
[291] Robbins and Dowty, 9.
[292] Bush and Lutz, 37.

must often overcome the picture of its culture during the early stages of the partnership formation rituals.

Cultural differences exist in every relationship. No two people have been shaped by reactions to the exact same experiences. They will therefore exhibit different understandings and behaviors in the face of similar current circumstances. Even a simple thing such as differences in the meanings and understandings of certain phrases or words can become detrimental to a relationship if members are unaware of these subtle differences and perspectives. Butler points out, "All of us have pre-conceived ideas of what certain words or phrases mean. Usually these are based on our experiences, not on dictionary definitions."[293] Newbigin illustrates the need to consider cultural context in language, explaining:

> In some cultures a dog is seen as a member of the household and an object of affection; in others it is primarily a scavenger and an object of contempt. The word 'dog' has distinctly different meanings in the two cultures, and the full meaning of the word can never be exhaustively specified.[294]

All of the partnership members' experiences and learned behaviors work toward the many cultural differences that must be considered for effective relationship building.

Church and Non-Church Partnerships

The church's inability to meet the ever-expanding holistic needs of a broken world has enabled a growing movement of non-church organizations to arise and begin to address areas of mission that have become neglected. Steve Corbett, Community Development Specialist for the Chalmers Center at Covenant College, and Brian Fikkert, Professor of Economics at Covenant College and founder and President of the Chalmers Center at Covenant College, suggest that while the biblical mandate to helping those in need (social service) is voluminous and somewhat clear, "the Bible gives Christians some freedom in deciding the extent and manner in which the local church cares for the poor, either directly or indirectly."[295] These non-church organizations are known by several names, such as parachurch organizations, relief organizations, holistic practitioners, and social compassion organizations. They can be government organizations or non-government organizations (NGOs). For purposes of this literature review, though not entirely accurate nor universally accepted, unless otherwise specified, the terms *parachurch* and *non-church* will be used interchangeably to denote non-church organizations that perform functions within a mission context.[296]

Parachurch organizations often find their origination in the holistic mission tasks of service and social responsibility. Padilla suggests also that they "find their reason for existence to the extent that they foster the church's organic growth and

---

[293] Butler, *Well Connected*, 254.
[294] Newbigin, The Gospel in a Pluralistic Society, 30.
[295] Steve Corbett and Brian Fikkert, When Helping Hurts: How to Allieviate Poverty without Hurting the Poor and Yourslf (Chicago, IL: Moody, 2012), 44.
[296] See previous definition of *parachurch*.

empower local churches for holistic mission."[297] Churches partnering with parachurch agencies gain access to valuable resources allowing them to address needs that they otherwise may struggle to meet. In his MTh dissertation, Jorma Kuitunen suggests that "Christian para-church development [organizations]… are holistic when they are… tools of holistic churches in their field of operations."[298] Padilla supports the collaborative nature of these arrangements between church and non-church organizations suggesting, "Service is better if it is integrated with other aspects of holistic mission, starting with the gospel of God's kingdom. Such integration frees the church to cooperate with secular entities for the common good, without neglecting Christian witnessing."[299]

Ringma suggests that "much of the concern and praxis of holistic mission is the domain of Christian development agencies and other parachurch organizations."[300] This assertion is noted in the previously cited study commissioned by Yamamori. Contributing to the Latin American study, Padilla reflects that "nearly all the projects are sponsored by parachurch organizations,"[301] an assertion that is consistent throughout the cases studied in other geographic areas.

Reflecting on these findings (and others), Ringma recognizes that parachurch organizations "can do much and are a rich resource… but they can't do everything and certainly cannot reflect the whole of God's missional concern for the world."[302] Accordingly, churches and parachurches must recognize their respective roles in a partnership relationship. Parachurch organizations tend to be specialists in a specific task or aspect of holistic mission, such as healthcare or education. As a result, parachurch organizations can generally take advantage of a greater array of resources and reach an economy of scale that a single local church can seldom attain. On the other hand, parachurch organizations must guard themselves from focusing solely on projects in isolation from the church, rather than being an agent of empowerment for the church to fulfill its holistic mission responsibilities.[303] As Kuitunen posits the parachurch organizations must get its Christian missional identity in congruence with the transformational missional Church.[304]

The interconnection between evangelism and social responsibility is not lost on mission leadership. Addressing the relationship between evangelism and social activity in LOP 21, the Lausanne Movement indicates that social activities "accompanies [evangelism] as its *partner*."[305] This LOP comment is not calling for organizational partnerships, rather suggesting that social activities can assist with evangelistic activities. In his Doctor of Ministry thesis for Northern Baptist

---

[297] C. René Padilla, "Holistic Mission in Theolgical Perspective." *Serving With the Poor in Latin America: Cases in Holistic Ministry,* Ed. Tetsunao Yamamori, *et al.* (Monrovia, CA: Marc Publications, 1997), 112.
[298] Jorma Kuitunen, The Missional Identity of Christian Development Organisations: Reflecting on the Evangelical Holistic Mission Debate as a Missional Identity-Strengthening Endeavor (MTh Dissertation, University of Wales, July 2015), 11.
[299] Padilla, "Holistic Mission in Theolgical Perspective," 115.
[300] Ringma, 435.
[301] Padilla, "Holistic Mission in Theolgical Perspective," 112.
[302] Ringma, 432.
[303] Padilla, "Holistic Mission in Theolgical Perspective," 112.
[304] Kuitunen, 66.
[305] Stott, *Making Christ Known,* 182, emphasis original.

Theological Seminary, Carlos Roberto De Oliveira evaluated this concept by looking at "holistic medical mission work" in Mexico and concluded that holistic Christian social activities (in this case, medical care) could play a key role in moving lost people toward God.[306] Like LOP 21, this work is not advocating an organizational partnership; rather, it is examining the role that Christian social activity performed through a medical missions team platform can play in enhancing evangelism and acceptance of the gospel message. De Oliveira goes on to describe several weaknesses of this manner of holistic mission done outside the church. Among these weaknesses, he includes the following:

- It is expensive and can often require resources not available locally.
- It is hard work, leading to long hours of serving the sometimes urgent medical needs. Missionaries can often work so hard at the physical that they compromise their own well-being as well as the holistic nature of the mission.
- It requires a high level of commitment from the missionary workers.
- It requires a means of follow-up, both medically and spiritually.
- Lack of discipleship.
- Lack of adequate facilities to do medical mission work.[307]

Mission leaders and scholars have begun to explore more formally the concept of partnership between churches and non-church organizations. In what Bush refers to as the "dawn of partnership,"[308] Article Eight of the Lausanne Covenant is entitled, "Churches in Evangelistic Partnership" and addresses the need for church partnership in mission. Article Nine of the covenant references the work of parachurch organizations. The Lausanne Movement also issued LOP 24, an extensive "handbook" on dealing with the relationships and related tensions between the church and parachurch organizations.[309] The predominant nature of this literature remains around partnering toward evangelism. For example, Stott offers his assessment of parachurch roles and responsibilities in his commentary of the Lausanne Covenant as that of specialty evangelistic, participating in activities such as Bible translation, Christian message mass media (television and radio) and Christian literature.[310] There are, however, missional authors that are beginning to explore mission partnerships in a more holistic manner, inclusive of other mission tasks beyond evangelism.

Myers uses the term *holistic practitioners* for "the Christians who promote basic transformational development."[311] He suggests that these practitioners are Christians with Christian character, and that they are professional. He explains

---

[306] Carlos Roberto De Oliveira, Breaking Down the Resistance to the Gospel Through Holistic Medical Missions: A Strategy for Reaching Resistant Rural Towns in Mexico (D.Min Thesis, Northern Baptist Theological Seminary, August 1999), 123–130.
[307] De Oliveira, 130–33.
[308] Bush, 4.
[309] Lausanne Movement, "Cooperating in World Evangelism: A Handbook on Church/Para-Church Relationships." March 1983. *Lausanne Occasional Paper No. 24.*
<https://www.lausanne.org/content/lop/lop-24> (accessed December 7, 2015).
[310] Stott, Making Christ Known, 35.
[311] Bryant L. Myers, "The Holistic Practitioner." *Serving with the Poor in Latin America: Cases in Holistic Ministry,* Ed. Tetsunao Yamamori, *et al.* (Monrovia, CA: Marc Publications, 1997), 136. He credits the term to Dr. Sam Kamaleson, former Vice President for Pastor's Conferences and Special Ministries at World Vision International, now retired.

professionalism when he writes, "God likes good work and so should we. We should never believe or act as if being a Christian is an excuse to be amateurish in our work."[312] Myers stresses the importance of spiritual formation in these holistic practitioners. He suggests that practitioner training should be "thought of as a kind of disciple-making—developing mature Christians with the best professional skills possible."[313]

Amy L. Sherman, a Senior Fellow at the Foundation for American Renewal, writes about collaboration between government and faith-based groups toward providing transformational services to those in need. She suggests that there is a need to move beyond a cost-saving "delivery system" model to more fruitful collaboration. The issue she maintains is that a simple cost-efficiency model "will not, in the long run, help the poor to help themselves."[314] She suggests that the collaboration model should build "not only on the cost-effectiveness of the faith-based ministries and churches... but on their unique strengths as religious organizations ministering holistically."[315]

Partnership Summary

Engel and Dyrness suggest, "A very different kind of missionary is required today—one who is willing to come in submission as an enabler, who serves by empowering others through an offering of much-needed gifts and skills that others do not possess."[316] There is a growing understanding that the world's holistic mission needs will not be met by people or organizations working in isolation; to do so will leave the harvest plentiful but the workers few (Matt. 9:37).

Many people doing mission in isolation share the same holistic concerns about the same groups of people. One ministry may desire increased health for a community, while another increased education. Such individual interests are not lost in partnership with others; they are rather reshaped into greater common goals for the shared common good. Both desire betterment of the community and social justice. Both are working together in order to share resources and to yield a potential result greater than the simple sum of the two (Eccl 4:9). As was remarked to Melba Padilla Maggay, "It's the common struggle that unites us; it's theology that divides."[317]

Mission leaders must be motivated by and motivated to the ultimate purpose of God's mission. It is this same purpose that motivates mission leaders to work together in collaborative relationships. Leaders must look beyond a view of their own ministries and ask how their gifts might be used to facilitate even greater missional gains when used in partnership with others in mutually shared mission.

---

[312] Myers, "The Holistic Practitioner," 133 and Myers, *Walking with the Poor*, 224.
[313] Myers, Walking with the Poor, 227.
[314] Amy L. Sherman, Restorers of Hope: Reaching the Poor in Your Community with Church-Based Ministries That Work (1997; repr., (Eugene, OR: Wipf&Stock, 2004), 206.
[315] Sherman, 206.
[316] Engel and Dyrness, 167.
[317] As quoted by Melba Padilla Maggay in "Engaging Culture: Lessons from the Underside of History," 67. Melba recounts a time when Sister Mary John Mananzan, feminist and President of the St. Scholastica College, made this remark to her while comparing notes on culture and activism in a conference on women's issues.

Plueddemann acknowledges the challenges and opportunities combined with a statement of hope when he writes,

> The good news is that leaders from around the world are partnering in ministry. We are all recognizing our blindness and are learning to be sensitive to the values of others. The continuing frustration often comes from the clash of leadership expectations between cultural values. Even though global cooperation will always be pestered by misunderstanding in this fallen world, a growing understanding, appreciation and harmony is possible and necessary.[318]

Perhaps Evelyn Eaton Whitehead, Developmental Psychologist (Ph.D., University of Chicago) whose work focuses on spiritual development in adult life and James D. Whitehead, theologian (Ph.D., Harvard University) who studies the interplay of religion and culture, summarize best the transformations that must take place to genuinely partner in cross-cultural mission endeavors:

> The promise of partnership stands as a challenge to us all. Personal transformation will be required as we open ourselves to the requirements of genuine interdependence. Structural transformation will be demanded as we bring our roles and rules into greater congruence with our deepest values. Through these transformations we will confirm again in our own time that ancient-yet-new image of the church: we are a priestly people called to be partners in the mission of Jesus Christ.[319]

While so much of mission seems stuck in denominationalism or theological division, secular organizations from sports teams to large complex businesses appear to understand that a combination of people and/or organizations with differing skills, talents and abilities working together is needed to produce greater results. Mission leaders have been slow to move from traditional means used to evangelize and minister to the masses, while at the same time the society has rapidly moved away from anything that resembles a Christian society. This rapidly changing secularized world demands more effective mission.

Summary

In this chapter, a review of relevant literature was presented for foundational understandings of holistic mission and Christian partnership in order to begin to form a foundational basis to evaluate Christian partnerships as a means to facilitate holistic mission.

First, literature was presented to understand the description, nature, and scope of holistic mission. This literature included a historical review of holistic mission, including the historic paradox between evangelism and social actions. Historical as well as contemporary views of holistic mission were presented to evaluate the richness of the various description of holistic mission and to establish a foundation

---

[318] Plueddemann, 212.
[319] Evelyn Eaton Whitehead and James D. Whitehead. *The Promise of Partnership: A Model for Collaborative Ministry* (Lincoln, NE: iUniverse.com, 2000), 176.

for determining a conceptual platform of mission as evangelism, formation, and service.

Next, literature was reviewed relating to Christian mission partnership. Partnership relationality was reviewed, stressing the need for strong vertical relationships with the Triune God and the Trinity as a model of interdependent relationships to be modeled horizontally. Partnership nature, form, and practical benefits, including relationships, roles, and motivations, were examined to understand how partnerships can be effectively created and maintained. Specific literature about mission partnerships between cross-cultural organizations and church and non-church partnerships was reviewed, illustrating the breadth of mission partnering possibilities.

Chapter 3

The making of a partnership

Introduction

This chapter lays the foundation for understanding the partnership between Total Health and the La Ceiba church and the characteristics that make it effective and successful. Chapter two examined the practical nature of partnership and revealed the many and various characteristics that scholars and partnership experts believe to be key principles for effective partnering. It is not surprising that the research data reflects a core set of practical leadership and partnership principles that were inherently foundational in the formation of Total Health and the resulting partnership. The Total Health board of directors consists of seasoned business executives, entrepreneurs, pastors, and doctors, all of whom are well versed in basic principles of working together. This chapter does not attempt to review each of these basic principles; rather it focuses on those principles that the study results show to be most significant to the success of the Total Health partnership.

The case study research findings revealed four principles that were consistently noted as key enablers to the Total Health partnership operational effectiveness and ultimate success: 1) having a common vision, 2) the authentic nature of the relationships between the partner members, 3) an interdependent and mutual relationship, and 4) the ability to work through cultural issues with sensitivity, patience, and grace.

This chapter will further define our concept of Christian mission partnership followed by a description of the Honduran context that gives rise to the need for partnership and the beginnings of the partnership collaboration.

Mission Partnership Further Defined

In its most basic terms, "partnership" is defined as "the ability to work together with another, sharing various resources, in order to achieve accomplishments which might not be achievable by working separately." The secular realm embraces this definition as a means to increased productivity and profitability.

Chapter two illustrates how several authors define partnership in a mission and ministry setting. Each of these definitions resembles the secular view of partnership with their general focus toward a more cost-effective and efficient means of accomplishing mission (primarily defined as evangelizing and serving). These definitions are problematic and incomplete if partnership is to facilitate holistic mission.

Inherent in Christian mission partnership is a significant tension between the mechanical/programmatic means of accomplishing tasks and the relational aspects of holistic mission. The mechanical view places priority on the desired quantifiable outcomes and the tasks to achieve those results. This narrow focus recognizes partnership solely as a way of adding resources as a means toward an end. A more holistic relational view recognizes the vast array of missional relationships created by the partnership that can exponentially expand the impact of the mission beyond the stated objective of the partnership. The following table illustrates and highlights the differences and incompleteness of the mechanical view versus the relational view of partnership.

Table 4 - Programmatic Partnership vs Relational Christian Partnership

Mechanical/Programmatic Partnership Focus	Relational Christian Mission Partnership Focus
• Places priority on the desired results and the tasks required to achieve those results – efficiency and productivity focused • Horizontal relationships over vertical relationships • Consumeristic – Mission recipients viewed as customers or targets • Dichotomy between "the Great Commandment" vs "the Great Commission" • Lacks a discipleship focus	• Kingdom focused – spiritual formation, discipleship, and spiritual maturity • Vertical relationship is primary – horizontal secondary • Holistic view of the interchangeable contexts of mission recipients and "missionaries" • Holistic mission – integrates "the Great Commandment" & "the Great Commission" • Recognizes discipleship opportunities throughout the missional partnership relationships

A definition of partnership must reach beyond the mechanical/programmatic aspects of achieving results and incorporate the holistic nature of the *missio Dei*. It must recognize that the supremacy of the vertical relationship provides for the effectiveness of the horizontal relationships ("apart from me you can do nothing" John 15:5). Accordingly, the following broadened definition of mission partnerships is put forward:

Mission partnerships are relationships of two or more people or organizations, who possess complimentary resources and skills, who have a common vision for Christian mission, and who, **orchestrated by the Triune God, join forces to participate holistically in God's mission.** The relationship of the partners to one another mimics that of the relationship of the Trinity through their unity with one another, their mutual love and respect for one another, and their mutual submission to one another.[320]

This definition broadens the mechanical definition of partnership beyond the accomplishment of tasks by recognizing the spiritual and relational nature of the mission partnership union in the context of holistic mission. In addition, this definition provides insights into the significant holistic mission value created by the relational nature of partnership and the broadened partnership aspects as depicted in the following table.

---

[320] Enoch Wan, *Diaspora Missiology: Theory, Methodology, and Practice 2nd Edition* (Portland, OR: Institute of Diaspora Studies of USA, Western Seminary, 2014:199-204.

Table 5 - Aspects of Relational Partnership vs Programmatic Partnership[321]

Partnership Aspects	Mechanical/Programmatic	Relational
Purpose	• Services to mission recipients, services related to felt or perceived needs	• Vertical and horizontal relationships, spiritual modeling, and spiritual & physical transformation
Focus	• Measurable goals • Quantifiable performance outcomes	• Building relationships into processes • Holistic mission
Strategy	• Efficiency oriented • Task and service oriented, transmission of mission tasks such as medical care and evangelism • Accomplishment focused	• Relational modeling • Relational teaching • Relational serving
Evaluation	• Statistical evaluation of productivity and performance	• Spiritual formation • Spiritual fruit
Goals	• Favorable outcomes • Ongoing plans & programs	• Vertical relationship – Glorifying God • Horizontal servanthood
Principles	• Systematic transmission of knowledge, skills, and services	• Relational modeling • Servanthood
Style	• Performance & efficiency • Managerial orientation	• Spiritual formation • Vertical & horizontal relationships
Procedures	• Organizational growth & expansion	• Kingdom orientation • Motivated by *missio Dei*.

This revised definition is not meant to diminish the need for successful mission tasks. Successfully completing that which God calls and directs the partnership to do remains critical. Revising the definition, however, does attempt to place mission tasks in their proper perspective relative to a relationship with God and God's full and complete mission. The relational nature of holistic mission requires such a dynamic view of mission partnership.

The Context and the Beginnings

The mission partnership between Total Health and the GCLA church in La Ceiba was born out of the tremendous spiritual and economical needs of the impoverished La Ceiba community and the desire of two men to minister to those needs. To

---

[321] Adapted from Wan, Diaspora Missions to international Students, 36.

understand these beginnings, one must first have a lens into the context of the community.

Honduras is a Central America country of approximately 9.2 million people. Its economy is one of the least developed in Latin America with more than 67 percent of all households living below the national poverty line. The rural areas are even more impacted, where 63 percent of those living in these areas experience extreme poverty.[322] Healthcare accessibility is primarily tied to one's income level. Those that can pay the prohibitive costs receive what care is available. Honduras citizens are entitled to government provided healthcare; however, widespread corruption and the weak national economy leave many without care. As recently as 1984, the ratio of doctors to the population exceeded 1 to 1,500.[323]

La Ceiba is Honduras' fourth-largest city and is situated on the Caribbean at the country's north border. Although it is a port community and boasts a tourist resort area, La Ceiba suffers from the same poverty and healthcare demographics as the entirety of the country.

Honduras was discovered by Christopher Columbus in 1502 and claimed for Spain. As Spain began its colonialization of Honduras, the indigenous people began to be baptized into the Catholic faith. As a result, the spiritual context in Honduras is predominately Roman Catholic. However, this has been progressing to evangelical and others as a result of intentional mission and evangelism. There are no reliable government statistics regarding religious affiliation; however, recent polls and surveys cited by the U.S. Department of State suggest that in 2002, the number professing to be Roman Catholic and evangelical Protestant was 63 percent and 23 percent, respectively.[324] More recently, in its 2018 Report on International Religious Freedom, the U.S. Department of State notes:

> The Roman Catholic Church estimates 63–65 percent of the population is Catholic. According to a 2016 survey by a local marketing research and public opinion company, 48 percent of respondents self-identified as evangelical Protestants, 41 percent as Roman Catholics, 3 percent as other, and 8 percent as unaffiliated.[325]

The impact of historical economic and spiritual impoverishment provides the primary impetus for holistic mission in Honduras. The country is poor and faces many physical needs that are not being met. In addition, Catholic colonialism resulting in a weak Catholic faith along with past indigenous religious practices have left the country spiritually deprived.

---

[322] Peter J. Meyer, "Honduras: Background and U.S. Relations." *U.S. Department of State, Congressional Research Service Reports (CRS) and Issue Briefs* (July 22, 2019). <https://www.fas.org/sgp/crs/row/RL34027.pdf> (October 10, 2019), 8.
[323] Tim Merril, ed. *Honduras: A Country Study* (Washington DC: GPO for the Library of Congress), 1995, 103.
[324] U.S. Department of State, *International Religious Freedom Report 2005: Honduras.* 2005. <http://www.state.gov/j/drl/rls/irf/2005/51644.htm> (December 29, 2015).
[325] U.S. Department of State, *2018 International Religious Freedom Report: Honduras* (June 21, 2019), <https://www.state.gov/reports/2018-report-on-international-religious-freedom/honduras/> (October 10, 2019).

Dagoberto Irias (Pastor Dago) was the lead pastor at the GCLA church in La Ceiba during the beginning of the Total Health collaboration. Born in Honduras, Pastor Dago was educated in the U.S. at the University of West Virginia, earning his Master's degree in forestry. A former member of the Honduran communist party, Pastor Dago came to faith while attending college. He returned to Honduras in 1989 to work as a forester in the abundant Honduran forests. Upon returning, he and his wife became active members of the GCLA church in the capital city, Tegucigalpa. Shortly thereafter, Pastor Dago moved his family to help with a small church plant in the La Ceiba community. In 1993, he was ordained and became part-time pastor of the church. By 1998, the church had grown to just 130 people.

Honduras experienced the devastating effects of hurricane Mitch in late October 1998. Over a two-day period, this slow-moving hurricane system made its way through almost the entire span of the country, leaving massive devastation in this already poor area of the world. It is estimated that more than 1.5 million people fell victim to the impact of the hurricane with up to 10 percent of the population becoming homeless.[326]

In the wake of the hurricane, Pastor Dago struggled to serve the many needs of the La Ceiba community. He and the church began welcoming and hosting short-term missionaries, primarily from the U.S., that were arriving to assist in the relief and recovery efforts. One such team was a short-term medical mission team sponsored by a church in New Jersey. Members of the community turned out in great numbers to be seen by the doctors and to receive care that they otherwise could not get. Pastor Dago recognized medical missions and healthcare as a great opportunity to present the church and to reach a higher number of people with the gospel message. People could receive both the spiritual healing and the physical healing that they desperately needed.

At about the same time, the Honduran government donated land to the church. Pastor Dago had visions of a church building, yet he believed that the community first needed a healthcare clinic. Simultaneously, the church received some funding from the New Jersey church to be dedicated to healthcare and a clinic building. Rapidly, a makeshift clinic was built that would provide the medical mission teams a more permanent place to practice. The clinic was completed in 1999, and the church began to host medical brigades whenever possible. These short-term teams brought doctors and much needed medicine, but the timing of the teams was sporadic and inconsistent.

It was about this same time that Jay E. Martin, MD, (Dr. Martin) a young Christian doctor in Columbus, Ohio, learned of La Ceiba's needs from the pastor of his church. An experienced medical missionary, Dr. Martin made the next trip to La Ceiba with his church and quickly felt the call to serve these people in great need. Subsequently, Dr. Martin began making regular trips on his own to serve in the La Ceiba clinic. While serving over the next several years, Dr. Martin became increasingly frustrated with the inability of short-term medical missions to increase

---

[326] United Nations Economic Commission for Latin America and the Carribean, "Honduras: Assessment of the Damage Caused by Hurrican Mitch, 1998." April 14, 1999. *United Nations Economic Commission for Latin America and the Carribean.* <http://www.cepal.org/publicaciones/xml/6/15506/L367-1-EN.pdf> (December 29, 2015), 9-10.

the overall level of health in the community. Short-term missionary healthcare, he believed, was not consistent enough to battle chronic diseases and to care for small traumas before they became emergencies. He began to search for a means of creating a more long-term solution.

Dr. Martin was equally concerned with the spiritual health of the community and the patients being served. He began to strategize ways to provide a consistent means of medical care using the newly constructed clinic building while also creating a strong relationship between the clinic and the church. Dr. Martin's desire was to support Pastor Dago's spiritual efforts while increasing the overall physical health of the community. Total Health was started with a purpose of supporting the church in La Ceiba by facilitating primary healthcare to the members of the community. Pastor Dago was immediately captivated by the idea and in 2004, a cross-cultural, mission partnership was born.

As pointed out earlier, parachurch organizations often find their origination in the holistic mission tasks of service and social responsibility. Likewise, Total Health found its origin in the mission to serve the La Ceiba community with primary healthcare. In addition, as Kuitunen suggests, Total Health recognizes its Christian identity within the missional goals of the La Ceiba church.[327] The organization was formed for just this purpose, to serve alongside the church, helping also to "foster the church's organic growth and empower local churches for holistic mission."[328]

Formed in 2004, the founding set of Total Health directors were comprised of two U.S. doctors (Dr. Martin and one other), an entrepreneur, a corporate executive (one of the authors), and a Latin American missionary pastor (Pastor Dago). This initial set of directors was well versed in leadership principles and experience, business and partnership practices, and Christian ethics. The group's experience provided the partnership with a foundation of the practical aspects of partnering.

The individuals in this initial group were selected by Dr. Martin based on the various experiences and skills that they could bring to the organization. However, common to each person selected were a set of common foundational Christian values and a heart to serve God's kingdom. This was not specifically related to mission work, rather a general heart to serve at whatever and wherever God called. One member, for example, had no mission experience at that time other than funding missions and hearing the stories. He had traveled little outside the U.S. and had experienced little diversity. He joined the organization not out of a great desire to help the impoverished people in La Ceiba, a desire that would come later. Rather, he joined with a heart to serve his brother in Christ toward success in his mission.

Common Vision

The partnership was born from the separate but common desires of Pastor Dago and Dr. Martin to holistically minister to the La Ceiba community. Their different backgrounds allowed these men to see the same needs from a different perspective, as well as how each of their gifts could be used to minister to those needs. Pastor Dago passionately wants to share the gospel with his community and will do whatever it takes to do so. He recognized the lack of community healthcare

---

[327] Kuitunen, 66.
[328] Padilla, "Holistic Mission in Theological Perspective," 112.

as not only a need of his community but also a means to show the gospel message in a tangible way. Dr. Martin, on the other hand, passionately wants to raise the physical well-being and health of the community. He recognizes, however, that physical health without spiritual health is not complete and is a false hope to the community. As a result, both Total Health and the La Ceiba church share a common vision of holistically ministering to the community. The name *Salud Total* (Spanish for *Total Health*) originated when the La Ceiba church first built the clinic building and is a reflection of Pastor Dago's desire to holistically minister to the community. Pastor Dago explains,

> After Hurricane Mitch we saw that the people were broken in every aspect: physically, emotionally and spiritually. It was not only a broken bone, people came just to cry on the shoulder of someone, it was suffering from a broken heart; and of course, they didn't know they were broken spiritually. And we saw the opportunity to serve them in every way. There are people that only needed to be heard about a child who is in a gang or a husband that has another woman. Our purpose is to be there for anything, and nobody leaves without being confronted with the Gospel.[329]

In a partnership relationship, each partner maintains its own identity and its own vision. Butler suggests that the "churches and other ministries involved must have their own clear mission statements and live by them. Otherwise, they will never understand how they 'fit in,' contribute to the overall picture, or benefit from the joint effort."[330]

A key component of the Total Health vision is to partner with Central American churches that desire a healthcare element to their vision of holistic mission. The common vision is the gospel message holistically expressed to the community in word and deed. Total Health does not enter a community to deliver healthcare without a means of spiritual care (i.e., the local church). Likewise, the local church desires that the healthcare partner place an equal emphasis on both the spiritual and physical care of the patient. The ultimate vision is the same: discipling people to Jesus Christ using evangelistic proclamation and acts of compassion. The roles and responsibilities of the partners are different yet interdependent in relation to achieving the ultimate vision. The partners are relying on one another to achieve the common goal of holistically ministering to a community in need.

In the Theological Preamble to the Lausanne Consultation's handbook, "Cooperating in World Evangelism," Stott suggests that the church and parachurch[331] exist in the "age-old tension between authority and freedom." He goes on to write that the committee suggests that for specialist organizations "independence of the church is bad, co-operation with the church is better, service as an arm of the church is best."[332] The Total Health board of directors has always practiced this concept and endeavored to make its partnership efforts consistent as an arm of the church. An early Total Health foreign missions vision document succinctly clarifies the vision, distinguishing the organization from a missionary

---

[329] Email correspondence with Pastor Dago Irias about the concept of Salud Total (Total Health).
[330] Butler, Well Connected, 320.
[331] In this case study, Total Health can be the "parachurch" reference for Stott's example.
[332] Lausanne Movement "Cooperating in World Evangelis," Theological Preamble.

organization. The document includes the clarification "We [Total Health] are a medical organization, but our work is done in partnership with missionary organizations [i.e., the local church] and allows them to effectively spread the gospel. We do not do any medical care outside of this type of partnership."[333] Partnering with Total Health allows the church to provide quality healthcare to its community in proximity to the church, thus the healthcare also becomes associated with the love of Christ through the church.

Plueddemann suggests, "The outcome of vision is transformed lives, demonstrating God's love in individuals and the church."[334] By recognizing their common vision, the mission leaders are motivated to partner, allowing Total Health and the church to combine resources and to impact the community in greater ways than either could do separately. Tizon illustrates that these "postcolonial global partnerships would demonstrate that the reconciliation the church offers to the world actually works!"[335]

Total Health's primary task is facilitating the provision of basic healthcare to residents in impoverished communities. Strategies are developed to best execute this task and the related results can be measured and analyzed. However, recognizing that the vision and goals of the organization must spring from God's ultimate purpose of leading people to a full relationship with God, one another, and all of creation, Total Health partners with a local church to ensure that the vision for spiritual care and the vision for physical care are equally aligned with God's holistic vision and mission. Working together allows the world to see unity in the Christian faith and puts the Christian works on display as living testimony.

God's vision is rarely quick and easy and not always flashy or immediately noteworthy. Yet here in the West, we live in a culture that longs for and chases the next best thing, the new and shiny. Many leaders are considered "visionary" because they dream up innovative ideas. The strong leaders, however, are those that not only start new ventures but see them through to completion. Being involved in the latest new adventure can be exciting, but most often it is better to treat the mundane to avoid the disaster.

Total Health got its start when its founder came to just this realization. On one of his earlier short-term medical mission trips, Dr. Martin treated a ten-year-old boy with a badly infected cut. It had started as just a small innocuous cut, but because the child had no access to medical care prior to Dr. Martin's arrival several weeks later it had become a dangerous infection that was spreading quickly. Dr. Martin realized that had there been a source of basic medical care available for this child earlier, administration of only fifty cents' worth of medicine would have avoided this disaster.[336] As he relates this story, Dr. Martin is fond of saying that "we [Total Health] treat the mundane to prevent the disastrous."

This is an example of a partnership motivated by a desire to build long-term capacity, not dependency. Facilitating needed primary healthcare alongside the other methods the church is using to minister to the community allows the

---

[333] Taken from the archived document "Total Health Foreign Missions Vision" written October 4, 2004.
[334] Plueddemann, 192.
[335] Tizon, 54.
[336] See the full account of Dr. Martin's story at www.totalhealth.org/our-story.

community's total well-being to strengthen. As the community's health and well-being increases so too does its ability and desire to provide value back to the community, thereby becoming less dependent. This not only provides transformational capacity to the community but is mutually creating capacity at the clinic through expanded medical services resourced by the community or when resources that are no longer needed are freed up to be allocated to other areas of mission need. The model is not without risk however, as the ever-pressing needs of the impoverished community tug at the heartstrings to provide relief. The partnership leaders are constantly faced with the challenge of focusing resources on developing long-term capacity versus providing short-term resources to meet immediate needs.

A Summary of the Relational Paradigm

The concepts of relationship are intertwined throughout the examples and explanations found in this book. The next sections deal specifically with aspects of relationship within the Total Health partnership. However, before proceeding to those sections we will take a brief excursion to introduce the important concept of the relational paradigm.

Neither holistic mission nor partnership happens without humans in relationship with other humans. In mission, one human "delivers" the mission to another human who "receives" the mission. More importantly, however is the human relationship with God and the work that God is doing in and through all the participants.

Embedded in the theoretical framework of partnership as a facilitator for holistic mission is that these relationships are the foundational reality for all that occurs. Wan captures the essence of relationship in his paradigm of relational realism when he stated," Ontologically, 'relational realism' is to be defined as the systematic understanding that "reality" is primarily based on the "vertical relationship" between God and the created order and secondarily "horizontal relationship" within created order.[337]

A relational paradigm in mission focuses on the relational networks between personal beings, both the vertical and horizontal relationships, and the missional interactions between them. Wan and Hedinger observe:

> The primary touch point for a correct understanding of reality is that <u>vertical relationship</u> (God and man within the divine-human relational network) is the fundamental issue of life: <u>horizontal relationship</u> (between created beings) is secondary. The Great Commandment is vertical and primary: to love God. The second commandment is horizontal and secondary: love your neighbor.[338]

Myers reinforces the primary importance of the vertical relationship:
The Holy Spirit empowers us for mission, leads us into mission, and is responsible for the results of mission. If there is to be any human transformation that is sustainable, it will be because of the action of the Holy Spirit, not the

---

[337] Wan, "The Paradigm of 'Relational Realism,'" 1.
[338] Wan and Hedinger, 38.

effectiveness of our development technology or the cleverness of our participatory process.[339]

Relationship and the relational paradigm will be at the forefront as we move forward through the remainder of this book. At the crux of holistic mission and partnership is the vast array of missional relationships across the spectrum of the holistic mission partnership. These relationships include not only the partnership members and those being served by the partnership, but also include each of their separate and overlapping spheres of influence. These relationships go beyond individual relationships and permeate the group and social interactions of all involved. In addition, as will be demonstrated in the next chapter, the individuals "receiving" the mission and those "delivering" the mission can change based on the context and the dynamics of those involved. These various horizontal relationships are evaluated using the relational paradigm as a theoretical framework, always recognizing the primacy of the vertical relationship.[340]

Partner Member Relationships

Most, if not all, partnership experts agree that the relationship between the partners is paramount to the effectiveness of the partnership. These experts, however, take varying views regarding the depth of these relationships. At the most basic level, the partners must be able to work together. The more practical partnership works of literature express practical ways to ensure that the members are communicating and resolving issues. Rickett, for example, advocates a concept that he calls "Alliance Champions," people within the partnership dedicated to working together on behalf of the partnership.[341] In general, this concept reflects a very businesslike perspective on relationship and is representative of how business schools might teach relationship. This concept, however, lacks an emotional bond of one member to another that is often reflected in effective mission relationships.

Effective horizontal relationships within the partnership should mirror that of a relationship within the Trinity. Each member of the Trinity has a distinct identity, a distinct relationship with one another, as well as distinct roles and responsibilities. God the Father is the grand architect of the mission, *missio Dei,* as he works through history to direct his plans. The Father sends the Son to reveal, inaugurate, and commission the mission here on earth. From an earthly mission perspective, the Son was sent by the Father to reveal and witness to the Father, and to demonstrate kingdom living as it is meant to be. Jesus was the incarnation of the Father's designed mission, and finally, the culmination of the Father's plan for redemption and reconciliation. God the Spirit is the continuing empowerment and influencer for the on-going earthly mission activities. The following table illustrates the partnership dynamics within the Trinity.

---

[339] Myers. Walking with the Poor, 84.
[340] For a thorough and complete explanation of the relational paradigm see Wan and Hedinger, 17-60.
[341] See Rickett, *Making Your Partnership Work,* 63–73. Rickett suggests that the Alliance Champion has seven key responsibilities for the partnership: building rapport, providing leadership, clarifying expectations, keeping things simple, keeping communications flowing, going the distance, and keeping God at the center. Other than keeping God at the center, these are very businesslike responsibilities and lack an emotional relationship factor.

Table 6. - Partnership Within the Trinity[342]

Relationship and Role	God the Father	God the Son	God the Spirit
Partner Relationship	Godhead Supreme	Obedient & Submissive to the Father, Sent by the Father	Empowers, Sent by Father & Son
	Ps. 2:2, 1 Cor. 15:28	John 5:30, 6:38-40, Phil. 2:6-8	John 14:26, Acts 1:8
Role in Created Order	Grand Architect & Designer	Reveal the Plans of the Father & Reign over Earth	Teach and Lead Believers
	Eph. 1:9-12	John 17:26, Eph. 1:22-23	John 14:26, Acts 13:2
Role in Mission	*missio Dei* - Grand Architect & Direct the Mission	Inaugurate & Define the Earthly Mission	Empowering Witnesses, Imparting Gifts
	The grand narrative of the entire Bible	John 20:21, Matt. 28:18-20	Acts 1:8, 1 Cor. 12:7

The success of the mission partnership is highly dependent upon the quality of the relationships between the partners. These relationships within the partnership should mimic those of the Trinity. There should be unity, the partners should enjoy one another, there should be a mutual respect for the others' roles and responsibilities, and a healthy submission to one another's authority as responsibilities are undertaken. With regard to the local context, the local church should play the role of mission architect. The local church knows the needs of its community and the best means to witnessing to the gospel message. The other partners should submit to this knowledge and experience. On the other hand, the non-church partner is most often a specialist in the type of ministry for which they are called (healthcare, in the case of this study). The local church should allow the non-church partner liberty in carrying out this aspect of the mission. The non-church partner, however, has the responsibility to ensure that its element of the mission activities provide witness to Christ and the gospel message. The table below illustrates the dynamics of the mission partnership roles and responsibilities as these roles mimic that of the Trinity.

---

[342] Parts of this table are adapted from Wan and Penman, "The Trinity: A Model for Partnership in Christian Missions."

Table 7. - Mission Partnership Roles and Responsibilities

Relationship and Role	Local Church Partner	Non-Church Partner
Partner Relationship	Must be included as a partnership leader.	Supportive to local church by using their Spiritual Gifts.
	Establish vision for local mission.	Provides specific ministry to support the needs of the local community as determined by the local church.
Role in Mission	Grand vision and biblical direction.	Supply specific ministry needs such as healthcare, education etc. in a display of Christian deeds.
	Determine how best to deliver the gospel message to the local context.	Insure that the ministry of deeds compliments the ministry of word and points to the local church and the gospel.

Relationships that mimic the Trinity go beyond a business-like working relationship. Sider, *et al.*, take the partner relationship further when they list "authentic relationship" as one of their three "absolute essentials" and call it an "indispensable principle" to partnership, especially those partnerships that cross cultures.[343] They describe authenticity as "a relationship that goes beyond toleration of one another"[344] and suggest a sign of this authenticity is that the relationships "go beyond the business of ministry as it begins to work itself out during the off hours."[345] Wan highlights seven relationship principles that can be derived from the model of the Trinity for the practice of mission and ministry partnership as illustrated in the table below:

---

[343] Sider, *et al.*, *Linking Arms, Linking Lives,* 66, 69–72. The authors list three "absolute, irreducible minimums" to partnership; deep reconciliation, authentic relationship, and collaborative action.
[344] Sider, et al., Linking Arms, Linking Lives, 70.
[345] Sider, et al., Linking Arms, Linking Lives, 72.

Table 8. - Partnership in Light of the Trinity[346]

Principles	Practice of Ministerial Partnership
1. Relationship	Know, confer, plan with one another
2. Unity	Spiritual unity leading unity of goal
3. Diversity	Difference in gifting and distinct roles
4. Interdependence	Not self-sufficient
5. Love	Self-sacrificial love within the Trinity and beyond
6. Peace	Harmony; freedom from anxiety and inner turmoil
7. Joy	Christians are to be joyfully serving God and others

Inherent in relationships that reach this level are all the common relationship attributes that a businesslike relationship strives to attain. Trust, honesty, and dependability, for example, are characteristics found in businesslike relationships. However, these characteristics can exist superficially and can break down easily in the face of adversity. Elmer suggests that some people believe that understanding people from another culture is a waste of time... These people see the job as a task to be done with little or no concern for genuine relationships with local people. A strong task orientation without first establishing friendships can lead to disappointing if not disastrous outcomes.[347]

Authentic relationships (using Sider's term) go much deeper than superficial relationships formed simply to do business with one another. These deeper relationships include the attributes of a loving brotherhood and sisterhood, deference to one another, and humility among and between the partner members. This creates a desire to see one another prosper, not just in the purpose of the mission but in their respective personal lives as well. It allows the members to see and think the best in one another even during times of conflict.

Bush suggests these are the types of relationships in line with the biblical partnership theme of Philippians, "Joy in Christian Partnership."[348] He goes on to illustrate that this relationship was marked by a love that Paul had for the Philippians, suggesting the intimacy of the partnership relationship is best characterized by Paul's closing words, "Therefore, my brothers and sisters, you whom I love and long for, my joy and crown... dear friends" (Phil. 4:1).[349] This is the type of relationships that exist to varying degrees between the Total Health partnership members.

The results of these deep relationships are manifest in several examples of how business is conducted in the Total Health partnership. For example, numerous examples of passive aggressive behaviors can be illustrated in both secular business as well as mission and ministry practice. These behaviors can be so pervasive as to taint one's perspectives regarding the motives of others. However, experiencing the authentic relationships with others within the Total Health organization and the

---

[346] Enoch Wan, *Diaspora Missiology: Theory, Methodology, and Practice 2nd Edition* (Portland, OR: Institute of Diaspora Studies of USA, Western Seminary, 2014), 200.
[347] Elmer, Cross-Cultural Connections, 13.
[348] Bush, "In Pursuit of True Christian Partnership," 5.
[349] Bush, "In Pursuit of True Christian Partnership," 12.

partnership allows one to move past whatever cynical thoughts they may have and on to appropriate realizations regarding the pure motives of those involved.

In another example, a specific project brought to the board for approval was denied. The discussions were honest and open, and though there was disagreement, there was no disrespect or ill will. In the end, each person involved participated with humility and deference to one another, with a clear focus on the partnership's calling and common vision.

The previous two examples illustrate these relationships as they are displayed in business situations. However, consistent with Sider's terminology and definition above as well as the implications Bush makes in his Philippians example, the relationships between the Total Health partner members span more than the business of the partnership into true Christian friendship. Perhaps the best illustration of the dynamics of these relationships is reflected in a story involving Pastor Dago and Dr. Martin, two founders of the partnership and now long-time friends.

In a freak accident, Pastor Dago fell and completely shattered his elbow. With available treatment in Honduras, his prognosis was limited. It was expected that Pastor Dago's elbow would be frozen in place and unable to bend, thus he would have limited use of his arm. Dr. Martin learned of the accident and asked Pastor Dago to send him the x-rays and other pertinent medical information.

Upon obtaining the information, Dr. Martin reached out to some of his medical colleagues in the U.S. for advice. Astonishingly, a surgeon, a hospital, and a medical team stepped in and volunteered to perform an operation to repair the shattered elbow at no cost. However, the surgery and related recovery would require that Pastor Dago remain in the U.S. for an extended period of time. To facilitate this treatment and recovery, Dr. Martin opened up his home to Pastor Dago, his wife, and his youngest son for as long as it would take to complete the surgery and rehabilitation. Pastor Dago remarks about this time, "what happened in those three months we spent in Jay's home is not a 'Ministry-business.' Jay, Roberta, their kids, the GPC family [Grace Point Church, Dr. Martin's home church] did something that in the regular world you don't see even within a blood-family."

Mission partnerships can certainly function on a businesslike relational level and a businesslike structure is required to efficiently manage the practical activities of the partnership. However, mission partnership and the ability to work together with one another gets its foundation from and flows out of friendships like these.[350] These relationships allow the partnership to move forward in genuine, trusting collaboration, avoiding the often political and individualistic nature of superficial business relationships. They allow the partner members to seek and see the best in one another as they work together toward achieving the common vision and goals. Though the work flows out of friendship, friendship is not the ultimate goal. It is a foundation on which to build. Friendships are formed for the good of the friends. However, friendships, in mission partnership are formed for the benefit of the mission.

---

[350] Sider et al., Linking Arms, Linking Lives, 72.

Mutuality and Interdependence

There was no formal written partnership agreement between the two organizations to form the partnership, nor does one exist currently. The relationship, however, cannot be described as an informal collaboration. The partnering members worked diligently to ensure that a clear set of responsibilities were established very early in the relationship, and though the group did not establish a formal set of guidelines per se, many of the practical foundational characteristics espoused by the "experts" are evident in the formation and evolution of the Total Health partnership. The collective experience of the partner members has consistently been a means of recognizing effective business, partnership, and mission principles.

A key aspect of developing these early set of responsibilities was the complementary concepts of mutuality and interdependence, especially in the area of economic support for the healthcare aspect of the mission. From the outside, the partnership can appear to be a simple funding arrangement, with the wealthy U.S. agency funding the ministry needs of the impoverished Latin American church. Given this funding relationship, Total Health would perceivably hold a structural power advantage in the partnership relationship. Lederleitner suggests that such a disparity of affluence can create a lack of mutuality in the partnership.[351] From a funding perspective, the partnership economics can seem unbalanced in regard to the funding Total Health provides via its donor base.

The partnership relationship is not without reciprocity, however. The church provides and bears the costs of maintaining the clinic facility, including economically quantifiable contributions such as utilities, building maintenance, and taxes. Thus, the economics of the mission are shared by the partners, not monetarily equally, but mutually burdened. As a result, both partners feel the economic burden of the mission and each is accountable to the other for their respective share of costs.

The leaders also recognized the importance for the community to have a sense of ownership in the clinic as well. They did not want the community to view the clinic as a "handout" from the wealthy North Americans. Over time, using the relationship principles for serving the poor put forth by Corbett and Fikkert,[352] the organization landed on a goal that economic support could be equally realized from three categories of participants: one-third from Total Health, one-third from the church, and one-third from the local community.

Corbett and Fikkert point out that working with the poor should provide a means of empowering the poor to make decisions about their life and how to use their resources, to act upon their decisions, and to evaluate the results of those decisions.[353] Accordingly, patients are expected to pay a small fee (approximates $2.00) for the doctor or dentist services at the clinic (those that cannot afford to do

---

[351] Lederleitner, 123.
[352] Per Corbett and Fikkert, the primary principles related to working with the poor and alleviating poverty deal with the recognition that poverty is a result of broken relationships caused by the fall of humanity. These relationships include the superiority complexes of those that seek to help the poor. Key principles include recognizing what the poor can contribute and allowing them to do so in order to alleviate shame and to build self-esteem.
[353] Corbett and Fikkert, 137.

so are still seen and treated). This helps empower the community to make their own decisions and evaluations of their medical needs. It is also important for the local community to recognize the value of the clinic service. Requesting payment for their medical services helps prevent abuses of the clinic services.

Economic support, however, does not always take the form of monetary contribution. Volunteer time supplied by the community provides just as meaningful economic value as monetary funding when it alleviates the need to pay for a service. See the table below for a breakdown of how the economics to support the clinic operations are shared.

Table 9. - Shared Economic Responsibilities for La Ceiba Clinic Operation

Total Health – U.S.	La Ceiba Church	La Ceiba Community
Funding for specific clinic staff and medications for the provision of primary care. A source of medical training and logistical support.	Provide the clinic facility, including maintenance, utilities, taxes, etc. Provide certain administrative functions such as payroll and HR administration.	Small payments for medical services (if possible). Volunteer services to the clinic. A means of protection for the clinic and the church.

Interdependence and mutuality extend beyond the economics. Each partnership member brings a set of gifts, talents, and knowledge that the other depends upon to fully execute the common vision. The U.S. organization relies on the La Ceiba organization for things such as local insights into patient care, local personnel administration, the needs of the community, language skills, and local logistics. The local La Ceiba church relies on the U.S. organization for things such as medical advice, sourcing of medicine and supplies, medical specialists (in the form of short-term medical mission teams), and other administrative actions.

The partnership leaders recognize the interdependence and the combined value of the partners toward evangelistic motives. This point was crystalized in a recent partnership leader meeting in La Ceiba, Honduras, when the current La Ceiba pastor stated that he views Total Health as an "equal partner" in evangelism and the spiritual care of his community. He also adds, "We [the La Ceiba church] see ourselves as a necessary component in the goal of Total Health." It is this interdependence between Total Health and the church that serves to mimic Jesus' healing ministry.

Mutuality does not end with the recognition of the gifts and talents that each partner brings to the partnership. There is also a mutual recognition of the needs that each partner may bring and how the partners can work together to alleviate those needs. The administrator position funded by Total Health can serve as an example.

The Total Health leaders realized that they would need an administrator to manage operations locally in La Ceiba, so the first position that they funded was an administrator position that managed the clinic, coordinated mission trips, and other related activities as required. However, as the La Ceiba church began to grow, this person also became a leader in the church and began to also spend time administrating various similar activities for them. The leaders at Total Health recognize that they are funding a position that is no longer fully devoted to their own organization. They continue to do so in the spirit of the partnership.

In a separate GCLA strategy and planning meeting (the GCLA umbrella organization, not the La Ceiba church), one of the GCLA leaders realized this situation and asked why Total Health was willing to do this. It was explained with affirmation that Total Health and the GCLA church were in this mission together. Funding this position benefits both partners and it is in the partnership's best interest that both partners grow stronger together. Being able to meet this need provides strengthening to the church that also benefits Total Health.

This mutual interdependency model is not without risks if not proactively planned and managed. Lederleitner warns against a model that assumes an interdependent partnership into perpetuity suggesting that "we [Total Health] cannot assume that we will always be able to fund" a share of the partnership. There should be an alternative backup plan should the funding dry up. If the structure is such that it is perceived to always need funding, i.e., never reaching independent state, the structure may not be sustainable. The question she suggests is "How would you have created the structure on your own" assuming no additional funding?[354] The partnership board of directors has discussed the sustainability of the current economic structure. However, given the extreme impoverishment of the La Ceiba community, it is difficult to imagine an independence scenario in the near future.

Working Through Cultural Issues with Sensitivity, Patience, and Grace

Cultural differences exist in every relationship and more so in cross-cultural relationships such as the Total Health partnership. Each member has been shaped by his or her own experiences and will therefore exhibit different understandings and behaviors in the face of similar current circumstances. These experiences and learned behaviors manifest in the cultural differences that must be considered and addressed for a partnership to effectively facilitate holistic mission achievements.

Anthropologists label people as cultural insiders or outsiders based on their relative relationship to a specific culture. In a cross-cultural partnership, however, members are at once a cultural insider and a cultural outsider within the partnership. They are insiders to their own culture and partnership specialty while operating as outsiders alongside those coming from another culture or perspective. Charles Kraft, American anthropologist, and Professor Emeritus of Anthropology and Intercultural Communication in the School of Intercultural Studies at Fuller Theological Seminary, suggests that the diversity of insiders and outsiders working together can strengthen both:

> [Insiders] have... an understanding that outsiders rarely attain, though insiders can often be quite naïve in their understandings and evaluations [of their own context]. Outsiders, however, if they learn to understand and appreciate the insider's point of view, can often be very helpful in the process of cultural

---

[354] Phone interview with Dr. Mary Lederleitner conducted Monday, November 20, 2017.

evaluation, for informed outsiders can often see certain things more clearly than the insiders themselves.[355]

The U.S. operating leaders of the Total Health organization are cultural outsiders to those that they seek to serve, as well as to those they serve alongside. As such, leading the organization requires deferring some of the leadership and decision making to those on the inside, to those with the inside knowledge. Gordon suggests that "those who live in the neighborhood [insiders] should be the ones to identify their own needs as well as determine what kind of help is necessary."[356] Local medical team leadership is paramount to the Total Health partnership. From the onset, the U.S. doctors and partnership leaders recognized that the local team has a more complete understanding of the medical needs of their own community and are more knowledgeable about local patient practices. As a result, the partnership has a structure of a local medical team that makes decisions based on the needs. This structure facilitates efficiency in things such as determining what medicines to purchase, thereby avoiding costly ordering mistakes and better serving the patient base.

Cultural differences can be reflected to some extent in almost all areas of human interaction, especially when that interaction crosses some form of major cultural border. The Total Health partnership crosses cultural borders as members from the U.S. and Central America partner with one another. The partnership also adds the complexities of a church partnering with a non-church organization. There are many differences between the Honduran (Latin American) culture and that of the U.S. Several of these more major areas of differences are captured in the following table.

---

[355] Charles H. Kraft, *Anthropology for Christian Witness* (Maryknoll, NY: Orbis, 1996), 76–77.
[356] Wayne L. Gordon, "Personal Words from the Authors," in Sider *et al.*, *Linking Arms, Linking Lives*, 24.

Table 10. - Latin American - U.S. Cultural Differences[357]

Cultural Difference Descriptor	Latin American Ranking	United States Ranking
Power Inequality Hierarchy vs. Equality	Trend toward hierarchy	Trend toward equality
Need for Structure Uncertainty Avoidance	Trend toward structure – low risk	Trend toward Less structure
Social Orientation Individual vs. Group	Highly group oriented	Highly individualistic (highest country studied)
Universalism-Particularism Rules vs. Loyalty	Trend toward loyalty	Trend toward rules and laws
Communication Explicit vs. Implicit	Highly implicit	Highly explicit
Space and Time	Close personal space - always enough time	Protective personal space - time is money
Formality	Trend toward formal interactions	Trend to more casual interactions

In the very beginning of the Total Health partnership, the partner members acknowledged that cultural differences exist. However, much like Butler suggests, the leaders did not recognize the full extent of these differences nor the nature of their manifestations.[358] Intellectually knowing that there will be cultural differences is much different than actually working through such differences.

Knowing that there would be differences, the team took steps to prepare to identify and work through them. The initial board of directors at Total Health included Pastor Dago to ensure that the Central American perspectives would be present in strategy discussions and the decision-making process. In addition, key strategy and planning meetings were held in Honduras in order to include other Central American leaders such as church leaders, medical professionals, and administrators. Taking these actions provided a foundation for recognizing and dealing with cultural issues as they developed.

However, as Maggay, suggests, "Increased cross-cultural contact does not necessarily lead to cross-cultural understanding."[359] The partnership members could fall into what Robbins and Dowty call the "ethnocentric fallacy - the idea that our beliefs and behaviors are right and true, whereas those of other peoples are wrong or misguided."[360] The partnership leaders fought against this fallacy with a humble spirit and, perhaps more importantly, approached one another as learners, seeking insights into one another's cultures and learning from mistakes along the way.

---

[357] Adapted from Thomas H. Becker, Doing Business in the New Latin America: A Guide to Cultures, Practices, and Opportunities (Westport, CT: Praeger Publishers, 2004), 116–36.
[358] Butler, "Kingdom Partnerships in the '90s," 20–21.
[359] Maggay, 62.
[360] Robbins and Dowty, 9.

Several of the partnership leaders (both U.S. and Central American) cite increased intercultural understanding and sensitivity as an area of growth in their lives as a result of being a part of this collaboration. Dr. Martin also readily acknowledges the "considerable grace" given to him from the Central American leaders when he began the process of starting Total Health.

Despite all of the planning and steps taken to avoid cultural difference issues, situations invariably occur. Years of experiences have so ingrained personal behaviors and responses that actions can take place instinctively, almost unknowingly. The manner in which these cultural issues can build upon one another and intertwine heightens complexity for the leadership team to manage through issues that arise. It takes time, effort, and experiences together to learn to mitigate and work through the deeper aspects of these learned differences.

One of the more difficult cultural differences to overcome in a partnership between the West and non-West can be the perspective of power equality. Power inequality relates to the degree in which a culture views various groups and the acceptance of the distribution of power and authority within them.[361] Thomas H. Becker, economic development authority and former President of the Business Association of Latin American Studies, observes that cultural rankings suggest that "relative to the typical Anglo, who tolerates authority, the average Latin respects authority, accepting as a given Latin America's large difference in power."[362] The Latin American culture expects that there is a hierarchy of power and has learned to respect those that are in authority. Society is viewed as a hierarchical pyramid, leadership at the top and the masses at the bottom. A person's place in the structure is dependent on birth, and the hierarchically structured society requires that each person recognize his or her position in society and his or her related dependency relationships.[363]

Whereas the Latin American person recognizes his or her place in the hierarchy, conversely, people in the U.S. view equality as an equal opportunity for all to move beyond a predetermined social status. Citing treatment of Blacks and women, Becker observes that though the U.S. culture makes a claim to equality it "does not mean that society always puts it into practice."[364] Even in hierarchical situations such as the workplace, those in the U.S. culture will make efforts to make the hierarchy appear more equal.

Further complicating matters is the issue that those in the U.S. typically are more adequately funded and may seem to be bringing more resources to the relationship. On the other hand, the Latin Americans view hierarchy as normal and accept it. However, the Latin Americans may be more knowledgeable about the mission and therefore expect a more equal part in the partnership.

Bush and Lutz illustrate how distorted this partnership equality picture might appear, writing, "To some, partnership resembles the famous 'safari stew' which

---

[361] Geert Hofstede, Gert Jan Hofstede, and Michael Minkov, *Cultures and Organizations: Software of the Mind: Intercultural Cooperation and Its Importance for Survival* Revised and Expanded 3rd Edition (New York, NY: McGraw Hill, 2010), 60-62. Becker, 117.
[362] Becker, 117. See also Hofstede, Hofstede, and Minkov, 58-59.
[363] Eugene A. Nida, Understanding Latin Americans: With Special Reference to Religious Values and Movements (Pasadena, CA: William Carey Library, 1974), 29.
[364] Becker, 127.

calls for equal parts elephant and rabbit: one elephant and one rabbit."[365] The U.S. is represented by the elephant with its vast resources, and the Latin Americans must deal with this large partner. However, Bush and Lutz suggest that partnership equality requires a new attitude and definition of equality, remarking that it "has little to do with size, amount of resources, or power. But has everything to do with attitude, values, and status."[366] Often money and resources result in a disproportion power distribution because they are overvalued. What is more important is a relationship built on true, trustful collaboration, where each member trusts that the other will listen respectfully without negative repercussions toward an expressed opinion. A significant learning experience occurred very early in the Total Health partnership that proved pivotal to highlighting these issues and moving the team forward to a much more effective functioning partnership.

Early in the partnership, a U.S. doctor approached Total Health with a desire to donate an x-ray machine for the La Ceiba clinic. The organization jumped at the opportunity to secure a valuable piece of medical equipment and accepted the offer. The team then set about the process of dismantling, shipping, and reassembling the machine in Honduras. After a lengthy process, the machine was operational in the Honduran clinic and ready to be used to serve the patients.

Fast-forward approximately twelve months. The x-ray machine is rarely if ever used. It sits in a room that is used more for storage than anything else. On the large x-ray table sits several boxes of supplies and miscellaneous items with no apparent purpose. The film room has been basically turned into a janitor's closet with few film supplies. In essence, the machine has become a large piece of unwanted equipment taking up space that could be used for something else. What happened?

The Total Health partnership leaders believed that they had addressed the power equality issue through the steps previously mentioned as well as open and honest conversations regarding decision-making responsibilities. What the leaders failed to realize, at least initially, was how deeply rooted the behaviors are that lead to this difference. They also failed to identify that behavior that may appear to be driven by power equality perspectives may in fact be entirely motivated by other experiences.

In this example, the U.S. team was excited about the possibility of increasing the clinic's ability to serve the patients with this new machine. The local medical team had not rejected the idea, and the U.S. team assumed that the locals were similarly as excited. On the surface, it appeared that the power issue had been addressed and that all parties agreed. However, there were deep rooted experiences beyond the power equality perspective that may have been driving behaviors.

The leaders of the La Ceiba church are used to short-term relationships. They are accustomed to churches and organizations working with then for short periods of time and then moving on. This insecurity plays into their behavior trait of a reluctance to say "no" to any idea, even the bad ones. They do not want to risk offending their partner, potentially resulting in the partner going elsewhere to serve someone more agreeable. Accordingly, they went along with the x-ray machine idea.

Had there been more discussion with an active listening approach from the U.S. team and some further investigation, the team would have realized some key

---

[365] Bush and Lutz, Partnering in Ministry, 48.
[366] Bush and Lutz, Partnering in Ministry, 48.

factors that were omitted in the decision-making process. First and foremost, the on-going operational costs of the x-ray machine would prove to be prohibitive to the clinic. The costs of the film development and supplies and incremental electricity costs were not factored into the decision. In addition, the lack of experience and infrequent use played into inefficiencies and even more incremental costs.

This situation could have damaged the relationships between the U.S. and the La Ceiba partners and resulted in a degradation of the future decision-making process. Each partner could easily have looked at their own disappointments and rationalized their own behaviors to the detriment of the others. However, the foundation of authentic relationship that they had been working hard to solidify served as a platform toward recognizing this as an opportunity to grow stronger rather than allowing it to drive relationships apart. These relationships allowed the partnership leaders to examine the situation, realizing that they all had the best of intentions, however, without the greatest of implementations. Viewing this as a learning opportunity and a means to get better, the partnership leaders came away from this experience with key insights into the biases and concerns that drive one another's behaviors and key learnings that would serve the partnership well into the future.

The U.S. team humbly acknowledged that their quest to "help" had blinded them to the realities of the La Ceiba context and the impracticalities of their actions within that context. It further crystalized the need to rely on local knowledge and experience in the development of plans and strategies. This experience also gave the U.S. partners a much greater appreciation of the depth of the La Ceiba leaders' desire to "please" the U.S. team. This desire stems not only from a power equality perspective but also from a mission partnership perspective. The La Ceiba leaders recognized the significant benefits to the community, and as a result, they wanted to take every step possible to maintain the Total Health relationship. Accordingly, there became a recognized need to reassure the La Ceiba leaders that Total Health was joining with them for the long-term in what Sider, et al., call a "real and faithful presence" in their community.[367]

The partnership leaders handled what could have very well been a divisive issue with sensitivity, patience, and tremendous grace. The experience taught the U.S. team the need for a more active collaborative approach that involves more thorough understanding of the local context and reinforced to the La Ceiba team the importance of their opinions and thoughts in the process, emphasizing that they are the experts in their community. In many ways, this experience was a significant building block to the future success of the partnership.

Evidence that these learnings were put into practice can be found in another example that has a somewhat different ending. The clinic building had been built as economically as possible. The building consisted of stark, unpainted cinder block walls, a concrete floor, and a metal roof. As the mission progressed, the La Ceiba team expressed a desire to enhance the appearance of the building and to make it more comfortable to the patients. There was a hesitancy on behalf of the U.S. partners to spend the money for the enhancements, citing other pressing needs. The discussion could have ended there if not for the culturally sensitive transformations related to past experiences.

---

[367] Sider, et al., Linking Arms, Linking Lives, 101.

Through the discussions, the U.S. partnership team was reminded of some of the objectives of holistic mission. The poor suffer from feeling devalued and marginalized and need to understand that they are made in God's image and are his children. They also need to believe that they are valued and can contribute to God's creation.[368] Holistic mission strives to reconcile this broken relationship with one's self and seeks to restore dignity and to remind the poor that they are made in God's image. The U.S. partners began to realize that a tangible way to do that was to show the patients that they are important enough to have a nice place to come to see the doctor.

Ultimately the money was spent, and the clinic appearance was enhanced. This outcome is reflective of the learnings gained through the x-ray experience. The La Ceiba team felt empowered enough to continue the discussion despite the initial rejection by the U.S. members. The U.S. members on the other hand exhibited a willingness to listen and an appropriate level of humility to recognize the true nature of the mission.

These are but two examples of cultural differences that the partnership leaders addressed and worked through. The favorable outcomes, however, can be directly attributable to the leaders' commitment first to authentic relationship. The work put into formation of authentic relationships created the foundation to effectively address these cultural differences.

Summary

The need for a mission partnership holistically serving the La Ceiba community is evident by its spiritual and economic impoverishment. The Total Health partnership was born out of the common vision and shared sense of mission to serve this community. The founders of the partnership recognized that the tasks were too numerous and too difficult to effectively address alone and that they are better together.

However, having a common vision, while imperative for partnership, is not a guarantee of success. Tizon writes that Christians involved in Western—non-Western ministry partnerships "must strive toward equality, mutual respect, an affirmation of diversity, a biblical understanding of the rich and the poor in God's economy, and a shared sense of mission."[369] Case study research into the Total Health partnership affirms that a common vision has been a key ingredient in the success of the partnership. The research also illustrates the great importance relationship plays in the success of the partnership in order to effectively execute the common vision. Relationship is the foundation that breeds the success of all the other principles. Without authentic relationships, interdependence, and cultural sensitivity would suffer. This chapter illustrates how the partnership leaders built a strong relational foundation that served as a platform for mutuality, interdependence and cultural sensitivity. This focus on relationship has provided the means for effectively handling historic partnership issues and decisions.

It is this relationship principle that extends outward beyond the partnership organization that then sets the stage for unique opportunities to facilitate holistic

---

[368] Myers, *Walking with the Poor*, 178.
[369] Al Tizon, "Personal Words from the Authors," in Sider, *et al.*, *Linking Arms, Linking Lives*, 26.

mission. As the relationships in a cross-cultural partnership begin to transform one another, they can also begin to transform others in both cultures. This is especially true as it relates to those in the West having a strong bias toward individualism and consumerism, which impedes Christian witness and discipleship.

Chapter 4

Partnership as a facilitator for holistic mission

Introduction

The case study that gave rise to this book asks the question "What are the dynamics (who, what, and how) of the mission partnership between the non-church organization Total Health and the GCLA church in LA Ceiba, Honduras that facilitates holistic mission and the related missiological implications of such a partnership?" To answer this question, the primary focus of the case study began with a view toward the clinic patients, those being "served" through the Total Heath partnership. The initial focus of the study was the related impact on this group as a result of the partnership between a specialist non-church organization (Total Health) and the local church and how this partnership cares for the patients both physically and spiritually.

As the study progressed, however, the evidence made clear that the scope and the impact of the mission partnership extend beyond the linear perception of a one-way, outward-focused mission. This became especially apparent as it relates to spiritual formation. Accordingly, the case study extended its focus to several other key missional relationships in order to gain additional missiological insights regarding how mission partnership facilitates a broadened perspective of holistic mission.

The case study found that significant holistic mission activities occurred throughout the myriad of intertwined relationships involved with and impacted by the partnership. Each relationship evangelizes, disciples, or serves at least one other relationship and likewise receives at least one of these elements from another relationship. The manner in which they evangelize, disciple, or serve differs from relationship to relationship and from time to time. Some are clearly intentional acts of mission and others are more witnessing by everyday way of life. However, it is the all-encompassing nature of the mission activities interworking throughout the myriad of relationships that provide unique opportunities for mission partnerships to facilitate holistic mission.

Research findings from this qualitative instrumental case study suggest three primary marks or characteristics of a Christian mission partnership that is achieving holistic mission. First, at its most basic level, the partnership must function as a true and viable partnership, illustrative of the practical benefits that make a partnership worthwhile and viable to each member. Second, there exists an array of relationships throughout the partnership and its constituents that promote an increasing level of spiritual formation and transformation throughout the relationships. And third, the actions of the partnership through Christian witness via its service and its proclamation displays the "new reality" that Newbigin suggests elicits questions that only the gospel can answer. In other words, the partnership mission activities point to Christ and open the door to the gospel discussion.

This chapter first begins, however, with a more thorough description of holistic mission in order to provide grounding to that which the research attests. Next the chapter examines the nature of the myriad of missional relationships inherent in a mission partnership, including those relationships involved in this study. The chapter then turns to the research findings related to each of the three holistic characteristics of an effective mission partnership: the practical benefits, the spiritual formative relationships, and the gospel-centered nature of the partnership actions.

Holistic Mission

Definitions can be derived from anyone that chooses specific words. Consider this fictional exchange between Alice and Humpty Dumpty:

> When I use a word" Humpty Dumpty said in a rather scornful tone, "it means just what I choose it to mean—neither more nor less." "The question is," said Alice, "whether you can make words mean so many things." "The question is," said Humpty Dumpty, "which is to be the master—that's all.[370]

The review of pertinent literature found in chapter two illustrates that holistic mission is often dichotomized between serving felt needs (horizontal/physical) versus saving souls (vertical/spiritual). To support these positions, authors and scholars generally reference "the Great Commandment" or "the Great Commission." This dichotomization, however, is a mischaracterization of holistic mission and it mischaracterizes Scriptures. The Great Commission passage, for example, is about much more than securing one's salvation and the related mission tasks. Most often, the Great Commission passage is used to define mission as the active outreach to save a lost world. Wan points out that, combined with Acts 1:8 and Matthew 24:14, the Great Commission traditionally is used to summarize what it means to do missions for God:

- What to do? (make disciples)
- How? (going, baptizing, teaching)
- Where? (Jerusalem, Judea, Samaria, end of the earth)
- When? (now to the end of time)[371]

However, the holistic mission discussion must begin relationally with what God's people are called to *be* before any description of what they are called to *do*. In other words, what does God call his people to be, before any discussion of the mission tasks people may be called to do? From a mission perspective, the Great Commission is both a call to be a disciple and the process of becoming a disciple.[372] Holistic mission integrates these vertical and horizontal dimensions of Christian mission, providing, as Myers describes, a "frame for mission that refuses the dichotomy between material and spiritual, between evangelism and social action,

---

[370] Lewis Carroll, *Through the Looking Glass, and What Alice Found There* (London, MacMillan and Co., 1872), 124. This example was inspired by Keith Ferdinando, "Mission: A Problem of Definition," *Themelios,* Volume 33.1 (Summer, 2008), 46.

[371] Wan, "Diaspora Missiology and International Student Ministry," 13.

[372] Michael J. Wilkins, *Matthew: NIV Application Commentary* (Grand Rapids, MI: Zondervan, 2004), 952.

between loving God and loving neighbor."[373] It encompasses both the vertical relationship with the Triune God and the horizontal relationships with others.

First and foremost, God calls his people to a person, Jesus Christ. The calling to belong to Christ (what God's people are called to be) is the essential relationship in the Christian faith and precedes any missionary calling of what God's people are called to do. Mark Labberton, President of Fuller Theological Seminary, says, "Call is primarily about who we are and what we do all the time. Call isn't measured by outcomes—but through the process of following Jesus in and through it all. In the end, call is about continuous formation into the likeness of Jesus Christ far more than it is about [what we do]."[374]

Wan clarifies, "Christian mission is *being* (God working in us), precedes *doing* (God working through us)."[375] What Christians are *doing* should be a natural outflow of their *being*. The call to follow Jesus is a call to a restored relationship with God, with other people, and with the world around us. It encompasses all of a person's being and doing. The call to a specific mission task (the doing) is secondary to the call to belong to Christ (the being).

Regarding the Great Commission missionary call to make disciples, Dallas Willard (1935–2013)[376] suggests,

> the first step... is to *be* his disciple and constantly to *be learning from him* how to live my life in the Kingdom of God now—my real life, the one I am actually living... Once we are disciples with some substance of the Christ-life, the person of Jesus himself, then we are in position to "bear wit-ness," to bring others to know, to bring them to awareness of reality.[377]

A witness is someone or something that can give evidence or attestation to a fact or event. Willard points out, "*Witnesses* are those who cause others to *know.*"[378] Christian witness then is the practice of providing evidence or attesting to the gospel of Jesus Christ so that others will know. By definition, this encompasses much more than evangelism via verbal proclamation. Not all are called to be evangelists (Eph. 4:11), but all are called to be witnesses (Acts 1:8). We do not have a choice but to witness to something; our lives witness to what we believe. The choice that we do have is to what or whom we will witness.[379] All aspects of a Christian's life and actions are meant to serve as a witness of the Christian faith. Likewise, the holistic integration of proclamation and social service is foundational to the definition of Christian witness used herein.

---

[373] Myers, "Another Look at 'Holistic Mission.'"
[374] Mark Labberton, *Called: The Crisis and Promise of Following Jesus Today* (Downers Grove, IL: InterVarsity Press, 2014), 135.
[375] Wan, "Diaspora Missiology and International Student Ministry," 24.
[376] Dallas Willard was an American philosopher also known for his writings on Christian spiritual formation. He was longtime Professor of Philosophy at The University of Southern California in Los Angeles, teaching at the school from 1965 until his death in 2013 and serving as the Department Chair from 1982 to 1985.
[377] Dallas Willard, The Great Omission: Reclaiming Jesus's Essential Teachings on Discipleship (New York, NY: HarperOne, 2006), 226.
[378] Willard, 225.
[379] Myers, Walking with the Poor, 312.

This concept of witnessing to God's glory gets its foundation first in the Trinitarian relationships. Jesus is sent by the Father (John 17:18, 20:21) and is obedient to and glorifies the Father (John 17:4, 1 Pet. 4:11). Likewise, the Holy Spirit is sent by both the Father and the Son, witnessing and glorifying both (John 15:26, 16:14). This aspect of "sending and submission, witnessing and glorifying" was then passed along to the disciples and Christians with Jesus' words "As the Father has sent me, I am sending you" (John 20:21).[380]

There are many views regarding the *missio Dei* and the ultimate purpose of mission, and these views are used by churches and mission practitioners to dictate the mission priorities. However, it is God's mission that sets the ultimate purpose, and his purpose does not change. To recognize mission as solely a human response to a set of God's commands reduces it to a programmatic act of obedience and allows it to be easily separated from God and his actions and purposes in history.[381] Mission, therefore, includes the vertical motivation and empowerment from God and a vertical relationship with God as the priority.

The mission tasks Christians *do* in mission are a result of their commitment to be Christ followers and the call to be witnesses to him that they follow; the doing springs out of the being. However, human endeavor to define God's purpose leads to selecting and designating specific mission activities as primary, essential, or having priority. Many of the proposed definitions of holistic mission, for example, begin with the concept of evangelism plus some other set of activities,[382] such as the debate between evangelism and social actions. Holistic mission does not attempt to designate activities to a primary or secondary position. To prioritize one activity over another, Bosch suggests, "implies that one component is primary and the other secondary… that one is essential, the other part optional."[383] Wan emphasizes this concept when he writes, "Sharing God's grace and mercies in charity and sharing the Gospel of salvation for spiritual conversion are not to be compartmentalized."[384]

Conversely, the broader scale of missions is to holistically live on mission horizontally through the power of the Holy Spirit as witnesses to God's truth and grace through Christ in the world, using both proclamation and actions in daily lives. Jesus taught his disciples how to do so and expected them to follow his service-minded example of love and compassion for others. Jesus called his disciples to follow him not only as an invitation to experience eternal salvation but also as a call to serve others.[385] Likewise, Wilkins suggests that discipleship should not be thought of solely in terms of personal spiritual growth, writing that "growth is important, but the goal of growth is service [to others]."[386] Countless biblical illustrations show Jesus acting compassionately toward others, demonstrating actions that were consistent with his teachings. He not only taught disciples that they should love their neighbor, he taught them how to love their neighbors. He demonstrated that by loving and serving their neighbors they were being a witness to him. Jesus' example provides appropriate illustrations of Christlike consistency of

---

[380] Adapted from Wan, "Diaspora Missiology and International Student Ministry," 16–17.
[381] Ott and Strauss, 61.
[382] Ringma, 440.
[383] Bosch, Transforming Mission, 415.
[384] Wan, "Diaspora Missiology and International Student Ministry," 22.
[385] Wilkins, Following the Master, 186.
[386] Wilkins, Following the Master, 68.

believing and being, of talking and doing for today's contexts. The goal of holistic mission is to allow God's mission to become the catalyst that directs mission activities.

It is against this backdrop of holistic mission versus mission tasks, and *being* a witnessing Christ follower preceding the *doing*, that this book progresses forward, not with yet another definition but rather to the more practical and secondary aspects of the activities of missions, or mission tasks. It is the effectiveness of the actions that manifest into fruitful holistic mission.

This is not to suggest the necessity of human evaluation of the performance of the mission tasks, rather the effective use of the gifts endowed by the Holy Spirit. For example, when a professor stands in front of the class in a seminary, that professor is first and primarily being a witness (the *being*). The professor is secondarily using the Spirit endowed gifts to teach the class (the *doing*). If teaching was not the Spirit endowed gift to that professor, the professor's witness would be less than effective.

Stetzer observes, "The making of definitions is in the nature of thinking. The describing of effective actions is in the nature of doing."[387] Accordingly, this book now turns to missions, the tasks involved in participating in God's mission. In other words, what are the activities, the things that Christians *do* as witnesses.

Stephen Neil (1900–1984)[388] said, "If everything is mission, nothing is mission. If everything that the Church does is to be classed as 'mission,' we shall have to find another term for the Church's particular responsibility for 'the heathen.'"[389] Neill seems to be suggesting that mission is only to deal with those that have not heard and accepted the gospel message, the unbelievers. By most accounts, this would be classified as a definition of mission that equals evangelism. Holistic mission does not subscribe to such a narrow definition of mission. However, neither does holistic mission subscribe to an 'everything' is mission reality. Holistic mission endeavors to focus on the interdependence of all mission activities without dichotomizing between the spiritual and physical dimensions of mission.

The spiritual and physical dimensions of mission are often labeled evangelism (proclamation or words) and acts of service and compassion (deeds). This assumes that proclamation equates to evangelism and sharing the gospel with everything else as some form of an action-oriented deed or service. This narrow description also serves to dichotomize the two, downplaying the integration of the two that a holistic mission approach demands. In addition, and significantly important, this simple categorization ignores the biblical call for discipleship and the importance of spiritual development, as both Hesselgrave and Myers point out.[390] Without sufficient spiritual development, mission activities of service and evangelism will be much less effective.

The church and its members are expected to play a significant role in serving the common good through actions to alleviate racism, poverty, and other social

---

[387] Stetzer "Responding to 'Mission' Defined and Described," 80.
[388] Stephen Neill was a Scottish Anglican missionary as well as a bishop and a scholar. He was an accomplished Christian historian known most notably for his work, *A History of Christian Missions*.
[389] Stephen Neill, *Creative Tensions: The Duff Lectures, 1958* (London: Edinburgh House Press, 1959), 81.
[390] Hesselgrave, "Redefining Holism" and Myers, "Another Look at 'Holistic Mission.'"

injustices. To do so requires a worldview that maintains a concern for these injustices and the common good. However, a post-Christian cultural formation immersed in a worldview of individualism, materialism, and consumerism is creating what Paul Borthwick, senior consultant for Development Associates International and Professor of Missions at Gordon College in Wenham, Massachusetts, calls "worldly Christians," a Christian who "accepts the basic message of salvation, but whose lifestyles, priorities, and concerns [worldviews] are molded by self-centered preoccupation."[391] These disciples may possess a strong theology and apologetic, but inadequate formation renders them weak in missional characteristics such as human empathy and relational skills, resulting in Christian witness that is weak and ineffective.

If Christian mission is not holistic in the sense that it facilitates formation of a Christlike worldview, it can lead to a distortion of the true gospel and may lead to an incomplete Christian conversion. Evident at only the formal religion level, people may begin to attend church, read their Bibles, and proclaim their identity as Christians, but the other dimensions of their worldview remain unchanged by the gospel.[392] In what is often described as a post-Christian Western culture, the resulting signs of a watered-down gospel, such as nationalism, prejudices and consumerism, are not hard to notice in many churches. An effective holistic Christian mission response is needed to counteract this post-Christian cultural formation. Accordingly, the view of holistic mission needs to be broadened to encompass a complete set of mission strategies inclusive of spiritual formation in order to effectively and holistically minister to a world with increasingly complex needs.

Evangelism and discipleship are two terms often used to describe spiritual formation. Evangelism is most frequently associated with verbal proclamation of the gospel message toward a goal of leading a recipient to a transforming decision for Christ. Discipleship on the other hand is used to reflect a post-conversion maturation process in which the disciple begins to reflect characteristics of Jesus. In addition, the historical debates regarding a definition for mission has at times focused on one element at the expense of the other (i.e., mission as evangelism).

The interactive nature of the holistic mission description, however, suggests that mission is less about getting someone over a somewhat arbitrary Christian boundary (i.e., evangelism for conversion) and rather more about inviting *everyone* (believer and non-believer) to take the next step toward a deeper relationship with Jesus. It allows for the outward nature of missional discipleship, avoiding the misconception that disciple-making happens only after conversion. Holistic mission recognizes a pre-conversion nature of discipleship that Beard suggests begins "at the point when a Christ-follower builds a relationship with another... discipleship is not limited to those 'already saved.'"[393] It also recognizes the discipleship nature of evangelistic activities. Wan and Hedinger point out, "God works IN the messenger as he is working through the messenger."[394]

---

[391] Paul Borthwick, *A Mind for Missions: 10 Ways to Build Your World Vision* (Colorado Springs, CO: NavPress, 1987), 13.
[392] Myers, Walking with the Poor, 345.
[393] Beard, 182.
[394] Wan and Hedinger, 64.

In addition, holistic mission recognizes that proclaiming the gospel is not solely a verbal activity. The Merriam-Webster on-line dictionary defines the verb *proclaim* as a) "to declare publicly, typically insistently, proudly, or defiantly and in either speech or writing (announce)," and b) "to give outward indication of (show)."[395] As noted in the second half of this definition, proclamation need not always be associated with verbality. To proclaim something means to make it known, verbally or otherwise. In support of the second part of the definition, Webster-Merriam uses the following sentence, "His manner *proclaimed* his genteel upbringing." In this example, a person's upbringing is proclaimed (made known) by the person's actions, not by his words.

Both Jesus' and Paul's ministry epitomized proclamation as the integration of words and deeds. For example, Luke chapter eight begins, "After this, Jesus traveled about from one town and village to another, *proclaiming* the good news of the kingdom of God" (Luke 8:1, emphasis added). Luke 8:4–56 then goes through Jesus' acts of proclamation.

The chapter begins with some verbal teachings and parables. It then moves into his actions: calming the storm, casting out demons, healing the afflicted, and ultimately raising the dead. Amidst all of this are references to the disciples and crowds who are seeing, hearing, and experiencing the "proclamation."

The integration of word and deed is further illustrated when Jesus instructs the man who was released from demonic possession to "Return home and tell how much God has done for you" (Luke 8:39). Chapter eight closes and chapter nine opens with Jesus giving "power and authority" to the twelve to cast out demons and to cure diseases and subsequently sending them out "to *proclaim* the kingdom of God and to heal the sick" (Luke 9:1-2, emphasis added).

Paul wrote,

> I will not venture to speak of anything except what Christ has accomplished through me in leading the Gentiles to obey God by what I have *said and done*—by the power of signs and wonders, through the power of the Spirit of God. So, from Jerusalem all the way around to Illyricum, I have fully *proclaimed* the gospel of Christ. (Rom. 15:18–19, emphasis added)

Holistic mission likewise "proclaims" the gospel both verbally and in action. Bosch suggests mission goes beyond the boundaries of the church to "the *world* God loves and for the sake of which Christian community is called to be the salt and light… Mission means serving, healing, and reconciling a divided, wounded humanity."[396] Myers likewise suggests, the "gospel message is an inseparable mix of life, deed, word, and sign. We are to be with Jesus (life) so that we can preach the good news (word), heal the sick (deed), and cast out demons (sign)."[397] Newbigin writes that "if the Church is faithfully living the true story, the evangelistic dialog will be initiated not by the Church but by the one who senses the presence of a new reality and wants to inquire about its secret."[398] This new reality is the

---

[395] https://www.merriam-webster.com/dictionary/proclaim.
[396] Bosch, Transforming Mission, 503.
[397] Myers, Walking with the Poor, 201.
[398] Lesslie Newbigin, *A Word in Season: Perspectives on Christian World Missions* (Grand Rapids, MI: Eerdmans Publishing, 1994), 152.

proclamations that are being made by the Christian actions as they go about the mission tasks. This cannot be complete without the verbal aspects because, as Newbigin points out, the "words interpret the actions."[399]

Holistic mission seeks spiritual transformation (conversion and discipleship) through the interdependent nature of all the mission tasks. This holistic view contrasts with the common view that delineates the processes of evangelism and discipleship and is often void of any types of service component. Spiritual formation within holistic mission integrates evangelism, discipleship, and service into an organic relationship-building process. It recognizes that hearing the gospel is not equivalent to being reached and transformed by the gospel.[400] Evangelism *and* discipleship (spiritual formation and transformation) are happening as the gospel is shared, displayed, and contextualized within the community.[401]

The nature of holistic mission does not emphasize one aspect above another: spiritual versus physical, formational versus transformational, words versus deeds. Rather, it emphasizes the interaction and integration of all mission tasks (i.e., evangelism, discipleship, and service) performed by Christian witnesses. It allows that these tasks often overlap as vertical and horizontal relationships are impacted throughout all mission activities. It does not equate the mission to the mission tasks, i.e., mission is not evangelism. It recognizes the validity of Bosch's contention that "mission and evangelism are not synonyms but, nevertheless, indissolubly linked together and inextricably interwoven in theology and praxis."[402] The same sentiment can be expressed of the other tasks; they are not mission in and of themselves but are completely interwoven in the praxis and theology of mission. The interdependency of evangelism, discipleship, and service might best be illustrated by the following:[403]

- Christian social engagement depends on the existence of Christians.
- A positive response to the gospel creates Christians – "How can they hear without someone preaching to them?" (Romans 10:14)
- Effective Christian discipleship leads to an obedient Christian life inclusive of the call to Christian social engagement.

These points illustrate that there is a multi-faceted aspect embedded within holistic mission that provides multiple missional outcomes for specific actions. For example, acts of service and compassion directed outward can also have an inward discipling impact on those doing the service, especially when the service is done in the context of a Christian community.[404]

To attempt to define mission by the task distorts the understanding of what constitutes true mission focus. If the essence of the Christian faith is a Christian's renewed and reconciled relationships with God, with other people, and with the world around them, then it stands to reason that mission should be described as the

---

[399] Newbigin, A Word in Season, 152.
[400] Mark Russell, "Christian Mission is Holistic." *International Journal of Frontier Missiology*, Volume 25:2, Summer 2008, 94.
[401] Flinn, 176.
[402] Bosch, Transforming Mission, 421.
[403] These points are adapted from Keith Ferdinando, "Mission: A Problem of Definition," *Themelios*, Volume 33.1 (Summer, 2008), 54–58.
[404] Flinn, 189–91.

action of working with God in this reconciling mission. In other words, holistic mission seeks to address the reconciliation of these three key relationships: vertical (God and people), horizontal (people and people), and circular (God, people, and creation),[405] and the acts of missions are the tasks used to pursue the mission.

Missional Relationships in Mission Partnerships

The previous chapter discussed the need for authentic relationships between the members of the mission partnership. However, holistic mission by its very nature involves many other relationships, most notably the relationships between those bringing the mission and those being served by the mission. A relational paradigm in mission focuses on the relational networks between personal beings, both the vertical and horizontal relationships, and the missional interactions between them. Wan and Hedinger observe:

The primary touch point for a correct understanding of reality is that <u>vertical relationship</u> (God and man within the divine-human relational network) is the fundamental issue of life: <u>horizontal relationship</u> (between created beings) is secondary. The Great Commandment is vertical and primary: to love God. The second commandment is horizontal and secondary: love your neighbor.[406]

Myers reinforces the primary importance of the vertical relationship:

The Holy Spirit empowers us for mission, leads us into mission, and is responsible for the results of mission. If there is to be any human transformation that is sustainable, it will be because of the action of the Holy Spirit, not the effectiveness of our development technology or the cleverness of our participatory process.[407]

Effective mission partnership, likewise, must begin with a relationship with the Triune God, the one who initiates and sustains the mission partnership. In John 15: 1–17, Jesus discusses how his followers have been chosen to bear fruit and tells them, "If you remain in me and I in you, you will bear much fruit; apart from me you can do nothing" (John 15:5). Likewise, Tizon advises that "the task of the reconciliation of all things [mission] belongs to God. The church announces it and models it; it doesn't bring it about."[408] Tizon acknowledges the horizontal importance, however, explaining that the "vertically reconciled become a horizontally reconciling force in the world."[409] Through their everyday horizontal relationships, Christians are expected to participate in commission with God's missional work so that, as Jesus said, "you might go and bear fruit—fruit that will last" (John 15:16). The effectiveness of a partnership in holistic mission starts first with the healthy relationship of the partners with the Triune God.

Wan illustrates the relational framework in the practice of holistic Christian mission with the following diagram:

---

[405] Tizon, 87

[406] Wan and Hedinger, 38.

[407] Myers. *Walking with the Poor,* 84.

[408] Tizon, 89.

[409] Tizon, 124.

Integrated Holistic Christian Missions: Practice

Practice:
Vertically: God's grace & love received, then
Horizontally: charity & sharing with others

GOAL:
- Reconciliation
- Redemption
- Transformation

Horizontal

VERTICAL

evangelism/discipleship
friendship / partnership

Figure 5. - Integrated Approach of Holistic Christian Mission in Practice[410]

Earthly Christian mission partnerships are made of those people that Jesus calls to bear fruit. Bosch points out that "God does not send 'ideas' or 'eternal truths' to the nations. He sends people, historical beings. He incarnates himself in his Son, and through his Son in his disciples. God becomes history, specific history, in the followers of Jesus en route to the world."[411] The partners are human beings in a horizontal relationship with one another to holistically serve others horizontally in the Triune God's mission, in the name of Jesus, with the power of the Holy Spirit.

The horizontal relationships involved and touched by a mission partnership are many and varied. These relationships stretch beyond just the outward-looking objectives of the partners, to the many others that may be involved in the mission, those touched in some way by the partnership or the mission activities, and the mission partners themselves. Butler recognizes this myriad of relationships in his list of fifteen critical partnership principles and suggests,

> Partnerships serve at least four constituencies: the people they are trying to reach/serve; the partner churches/ministries with their own staffs and vision; the partner funding and praying constituencies behind each of these ministries; and, eventually, the partnership itself with its growing expectations. There are many more players around the table than we often acknowledge.[412]

Wan and Hedinger illustrate this with a conceptual relationship framework that depicts the various relationship dyads (both vertical and horizontal) inherent in sending and preparing intercultural workers.[413] A similar framework for the Total Health partnership identifies a number of relationships (vertical and horizontal)

---

[410] Wan, "Diaspora Missiology and International Student Ministry," 22.
[411] Bosch, *Witness to the World,* 70.
[412] Butler, *Well Connected,* 320.
[413] Wan and Hedinger, 40. Pages 38–50 explore and explain the authors' view of the seven key missionary relationships.

inherent in its mission activities. Most notably are the horizontal relationships between those being served by the partnership and those that are serving within the partnership. Other notable horizontal relationships within the partnership include the donors, short-term missionaries, other churches, and other related organizations.

Less noticeable, however, are the intertwined relationships between those within the partnership and those outside the partnership. The nature of the partnership provides unique, expanded missional opportunities to witness far beyond the stated partnership activities. As Christians from the partnership, as well as those non-Christians impacted by the partnership, go about into their other relational community groups and spheres of influences, new and different relationships are formed with other Christians as well as non-Christians. These relationships often become the beginning of new spiritual formative relationships, enhancing Christian spiritual formation between believers and allowing nonbelievers to see and experience Christlike behaviors and kingdom living. These horizontal relationships, working through the power of the Triune God, provide opportunities for holistic mission witness (evangelism, discipleship, and service) throughout an exponentially expanded network of relationships (see Figure 6 below).

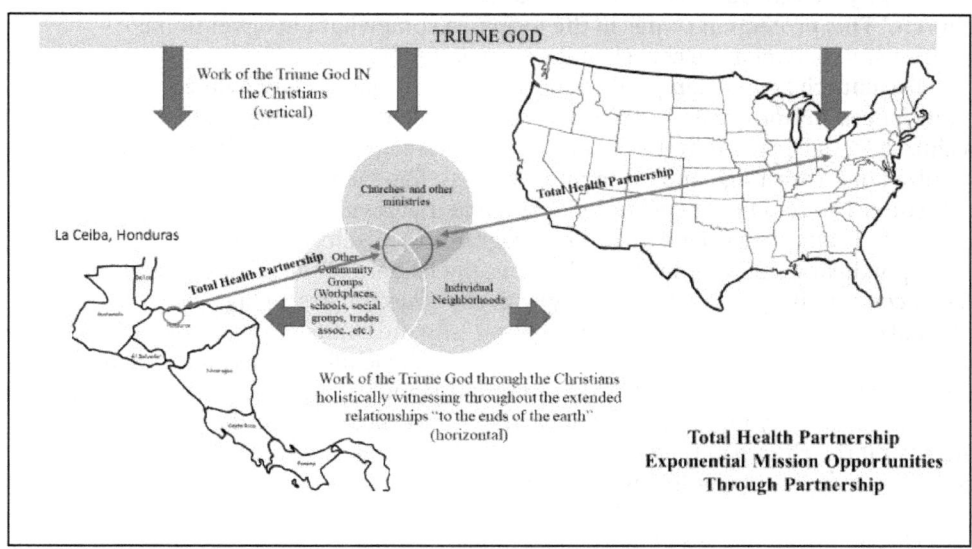

Figure 6. - Total Health Partnership Missional Relationships

In the epilog chapter of *Common Fire*, the authors focus on twelve specific "sectors" of society that they suggest can "make a strategic contribution to the formation of a shared moral compass."[414] Nonprofits, they suggest, "are key settings

---

[414] Daloz, *et al.*, *Common Fire*, 213. The twelve sectors cited are households (children, youth, and family); schools; higher education; the professions and professional education; religion; arts and

in which commitments to the common good can ferment and mature," and the authors challenge nonprofits to build commitment to the larger common good as part of the organization's mission and to pave the way for this commitment among the organization's relationships.[415]

Total Health sees itself as such a non-profit organization called out in the *Common Fire* study. The organization is cognizant of the diversity of its relationships and considers its mission more holistic than meeting just physical needs in Central America. While formalizing its vision and strategy, Total Health recognized, as the *Common Fire* authors suggest, that the organization, in partnership with the church, could play a role in the spiritual formation and well-being of its key relationships, including those in the U.S. As a result, the organization has prioritized "facilitating spiritual health" as a priority and key value component of its vision and has framed this part of its vision to include all of its various relationships.[416]

Perhaps one of the most revealing examples of the relational impact of the Total Health mission partnership is found in an unusual relationship with a local gang in the La Ceiba community. Referring back to the previous chapter's section "Mutuality and Interdependence," Table 9 depicts how the costs of the La Ceiba clinic are shared between Total Health, the church, and the community. One of the community's contributions is shown as a "means of protection for the clinic and the church." This protection comes in the form of a somewhat unconventional relationship between the church and a local gang.

The church is not exempt from the far-reaching gang related violence experienced in Honduras. A series of rival gang related activities led to the death of a church leader (caught in the cross-fire of the rival gangs) and subsequently resulted in Pastor Dago and his family having to flee the country due to threats of extortion. The remaining church leaders made it known to the community that they planned to relocate the church and its programs to a "safer" location.

Upon hearing about the church's plans, the leaders of the primary gang in the La Ceiba community called for a meeting with the church. These gang leaders recognized that many in their families, especially the children, were served by the church, the clinic, and the other programs. The gang leaders communicated that they valued the church as part of the community and what the church was doing for their families. They indicated that they were not responsible for the past activities and that if the church agreed to remain in La Ceiba and continue to serve the community the gang would ensure their safety and protect them from the other gang violence.

This arrangement is a glimpse of an unusual, yet culturally necessary, relationship in which unlikely members of the community (in this case the gang) meet a need of the partnership in a unique and unorthodox manner. Most importantly, however, it also illustrates the breadth of the community and the measure in which the partnership's mission is permeating that community. The

---

media; public policy; business; nonprofit organizations; the health and therapeutic community; foundations and philanthropy; and the readers of the book.
[415] Daloz, et al., Common Fire, 235–237.
[416] Taken from an internal Total Health vision and strategy map created in 2017 and updated in 2018.

gang leaders value how their "people" are being served and cared for so much so that they are willing to protect the church and the clinic. They offer this protection even with the recognition that others whom the gang might consider adversaries are also being cared for. The gang "culture" is prevalent in Honduras, and this illustration represents one case in point of the unique and expanded missional opportunities to be a gospel witness far beyond the stated partnership activities.

Practical Benefits to Mission Partnership

For a Christian partnership to effectively facilitate the achievement of holistic mission, it must first simply be an effective functioning partnership. Doing so requires that the partnership mutually benefits from each of its member's mission activities and makes each member better. The partnership between Total Health and the La Ceiba church renders each one's mission activities more cost effective, more efficient, and therefore, more missionally effective. In addition, as will be discussed in the next section, partnership members play a part in one another's spiritual growth through the missional and personal relationships built though their participation.

The attributes that make the Total Health partnership functionally effective are addressed in the previous chapter. These attributes, such as common vision and mutual interdependence, are essential elements to the success of the partnership and lead to the practicality of effectiveness.

The practical benefits serve to improve each organization's operations and ministry beyond the obvious funding relationship. In a partnership relationship, each organization maintains its individual identities and vision, yet is dependent upon one another for the maximum success of the holistic mission. The key to effectiveness is that by working in tandem, each member's mission realizes incremental benefits from the partnership. The table below provides a view into the practical ways that each member benefits from being a part of this partnership model.

Table 11. - Practical Partnership Benefits

Benefits the Church Receives	Benefits Total Health Receives
• Funding for clinic staff. • Medicines for patients. • Medical training. • Periodic S-T mission teams. • Funding for special ministry projects. • Access to U.S. contacts. • A reason for the community to visit the church complex.	• Clinic facility to serve the patients. • Local human resources expertise and payroll management. • Language translators. • Access to local contacts. • Local Christian medical professionals. • S-T mission team coordination. • Local (La Ceiba) medical knowledge.

The initial Total Health medical mission model was a somewhat minimalist partnership model. The initial model called for Total Health to utilize the clinic facility provided by the church as a platform for medical missions by U.S. medical mission teams traveling to La Ceiba on a monthly basis. The medical professionals would primarily serve the patients physically, with the church available for spiritual care as well.

This is a model of missions that bears some similarity to the holistic medical missions model studied by De Oliveira,[417] with the significant exception that De Oliveira's model was done entirely outside the local church. Spiritual care was the responsibility of the Christian medical professionals administering the physical care. De Oliveira noted several weaknesses to this model, many of which are negated through the practical benefits of the partnership model in place between Total Health and the La Ceiba church. The table below illustrates four specific weaknesses noted by De Oliveira and how the weaknesses are negated by partnership.

Table 12. - Holistic Medical Mission Weaknesses Mitigated by Partnership

Weakness noted by De Oliveira[418]	Partnership Solution
Medical missions are expensive. (Monthly medical mission teams could cost up to $90,000 annually in travel costs alone.)[419]	Total Health can fund an entire year of clinic operations, including a local doctor, assistant, and full year of medicines for approximately $35,000 annually.
A means of local follow-up is required, both physically and spiritually, after the missionaries leave.	The local church is there to provide spiritual care. The local medical professionals are there every day.
Lack of discipleship for new believers.	The local church is available for discipleship of new believers. In addition, the myriad of relationships provide discipleship beyond new believers to a higher level of maturity (to be discussed in the next section of this chapter).
Lack of adequate facilities.	The local church provides the facility. This weakness would also be negated in the limited partnership model initially contemplated by Total Health.

This table illustrates the significant value of partnership to the cost-effectiveness and efficiency of the mission activities. Utilizing local medical professionals rather than traveling missionary professionals is clearly a more cost-effective manner of medical care. The care is less costly and, at the same time, more readily available and consistent. In addition, the local team is there for follow-up. This ensures that the patients are cooperating in their care with regular visits and maintaining their medications. The local staff also has other local contacts and connections for patient referrals for the instances in which a patient requires a level

---

[417] De Oliveira. "Breaking Down the Resistance to the Gospel Through Holistic Medical Missions."
[418] See previous discussion in chapter two and De Oliveira, 130–33.
[419] Assumes a 5-person team monthly at $1,500 per person, an average experience per Total Health teams.

of care not available at the clinic. Given the nature of the Honduran culture, a referral from another respected local physician can be a matter of life and death for the patient. In addition, Total Health can rely on the local medical professionals' knowledge of the local health concerns. Disease states and various chronic ailments can be much different in Honduras than in the U.S. Partnering with local knowledge prevents costly mistakes such as purchasing medications that go unused.

Total Health also receives administrative benefits by partnering with a local organization. Total Health relies on the church to maintain the human resource function for the organization. The clinic staff becomes employees of the church, and the church manages the intricacies of the Honduran payroll and employment laws and regulations. Re-creating this administrative function would be a costly endeavor for any U.S. organization.

This model of partnership provides the church with the ability to serve and minister to its community in ways that it otherwise could not afford. Partnering with Total Health provides it the wherewithal to offer a medical ministry staffed with Christian medical professionals who live in the local community and attend the local church. Previously, the best that the church could manage was periodic medical mission teams with a makeshift set of supplies. In addition, this medical staff has direct access to U.S. medical knowledge via the Total Health doctors that can provide added insights to patient care.

Perhaps even more significant than cost savings and efficiencies in the medical care aspect of the partnership are the advances in the spiritual growth and transformation goals of the partnership. The church can offer a level of spiritual care that would be impossible for a periodic medical mission. As noted in the table above, lack of spiritual follow-up and discipleship of new believers is a weakness of a holistic model done outside a church partnership.

A community healthcare clinic associated with a church adds an element of efficiency to the church's mission that is difficult to consistently replicate. Not unlike Jesus' healing ministry, it gives the community a reason to visit the church complex. People come to the community clinic to be healed physically just as people flocked to Jesus to be healed. Jesus' healing ministry illustrated both his compassion (Matt. 14:14) and his power (Matt. 8:17). Jesus had power equal to his compassion, and his healings reflected evidence that he was God in human form. Likewise, the compassionate care in the clinic bears evidence to the healing power of Christ and Christ's love in human form.

When patients interviewed were asked why they come to the clinic, each patient expressed some sentiment related to how they were treated. They used words such as love, compassion, blessings. Each of the staff interviewed explained that she tries to love the patients in the same way Christ would love them. This is evidence that is seen and experienced by the community every day. This kind of love softens and prepares the heart for the Holy Spirit's work.

Spiritual Formation through Mission Partnership Relationships

Christian mission partnerships have a unique opportunity to facilitate holistic mission extensively through the myriad of relationships that intertwine throughout the partnership and its constituencies. These relationships missionally provide the opportunity for increasing levels of spiritual formation and transformation not only to those that the partnership serves (i.e. the clinic patients) and to one another but also reaching out into other relationships impacted by those within the partnership. Using a holistic approach of words, deeds, and signs, holistic mission endeavors to move people within this vast array of partnership relationships to a closer relationship with Christ.

One's worldviews, values, and beliefs are formed over time through the internalizing and interpreting of the influences and experiences through one's relationships. Worldviews are formed through family, friends, church, vocation, and many other daily relationships and experiences throughout one's life. The vast set of relationships found within a Christian mission partnership such as the subject of this case study can play a significant role in forming and interpreting these life experiences from a gospel perspective.

The Total Health partnership has a clear focus on spiritual health, including spiritual transformative conversions to a decision for Christ. This is clearly apparent related to the clinic patients, the primary target group of the partnership. The partnership employs an evangelist to be on staff and she is intentionally placed in the patient rotation process. In other words, at some point in the patient's visit, the patient will speak with the evangelist. Over a series of visits, the evangelist gets to know the patients and their families. Conversations take on a relational nature rather than a preaching nature. Patients interviewed expressed it as "hearing the word of God" and "hearing about the Bible." It is an interesting note that no patient complained during the interviews about talking to the evangelist. Rather, several expressed that it was just another way that the clinic shows its love for the people.

The evangelistic reach of the partnership also extends beyond that of the patients being served. Sider, Olson, and Unruh suggest that Christian mission partnerships "expand a church's opportunity to form evangelistic relationships beyond those being served... offering a unique avenue of reaching co-laborers in social action with the gospel."[420] Beyond the clinic patients, there are many other unbelievers that get involved and come into contact with the gospel through the operations of the partnership, both in Honduras and in the U.S. For example, non-Christian U.S. doctors participate with Total Health from a compassion/benevolent perspective, often with little regard for the spiritual aspects of the mission. They recognize that they will be working with a Christian organization partnering with a church, but their focus is solely on physical healthcare. These doctors are exposed to the gospel message as they participate, whether it is through discussions with the U.S. team or actual travel to Honduras to serve in the clinic. Pastor Dago tells the story of a non-Christian who came to serve in the clinic saying they "get discipled even if they are not Christians." In this particular case, the person returned to the U.S. and later wrote to Pastor Dago saying, "Because of what you are doing, I know it's from the Lord, and I want to accept the Lord."

Transformations, such as Christian conversion, are often characterized and illustrated as a miraculous change occurring at a specific given point in time. People are known to give testimony to the moment that they accepted Christ, often citing the exact date and time, and videos of Billy Graham altar calls have shown thousands of such conversions. However, many decisions that appear to be in-the-moment transformations have been influenced by past events and experiences that

---

[420] Sider, Olson, and Unruh, 225.

involve multiple relationships and multiple forms of communication over a period of time.[421] For example, Saul's transformation on the road to Damascus (Acts 9) is often thought of as a miraculous instant transformation.

However, it is important to recognize the influences of Saul's context. He certainly would have had much knowledge about Jesus. Saul was alive during Jesus' ministry, though the scriptures give no indication that he ever met Jesus prior to the road to Damascus. And, though we do not know from Scriptures, he likely had the occasion to hear the Apostles speak while the Apostles were on mission. Having studied under Gamaliel, (Acts 22:3), Saul would have been aware of Gamaliel's intervention on behalf of the Apostles to the Sanhedrin (Acts 5:34–39). Saul was a "young man" when he heard Stephan testify (Acts 7:58 – 8:1). These relational experiences and influences provided Saul a background from which to draw when he faced the supernatural meeting with the Lord Jesus.

In one of his "Partnership in Practice" sections, Butler illustrates a somewhat similar contemporary example of a woman that was raised by religiously indifferent parents and who was for years taken to church and Sunday school by an aunt. The aunt spoke to her about spiritual matters and prayed for her continuously. It was not until sometime in the woman's adulthood that she accepted Christ while watching Billy Graham on television. Butler points out, "There had been hundreds of conversations between the aunt and her niece, hundreds of prayers by the aunt, and all those Sunday school visits… There had been all of the ongoing letters of support and prayer." Butler then ends with the question, "Who was the evangelist? Billy Graham, who never met the woman? Or the faithful aunt?"[422]

In a similar way, the consistent gospel presentation through the Christian partnership relationships gives unbelieving participants a background and a context to understand and process the supernatural work of the Holy Spirit. It provides meaning to the convictions they are feeling. The action-oriented nature of these missional horizontal relationships led by the Spirit allows the gospel message to be experienced and observed (salt and light) by the surrounding world. Just as living and learning from Jesus for three years provided meaning for the Apostles to the Pentecost event, actions of today's Christians, holistically witnessing through life, word, and deeds, provide context for God's current supernatural work.

Spiritual transformation in holistic mission extends beyond conversion to ongoing discipleship.[423] De Oliveira cites a lack of ongoing discipleship as a weakness to a medical missions strategy performed outside the local church when he states that if they "do not have people in the church that can teach new believers about the foundation of the Gospel, our work is worthless."[424] The relational nature of the Total Health partnership with those it serves and with one another within the partnership provides a unique platform for Christian discipleship that spans the spectrum of Christian maturity, pre-conversion to long-time Christ follower.

---

[421] Butler, Well Connected, 59.
[422] Butler, *Well Connected*, 61–62.
[423] Discipleship in this context is meant to illustrate post-conversion discipleship. As previously noted, we subscribe to the premise of pre-conversion discipleship or spiritual growth. Discipleship is not limited to converted Christians. See "Holistic Mission" section earlier in this chapter.
[424] De Oliveira, 131.

The significance of the partnership relationships in discipleship is found in the context of community.[425] A community can be described as a self-organized network of people with a common purpose, cause or interest.[426] While the partnership and the whole of all its relationships can be described as a type of community, there are other community sets inherent within the myriad of the relationships such as the clinic staff, the board of directors, etc. For example, one of the clinic staff refers to the staff group as a "sisterhood," saying, "We are not just co-workers; we are like sisters" (it should be noted that all of the clinic staff at this time are and historically have been female).

Communities that come together for mission purposes can be described as "missional communities." Flinn defines missional communities as "intentional networks of relationships bound together for the purposes of expressing the love of the Triune God in both word and deed to those outside the Christian faith, caring for one another, and discipling all people continually toward Christlike transformation."[427] At the heart of these communities is the missional goal of "discipling people to Christlikeness as observable examples of loving God, loving one another, and loving our neighbor."[428]

Researchers are confirming that deep personal transformation does not happen simply through rational educational study but is "equally dependent on relational ways of knowing."[429] Edward W. Taylor, Associate Professor of Adult Education at Penn State University-Harrisburg, suggests that "it is through establishing trustful relationships that individuals can have questioning discussions wherein information can be shared openly, and mutual and consensual understanding be achieved."[430] These formative relationships serve to foster and facilitate the transformation education process. Wan argues, "Human understanding is best comprehended and experienced in relational networks."[431] Beard comments, "The community itself is fundamental for the shaping of the disciple's identity as it becomes a context of transformative experience. Throughout the spiritual-formation process, community is present, interactive, and formative."[432] These community relationships influence and shape what one believes about the world in which they live and their ultimate purpose and role within it. A Christian worldview is shaped and transformed through the continued holistic mission of these relationships.

To establish a framework for insights into the Total Health partnership platform for discipleship and spiritual formation, a brief grounding in the nature of relational discipleship is in order.

Jesus said that to be a disciple is to become like the Master (Matt. 10:24–25; Luke 6:40). The essence of discipleship is teaching the disciples to obey all that

---

[425] See Flinn, "Missional Community as Context for Disciple-Making" for more in depth review on the foundations of discipleship in the context of community.
[426] Flinn, 172.
[427] Flinn, 175.
[428] Flinn, 199.
[429] Edward W. Taylor, "Analyzing Research on Transformative Learning Theory," in Jack Mezirow & Associates, *Learning as Transformation: Critical Perspectives on a Theory in Progress* (San Francisco, CA: Jossey-Bass, 2000), 306.
[430] Edward W. Taylor, 307.
[431] Wan, "The Paradigm of 'Relational Realism,'" 1.
[432] Beard, 190.

Jesus had commanded, such that the disciple is transformed toward a Christlikeness. Wilkins describes this as

becoming like the master includes going out with the same message, ministry, and compassion (Matt. 10:5ff.), practicing the same religious and social traditions (Matt. 12:1-8; Mark 2:18-22), belonging to the same family of obedience (Matt. 12:46-49), exercising the same servanthood (Matt. 20:26-28; Mark 10:42-45; John 13:12-17), experiencing the same suffering (Matt. 10:16-25; Mark 10:38-39), and being sent in the same way into the world (John 20:21).[433]

One of the best insights into "all that Jesus commanded" is the all-inclusive nature of three significant commands that Jesus specifically described. The first two come from Mark's gospel, "Love the Lord your God with all your heart and with all your soul and with all your mind and with all your strength. The second is this: Love your neighbor as yourself" (Mark 12:30-31). Later, Jesus gave his disciples a new command, saying, "A new command I give you: Love one another. As I have loved you, so you must love one another" (John 13:34).

These commands are relationally action oriented. The word *love* in these commands is not an emotional state but an action that is directed to someone other than one's self. Implied in these verses are two elements of Christian formation: the loving service and care for one another done in Jesus' likeness and the observation of this love by others. Both elements serve to positively influence spiritual formation, especially when done in community with others. These three commands reflect an action-oriented, missionally balanced life that Jesus himself lived and taught with his words and his actions.

Timothy Keller, American pastor, theologian, and Christian apologist and founding Pastor of Redeemer Presbyterian Church in New York City, New York, suggests that "all people need theological education to 'think Christianly' about everything and to act with Christian distinctiveness."[434] This "theological" education, however, is not seminarian type book learning. Though book learning and Bible study are a part of it, disciples must move beyond biblical intellectual knowledge of what Jesus commanded and on to the practical application of this knowledge into faithful acts of obedience to his commands. The Apostle John suggests that keeping Jesus' commands is the evidence of a true believer,

> We know that we have come to know him if we keep his commands. Whoever says, 'I know him,' but does not do what he commands is a liar, and the truth is not in that person. But if anyone obeys his word, love for God is truly made complete in them. This is how we know we are in him: Whoever claims to live in him must live as Jesus did. (1 John 2:3-6)

In other words, a true disciple's outer actions should reflect the inner reality of the disciple's transformation in Christ.

A life of obedience does not happen automatically; disciples must be taught how to obey (Matt. 28:20), and obedience is not easily taught. Experts and consultants cannot tell someone specifically how to love his or her neighbor; for example, they

---

[433] Michael J. Wilkins, "Disciple, Discipleship," *Evangelical Dictionary of World Missions*, Ed. A. Scott Moreau (Grand Rapids, MI: Baker, 2000), 279.
[434] Timothy Keller, Center Church: Doing Balanced, Gospel-Centered Ministry in Your City (Grand Rapids, MI: Zondervan, 2012), 259.

can only provide examples of how this has looked in other contexts. Describing what Jesus meant by, "As I have loved you" is difficult to put into words. The characteristics of this love can be captured in two important ways that God loves: He loves us first (1 John 4:19), and while we were still sinners Christ died for us (Rom. 5:8).

Gary M. Burge, Professor of Bible, Theology, Archaeology, and World Religions at Wheaton College, suggests that the newness of the command is not that the disciples are to love one another; rather, it is how they are to love one another "with the sort of love modeled by Jesus":

> Love characterizes Jesus' relationship with God (John 14:31), and love characterizes God's relationship with Jesus (John 3:35; 15:9-10). Jesus' love is manifested in his obedience to the Father's will ("the world must learn that I love the Father and that I do exactly what my Father has commanded me," John 14:31). Therefore disciples are to reflect the sort of love known to Jesus—a love expressed through committed obedience. "As I have loved you" points to Jesus' most immediate act of love (the footwashing) and means that to truly love another, we must pursue a life of servanthood and sacrifice.[435]

However, from a discipleship perspective, it remains difficult to further reduce this kind of love into words. Jesus' love has been described using phrases such as unconditional, forgiveness, accepting one another, honoring one another, bearing one another's burdens, praying for one another, serving one another, encouraging one another, forbearing one another, being subject to one another, and the list could go on. Jesus ultimately describes his love as, "Greater love has no one than this: to lay down one's life for one's friends" (John 15:13).

Despite all of these descriptions, complete understanding of loving like Christ is an elusive idea. It is a bit like taking my wife shopping for furniture. She cannot describe what she is looking for but tells me, "I'll know it when I see it."

So it is for the love of Christ: It is known when it is seen. For example, when Jesus washes his disciples' feet, he takes on one of the lowliest servant's task and models his servanthood love. Through the act of foot washing, Jesus is teaching and discipling in order to make fully observable and understandable what he means when he says, "For even the Son of Man did not come to be served, but to serve, and to give his life as a ransom for many" (Mark 10:45). This is consistent with Jesus' manner of teaching his disciples through tangible, real-life demonstrations. Jesus not only taught disciples that they should love their neighbor; he taught them how to love their neighbor. Likewise, demonstrating and modeling loving behavior toward others is the primary means of discipling and teaching the Christian concept of Christlike love for one another.

This type of discipleship is best done in a group with others, a community. The concept of a mission partnership in the context of a community was introduced earlier in this chapter. The community context becomes most effective when the primary means of discipleship is modeling certain actions. Although there are many scenes of Jesus teaching in a traditional verbal, lecture format (The Sermon on the

---

[435] Gary M. Burge, *John: The NIV Application Commentary* (Grand Rapids, MI: Zondervan, 2000), 376.

Mount in Matt. 5–7), Jesus' primary teaching took place in the community (in a boat, along the road to Jerusalem, at a well, etc.), where he could actively demonstrate the implementation of his words to both his disciples and to the crowds. Jesus moved beyond the passive knowledge-transfer model to an all-encompassing demonstrative model that credibly reflected his message in his everyday life, an exemplary life that was observed by others. Jesus not only proclaimed and explained God's kingdom, he was the very embodiment of all he proclaimed.

Jesus did not come into the world only to talk. A complete integration of his words and works made Jesus' credibility high and caused the people to say, "He taught as one who had authority, and not as their teachers of the law" (Matt. 7:29).[436] His was a method of *participating discipleship* with his followers.[437] Jesus set forth the mission and provided his disciples with the opportunity to experience the things he demonstrated and taught.

The Bible provides a remarkable illustration of a community of disciples formed in the early church (Acts 2:42–47). The community provided the environment that allowed the disciples to maintain a clear focus on Christ, to continue to grow in their faith, and to serve one another. In the process, additional disciples were made.[438] Christians today must be likewise provided with an environment to practice and experience their obedient faith. The community of relationships in the Total Health partnership provides a similar environment, allowing for appropriate demonstrations of Christlike consistency of believing and being, of talking and doing.

Serving and participating in the Total Health partnership provides an environment and a context for active transformational learning and spiritual formation. Experiences happen in real-time and are demonstrated and modeled in the contexts of real relationships. Real-time demonstration provides for real-time involvement, thus real-time learning. These experiences provide real-life examples that disciples can internalize and imitate. Paul exhorts the church in Philippi to "Join together in following my example, brothers and sisters, and just as you have us as a model, keep your eyes on those who live as we do" (Phil. 3:17). The nature of these partnership relationships gives participants (disciples) the opportunity to see and experience an obedient life demonstrated in action so that they may know how to imitate such a life. As importantly, the community also gives disciples the opportunity to exhibit and practice these characteristics in their own lives for others to imitate.

This aspect of serving within the Total Health partnership community gives participants a means of gaining spiritual insights and learnings from others as they do their best to serve in God's image. As people serve together, whether it be at the

---

[436] Butler, *Well Connected*, 255.

[437] This was a Hebrew rabbinical form of discipleship that involves life-on-life teaching. It is oriented toward understanding life situations and applying Godly principles accordingly. This may be considered in contextual comparison to that of the Greek Academy, which are reflective of modern-day schools and academies. Though there may be differences between rabbinic discipleship and Jesus' methods, life-on-life participation and observation are primary to both. See Alan Hirsch, *The Forgotten Ways: Reactivating the Missional Church* (Grand Rapids, MI: Brazos Press, 2006), 120–125, for discussion of the rabbinic vs. academy models of discipleship and leadership training.

[438] Wilkins, Following the Master, 273.

clinic, the board of directors, or within some other function of the partnership, the participants have a group of relationships that the Holy Spirit uses as a tool to foster and facilitate transformation to a deeper relationship with Christ. Transformation occurs as Christians share their kingdom-life experiences (both good and bad) in the relational environment of the everyday actions of life and service.[439]

Obviously, the Total Health partnership does not have Jesus on earth doing the modeling, so actions and models are less than perfect. It does, however, have a group of mature and maturing Christians demonstrating and modeling their love for one another in many practical ways. Accordingly, love for one another within the Total Health partnership relationship context is best experienced through various actions and anecdotes that occur in the everyday life of the participants.

Community life discipleship has the advantage of more than one person developing another. Every person has the opportunity to be a model of love while also having the opportunity to experience the love of another. This is tangible movement from intellectually learning what should be done and moving toward a life of faithful, obedient action.

Evidence of this community life discipling process was apparent in the research findings. As part of the research interview process, the clinic staff was asked if there is something that they may have learned from others that they serve with in the clinic. The responses overwhelmingly centered around learning to love and serve one another and others. The following are some of the responses:

- "I learned to love the patients. I realize it is their disease that is driving their meanness, not them as a person."
- "I learned the power of prayer."
- "I learned love for the patients."
- "I learned to see people's needs."
- "I learned to serve without a desire for a payback."
- "I didn't like to be around people. Here I have learned about relationships and how to be a friend."
- "I have learned what serving is about, and what it means to serve correctly. How to serve in love."

Recognizably these are the words of the staff speaking about what they believe they have learned in answer to an interview question. However, proof that the staff has put into practice what they learned is reflected in the responses received from the patient interviews. Most of these patients are the very poor of the community and, similarly to biblical times, are considered the outcasts of society. However, overwhelmingly, the patients included comments in their interview responses that indicated how they had been treated by the staff, not as an outcast or a person unable to pay for service, but as a human in need of care. Often, the patients described how the staff "loves" them. The clinic patients consistently contrasted the personal loving care they received at the Total Health clinic with the impersonal, sometimes inhumane care they received at the local public facilities.

The clinic staff embraces their vocation as a mission or ministry to share the love of Christ rather than primarily that of a medical provider. The Christ-like love and compassion that the staff has for the patients is evident to even the most casual observer. Bellah suggests that a "deep concern for justice and the common good

---

[439] Flinn, 198.

[such as displayed by the clinic staff] as part of one's character is not an add-on that can be attained from a one-shot course in ethics. Rather it is a matter of what has been traditionally called formation."[440] People with this commitment are "formed little by little, step by step, to become the kind of citizens they are."[441] These are the external actions that reflect the evidence of an internal transformation made possible by the work of the Holy Spirit through the holistic mission activities of the Christian mission partnership.

All the while, these actions are being observed, not only by the patients and the partnership team, but also by the outside, non-Christian world. Jesus knew that his disciples' actions would be watched and judged by the world. He commanded them to love one another in his likeness, and he wanted their love to be on display for the world to see (John 13:35). It was by the disciples' observable actions of love that the crowds would be able to identify them as Christ's disciples.

When non-Christians comes into contact with a Christian group, whether it be a church or some other form of Christian group such as a Christian community healthcare clinic, their first observation should be of the loving nature of the group. Non-Christians should recognize this as something different from the world that surrounds them. Keller suggests, "We [Christians] will have an impact for the gospel if we are like those around us yet profoundly different and unlike them at the same time, all while remaining very visible and engaged."[442] Burge suggests that the story of people who have given themselves to Christian service often "begins with an overwhelming encounter with God's goodness, which never fades for them."[443] He observes,

> Nothing so astonishes a fractured world as a community in which radical, faithful, genuine love is shared among its members. There are many places you can go to find communities of shared interests. There are many places you can go to find people just like yourself... But it is the mandate of the church to become a community of love, a circle of Christ's followers who invest in one another because Christ has invested in them, who exhibit love not based on the mutuality and attractiveness of its members, but on the model of Christ, who washed the feet of everyone (including Judas).[444]

The understanding that Christian love is noticeably different from that of the culture dates back to the early days of the church. In chapter 39 of his work, *The Apology of Tertullian*, Tertullian contrasts Christians' love for one another with that of the Roman culture of his time. He writes,

> But even the putting into practice of so great a love as this brand us with a mark of censure in the opinion of some. "See," say they, "how they love each other!"—for they themselves hate each other; and, "how ready they are to die for each other!"—for they are more ready to kill each other.

Francis Shaeffer (1912–1984)[445] suggests that "without true Christians loving one another, Christ says the world cannot be expected to listen, even when we give

---

[440] Bellah and Tipton, 440.
[441] Daloz, et al., Common Fire, 210.
[442] Keller, 282.
[443] Burge, 381–82.
[444] Burge, 387.
[445] Francis Shaeffer was an American Evangelical Christian theologian, philosopher, and Presbyterian pastor best known for establishing the L'Abri community in Switzerland.

proper answers." He goes on to write, "But after we have done our best to communicate to a lost world, still we must never forget that the final apologetic which Jesus gives is the observable love of true Christians for true Christians."[446] Flinn observes that "Jesus' disciple-making methods exhibit a principle understanding that the observable demonstrations of his message by the transformed lives of his disciples carry more weight with the crowds than that of theological knowledge and education."[447] Jesus understood that people observing his followers loving one another is a pronounced picture of how actions can speak louder than words ever can. People are brought to faith in Christ in many ways. However, ultimately there is an aspect of a contagious joyfulness reflected in the lives of believers that cannot help but to communicate itself.[448] These external actions, sometimes referred to as fruits, provide a glimpse into the beauty of the Christian life. Jesus was warning about false prophets when he said, "By their fruit you will recognize them. Do people pick grapes from thornbushes, or figs from thistles?" (Matt. 7:16). The same can be said for "good fruit" (c.f. John 13:35). The Christian life can be recognized by its observable good fruits.

The Fruit of Spiritual Formation

The outcome of discipleship is what is known as bearing fruit. The term *to bear fruit* generally means "to yield positive results." Bearing spiritual fruit is often thought of as the outward actions that God does through his people. Caring for orphans and widows (James 1:27), for example, might be considered a fruit-bearing activity. However, this chapter earlier reflected on the concept that God works in his people before he works through his people. Beard writes:

> Disciples are made [transformed] when information moves from a surface knowledge to affecting the believer from the inside out, in addition to behavior moving from something that is external in nature to activities and actions that spring forth from the very being of the believer.[449]

It is who and what a person is becoming that precedes and manifests what a person will do. Before there can be a focus on what God is doing through a person (external fruit), there must be a focus on what God is doing in a person (bearing internal fruit). The nature of one's internal attitudes or characteristics leads to the nature of one's outward actions. The types of actions that spring from the internal fruit depend on the nature of the internal fruit. A person might be doing many good things externally but internally may be less than pure. When pressed, it is the true internal nature that will become exposed. The following fictitious situation serves to illustrate:

> Imagine you're holding a cup of coffee when someone bumps into you, causing you to spill your coffee. Why did you spill your coffee? It was not because someone bumped you, but because that was what was in your cup. You didn't

---

[446] Francis A. Schaeffer, *The Mark of the Christian* (Downers Grove, IL: InterVarsity, 1970), 29.
[447] Flinn, 198.
[448] Lesslie Newbigin. "Cross-currents in Ecumenical and Evangelical Understandings of Mission," 148.
[449] Beard, 179.

spill tea. You didn't spill grape juice or soda. You spilled coffee because coffee is what was in your cup. If you'd had tea in your cup, it would have been tea that spilled out. The point is, whatever is inside your cup is what will spill out of your cup if bumped or shaken. We are each a vessel, not unlike a cup. Looking from the outside, no one can know what we "contain." But when events of life bump up against us or shake us up, whatever is inside will likely come spilling out. So, we must ask ourselves, "What's in my cup?" Is it love, joy, peace, patience, kindness, goodness, faithfulness, gentleness, and self-control? Or is it anger, bitterness, anxiety, impatience, mean-spiritedness, ill will, faithlessness, harshness, and lack of discipline? We might present to the world that we are full of one thing when really, we are full of another. It's easy to fake it when nothing is bumping into us or shaking us up. But bring on a little trial, a little temptation, irritation, conflict, inconvenience, etc., and what's inside our heart of hearts will come spilling out.[450]

A person becomes spiritually transformed as the Holy Spirit manifests changes in his or her character into the fruit of the Spirit: love, joy, peace, forbearance, kindness, goodness, faithfulness, gentleness and self-control (Gal. 5:22–23). These are not actions, rather internal attitudes or characteristics of one's persona that lead to an outward display of fruit. Jesus provides the perfect example of inner fruit that yield outward actions. There are several passages in Scripture that express Jesus feeling "compassion" toward someone with a need (Matt. 30:32–34; Mark 1:40–42) or toward the crowd (Mark 6:34; Mark 8:2; Matt. 14:14). One such passage seems to point specifically toward a call to action in mission:

Jesus went through all the towns and villages, teaching in their synagogues, proclaiming the good news of the kingdom and healing every disease and sickness. When he saw the crowds, he had compassion on them, because they were harassed and helpless, like sheep without a shepherd. Then he said to his disciples, "The harvest is plentiful but the workers are few. Ask the Lord of the harvest, therefore, to send out workers into his harvest field." (Matt. 9:35–38)

Jesus' compassion always leads to action, whether healing, feeding, providing, praying, or calling others to serve. Growth and nurturing the fruit of the Spirit is an ongoing process that takes time. It is analogous to a tree or plant that becomes noticeably fruit bearing only after several seasons of growth and care. Observable fruitfulness is the outcome of abiding in Christ, "Apart from me you can do nothing" (John 15:5), manifested through the interior work of the Holy Spirit, or fruits of the Spirit (Gal. 5:22–23). It is the outward actions resulting from the inward condition of a person's heart. From the abiding love of the Triune God flow the outward actions of recognizable fruit. Burge suggests, "Fruit then becomes a sign of spiritual life and vitality… not evidence by which we demonstrate that we belong in the vineyard."[451]

There can be no doubt that the Bible calls for believers to serve the poor and oppressed as an element of external fruit. Studies have been done regarding the sizable number of biblical passages that reference serving the poor and doing

---

[450] Adapted from the website "IllustrationExchange," https://illustrationexchange.com/illustrations?category=91, accessed 9/30/2019.
[451] Burge, 426.

justice. Jim Wallis describes a time when he and his fellow seminary students set out to explore the Bible's passages about the poor, finding several thousand such passages. One of his colleagues proceeded to physically remove those scriptures referencing justice and the poor, leaving little resemblance to what we would recognize as the Bible. In Wallis' words, "the Prophets were decimated, the Psalms destroyed, the Gospels ripped to shreds, and the Epistles turned to tattered rags."[452]

Richard Stearns went even further by penning a book built on this demonstration. Stearns left a successful career as a CEO to serve the poor by leading the compassion agency World Vision. Referencing the title of his book, Stearns says that unless we faithfully serve the poor, there is a "hole in our gospel."[453] The table below lists just a sampling of the verses that call for Christian action and service to those in need.

Table 13. - Bible Verses Supporting Christian Action of Compassion

Bible Passage	Reference
And let our people learn to devote themselves to **good works**, so as to help cases of urgent need, and not be **unfruitful**.	Titus 3:14 ESV
All Scripture is God-breathed and is useful for teaching, rebuking, correcting and training in righteousness, so that the servant of God may be thoroughly equipped for every **good work.**	2 Tim. 3:16–17
Let us not become weary in **doing good**, for at the proper time we will reap a harvest if we do not give up. Therefore, as we have opportunity, let us **do good** to all people, especially to those who belong to the family of believers [love one another].	Gal. 6:9–10
There will always be poor people in the land. Therefore I command you to **be openhanded** toward your fellow Israelites who are poor and needy in your land.	Deut. 15:11
As the body without the spirit is dead, so **faith without deeds** is dead.	James 2:26
And let us consider how we may spur one another on toward **love and good deeds.**	Heb. 10:24

Bearing fruit through good works calls for Christian engagement of and commitment to the world in which one is planted. It is becoming bearers of grace to one another, both inside and outside the community of believers, and developing a Christlike compassion for others, something often referred to as a compassion for the "common good." Christians should be known as those who use their gifts to work for the common good of all (1 Cor. 12:7).

The researchers for the *Common Fire* study note that a particularly important relationship experience in the lives of those committed to the common good is engagement with those that are significantly different than themselves. They call

---

[452] Wallis, *Faith Works*, 71–72.
[453] Richard Stearns, *The Hole in our Gospel* (Nashville, TN: Thomas Nelson, 2009). The title of Stearns' book stems from the result of Wallis' Bible cutting activity.

this "a constructive engagement with otherness"[454] and state that it is, "the single most important pattern they found in the lives of people committed to the common good."[455] Otherness need not be described solely as ethnic or nationality differences but encompasses differences in economic or social status, mental or physical capabilities, or any number of significant differences that can differentiate people from one another. It is not simply the encounter with someone different that yields transformation. To be a transformative experience, the engagement must be "constructive," an experience that begins to transform one's thinking.

The Total Health partnership provides this constructive encounter with otherness throughout its community of relationships. Examples of otherness found within the partnership relationships are illustrated in the table below.

Table 14. - Examples of Otherness

Examples of Otherness Within the Total Health Partnership
Poor and non-poor
Highly educated and less educated and uneducated
Christian and non-believer
U.S. and Honduran
Medical staff and patient

These relationships are often generalized as differences between those in the U.S. and those in La Ceiba. Such generalizations, however, miss the gravity of the disparity. Each of these differences (with the exception of U.S. and Honduran) fully exists within each of the nationality and ethnic cultures.

A transformative engagement with others helps people develop a cultural consciousness, "the recognition that we dwell in cultures—patterns of human behavior shaped by a particular community or population over time."[456] These cultures need not necessarily be defined solely by ethnicity or nationality. Everything one does is shaped by one's surroundings and the related experiences one has within those surroundings. Behaviors, motivations, and expectations are molded by this phenomenon labeled culture. However, as Hiebert points out, there is often an unawareness of one's own cultural biases and the impact these biases can have on one's behaviors.[457] Transformation begins to occur as previous cultural boundaries are challenged, allowing for a renewed view of one's self and the world.

Those participating in mission tasks to serve the poor, for example, often realize just how spiritually and relationally impoverished they themselves are in comparison to those they had planned to help and those with which they are partnering to serve. For example, Dr. Martin has lamented about how partnering in mission with churches in Latin America led him to realize the limits of his own faith. Recalling his experience in Latin America, he noticed the different reactions to difficult situations. When something such as a church air-conditioner breaks down

---

[454] Daloz, "Transformative Learning for the Common Good," 110.
[455] Daloz, et al., Common Fire, 63.
[456] Daloz, et al., Common Fire, 116.
[457] Hiebert, 62.

in the U.S., the church leaders immediately start soliciting the funding for a new replacement.

The same situation in an impoverished church in Latin America elicits a much different response, bringing the people first to their knees in faithful prayer. There is no money to solicit; only God can provide. Dr. Martin's point of the story is that having experienced partnership with those of another culture, he gained a new perspective of his own lack of faith. His newfound self-awareness was a formative discipling impact of partnering cross-culturally.[458]

This need for self-awareness extends also to those being served by the partnership. At the essence of the gospel is a right relationship with God through Jesus Christ. The need is the same for both the poor and the non-poor. However, the related issues of a transformed self-identity are different. Those being served are generally extremely impoverished people living in an economically oppressive nation. They are considered societal outcasts and suffer from feeling devalued and marginalized. This group of people needs to understand and believe that they are made in God's image, that they are his children, and that they have value and can contribute to God's creation. The non-poor on the other hand may have an overstated self-worth. They too need to understand that they are made in God's image, but they also need to understand that they are not God. Ridding themselves of their "god-complexes," the non-poor must understand and believe that the things they possess are meant to be shared, not used for control.[459] Tizon writes that the "church engages in the ministry of reconciliation when it at once cares for and empowers the poor and exhorts the rich to denounce Mammon and to shift their gaze and resources toward the world's most vulnerable."[460]

Jesus ministered to both of these contexts, the poor and oppressed as well as those like the "rich young ruler," bearing fruit in each one. It is in this same context that the Total Health partnership seeks to serve those in need, both the spiritually poor and the materially poor. Total Health actively partners with the church in these mission tasks as it seeks to both care for the poor through provision of primary care while at the same time discipling those that participate with them in providing that care, including those wealthy participants from the U.S. with regard to biblical aspects of poverty and relationships.

Short-Term Mission Trips

Short-term mission trips done within the Total Health partnership are a significant discipleship activity that warrants a separate section. These trips, done in partnership, can foundationally build upon the already vast network of relationships and provide even more opportunity for spiritual formation and relational reach.

As suggested earlier, a most important element to the formation of a worldview committed to the common good is a "constructive engagement with otherness." Daloz suggests four critical conditions required to facilitate the steps toward a

---

[458] This story is paraphrased from a message given to Grace Point Community Church in Lewis Center, Ohio, on September 4, 2016, by Jay E. Martin, MD, President of Total Health, and is included with permission.
[459] Myers, Walking with the Poor, 178.
[460] Tizon, 15.

transformative constructive engagement of otherness: the presence of the other, reflective discourse, a mentoring community, and opportunities for committed action.[461] The nature of the cross-cultural relationships within the partnership provides the partnership a unique opportunity to work within these conditions and to missionally facilitate this most important engagement with otherness experience. Nowhere is this more prominent than in the way Total Health and the church relationally organize and coordinate short-term mission trips together.

There are thousands of short-term mission trips taken each year. The predominant attitude of these trips is the view of the missionaries traveling to "help" the less fortunate. Total Health recognizes that there are much more cost-effective ways to aid these communities (such as community healthcare clinics). However, the organization also recognizes the value these trips can provide to the spiritual health and worldview transformation of the travelers. When viewed with a lens toward spiritual formations and transformative learning, Total Health short-term mission trips provide a structure for facilitating a "constructive engagement with otherness" that has been deemed important to transformation toward a commitment to the common good.

First and foremost, the trip provides the presence of the other. By design, the trip takes the team to a part of the world that by most measures is significantly different than their home. The Total Health trip then takes this a step further. The team members are split into small groups and housed in the homes of host families within the local community. The host family cares for the missionary travelers during the extent of their stay. This provides missionary travelers a fishbowl view of the local culture. The travelers can begin to experience not only the difference, but also the similarity to that of their own culture. Often a connection is formed during the trip that, thanks to the ease of current media communications, continues well past the end of the trip.

In the process of learning about the "other," travelers also gain invaluable insights into their own ethnocentricity. Borthwick suggests, "We need firsthand experience in other cultures and with other ethnic groups to grow beyond our racism, false stereotypes, and narrow world views."[462] A short-term mission trip to another part of the world provides travelers with experiences that exceed the borders of their normal. The transformative learning process is initiated as the experiences begin to create fundamental questions to previously held assumptions regarding what the travelers are seeing and experiencing. Robert J. Priest, Professor of Missions and Intercultural Studies and Director of the Ph.D. program in Intercultural Studies at Trinity Evangelical Divinity School, and Joseph Paul Priest, researcher, suggest,

> [short-term mission trips] also represents an awesome opportunity to help large numbers of ethnocentric North Americans develop global awareness, helping to shape the conscience of North American churches and of a nation with reference to global issues, from the environmental pollution to immigration, to

---

[461] Daloz, "Transformative Learning for the Common Good," 112.
[462] Borthwick, A Mind for Missions, 83.

AIDS, to the global sex trade, to global poverty, to Darfur, or the third world debt.[463]

The ability to reflect on these experiences is a key part of the learning process, and transformative learning scholars suggest that reflection works best when done in discourse with others. Mezirow defines discourse as "the process in which we have an active dialog with others to better understand the meaning of an experience."[464] By definition, a Total Health mission trip involves a team of other people with which to dialog. In addition, the team leader will be a veteran short-term missionary, with experience in the host culture. Team members are encouraged to reflectively journal their thoughts at the end of each day, specifically those experiences that raised questions. Each morning the team meets to discuss and reflect on the events of the prior day, allowing for a "reflective discourse" of their experiences.

A Total Health trip also ensures that there will be several local people involved in these morning sessions. These people are from the local community and are experienced working with short-term missionaries from other countries. They understand many of the cultural biases these travelers bring with them. This allows the travelers to process their thoughts and experiences not only with people from their same culture but collectively alongside people other than themselves. Daloz proposes that "transformation proceeds from the progressive taking-in, digesting, and reconstructing of perspectives different from our own,"[465] and having people other than the team members involved in the reflection sessions helps to provide these diverse perspectives.

Action is the visible reflection of transformation, and Daloz states that "The opportunity to act on one's evolving commitments, to test and ground one's growing convictions in action, is vital."[466] A short-term mission trip is an excellent way to provide an experiential learning experience. For example, many of the Total Health mission teams are made of students, often in the medical field (nursing, residents, physician assistant, etc.). These short-term mission trips provide the students the opportunity to experience and practice medicine in a way that they may not get in the U.S. Bellah suggests that studies have shown "where service learning is integrated with actual course work, where it is done together with others, and, above all, where it takes place in a context on ongoing reflection about the meaning and value of the work, it can have life-changing consequences."[467]

This "engagement with otherness" through the Total Health trip provides the students a platform for the transformative learning process to occur. They see something different, yet similar, to their normal experiences. As the students go through the experiences, they can begin the transformative learning step of reflecting on the differences and similarities in the contexts and how this might

---

[463] Robert J. Priest and Joseph Paul Priest, "They See Everything, and Understand Nothing: Short-Term Mission and Service Learning." In *Missiology: An International Review* Vol. XXXVI No. 1, 2008, 67.
[464] Mezirow, 14.
[465] Daloz, Transformative Learning for the Common Good, 115.
[466] Daloz, Transformative Learning for the Common Good, 117.
[467] Bellah and Tipton, 445.

serve to reshape their prior convictions and worldviews. It can be a very powerful sense of reality to experience the same desires to treat the medically ill but to do so without the Western entitlement mentality of having the "best of everything" at one's fingertips.

Each short-term mission trip offers a unique experience and a different opportunity to engage with otherness. Priest and Priest suggest, "America's future pastoral leaders will have acquired many of their understandings of 'social others' and of the wider world in the context of short-term mission trips."[468] These short-term trips are not moments-in-time transformations; rather these "successive experiences over time create a way of being in the world which is continually open to rediscovering that 'we' and 'they' share common bonds."[469] Multiple mission trip adventures allow travelers to build on each experience, learning something new each time, furthering transformation and commitment.

The Importance of Spiritual Formation to Mission Practice

Spiritual formation plays a vital role in the ongoing practice of holistic mission. Human capacity to "do" mission is not limitless and those practicing mission invariably reach a point of diminishing effectiveness. This is analogous to fruit trees that reach a limit and must be pruned (transformed) in order to thrive. Trees that are regularly pruned produce fruit with a higher sugar content and consistent ripening. It is the same for those on mission. When one's limits are reached, new transformation is required.

Human learning comes from the life-long recursive cycle of integrating information and experiences, evaluating and interpreting feedback from experiences, and allowing the cycle to continually guide future actions. Each new action brings new experiences and new learnings. Additionally, each cycle provides a new level of transformation to the learner. Ruth Haley Barton suggests a similar recursive transformation process inherent in missions as depicted in the figure below.

---

[468] Priest and Priest, 55.
[469] Daloz, et al., Common Fire, 71.

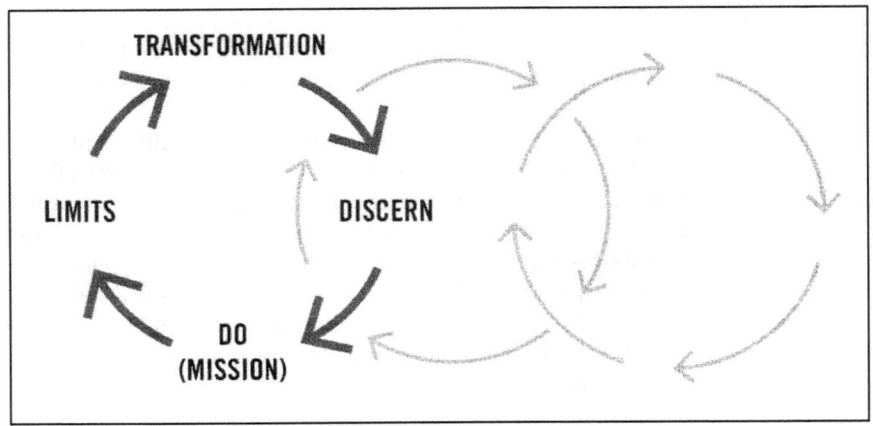

Figure 7. - Transformation and Mission[470]

An appropriate level of Christian spiritual transformation must take place before embarking on mission tasks. This occurs through the work and power of the Holy Spirit as he works through the community of relationships of the one being transformed. As transformation occurs, there is a level of discernment regarding what God is doing and how one might participate. This leads to the "doing" of missions.

Invariably, one reaches the limits of the mission or a plateau in its effectiveness. This point in the cycle might be due to changing circumstances or needs within the mission context. It could be just as likely that God, the designer of the mission, desires that the mission take a different direction. At this point, the mission practitioners must enter a phase of continued and focused transformation in order to reach a level of discernment regarding the future mission path.

The Total Health partnership leaders found themselves in just such a cycle at a crucial point in their mission in La Ceiba, a point they call their "Tower of Babel" experience. At that time in the history of the organization there was just the one clinic partnership in La Ceiba. The clinic had added staff and additional services as it continued to grow. The team continued to investigate opportunities to expand in La Ceiba. However, a series of violent gang-related actions in the community and specifically against the church leaders put the future of the clinic in jeopardy.

The team came together as a community of believers and began to pray together. What quickly became evident was that perhaps the mission in La Ceiba had reached a limit. Not a limit in which God's mission was completed and the clinic was no longer needed, rather a limit to the extent to which God wanted the team to expand. Prophetically, the team realized that the violence was what it took for God

---

[470] Printed with permission from Ruth Haley Barton, www.transformingcenter.org. Ruth Haley Barton, "Transformation and Mission Diagram," *Becoming a Transforming Church* Retreat, September 2017. ©Ruth Haley Barton, Wheaton, IL USA. Not to be reproduced without express written permission from Ruth Haley Barton, author.

to get their attention to his desire to move the mission forward in other geographic areas.

Walking through that stage of transformation as a team was a gift to one another. Each member brought his or her spiritual gifts to the stage, none more so than one of the Total Health directors that seems to have a gift of prophesy. Since that time God has blessed the obedience of the team and provided for the mission partnership platform to be expanded and to serve in multiple new countries with multiple new clinics.

Attesting to a "New Reality"

The ultimate measure of effectiveness of holistic mission is its ability to point to Jesus Christ in all elements of its tasks. Or, as Newbigin might ask, does the mission attest to a new reality that provokes the questions that require the gospel answers and that allows for the supernatural working of the Holy Spirit?

One of the Total Health directors noted a story of his grandchild who was attending a baptism at a local beach in the town. One of his grandchild's friends happened to be at the beach also and began quizzing him about what was happening. The director's grandchild explained the baptism, including that it is a public display of a person's belief and faith in Jesus. The friend then asked, "Who is this Jesus?" The director commented, "That is why Total Health exists, to get people to ask, 'Who is this Jesus?'"

Previous sections of this book have examined how the service element of the partnership points to and reflects the love of Christ. The medical care includes evangelism through proclamation as well as a clinic staff that embrace their mission to share the love of Christ. The church is in close proximity to the clinic, and church leaders are frequently seen in and around the clinic. There is basically nothing that happens in the La Ceiba context that does not somehow point to Jesus.

The U.S. aspects of the partnership, however, have had to mature into this. Total Health is an organization that was formed as a charity under the U.S. tax laws. There was some concern at the time about the nature of incorporated faith-based organizations. In addition, being novices to this type of mission organization, the leaders were uncertain about the ability to raise funds as a faith-based organization versus that of a medical provider organization. As a result, the organization positioned itself more as a medical provider than as a mission or ministry. This is evidenced by the wording selected in the early mission and vision statements:

> Our [Total Health] vision is to provide consistent and quality healthcare to the severely impoverished in La Ceiba, Honduras, and its surrounding communities.
>
> Total Health is a Christian based organization that is designed to deliver healthcare to impoverished people in partnership with churches in the third world... We are a medical organization, but our work is done in partnership with missionary organizations and allows them to effectively spread the gospel. We do not do any medical care outside this type of partnership.[471]

---

[471] Excerpts taken from two separate vision documents drafted in 2004 as part of the Total Health incorporation process.

The faith element was never denied and always existed just under the surface. The fact that the organization partnered with a church in a different demographic and delegated much of the service to the locals garnered notice, however. Sider, Olson, and Unruh suggest that "when Christians of different denominations, races, and socioeconomic backgrounds come together around the banner of holistic ministry, people take notice. Such ministry partnerships are a living testimony to the reconciling power of the gospel."[472] The visible act of partnership between disparate groups was noticed and began serving as a powerful illustration of God's people working for God's mission.

As the team matured spiritually, they began to recognize that they could have a spiritual impact not only in La Ceiba but among the U.S. relationships as well. As a result, they began to position themselves more as a partner in holistic mission with a specialty of medical care. The spiritual aspects of the mission were brought more to the surface. Consider the changes in the various mission and vision statements:

Transform physically, emotionally and spiritually impoverished people and their communities by delivering primary care medicine along with related activities in partnership with Christian nationals.

Facilitate spiritual development of those we serve and our partners... use Total Health communication tools (i.e., newsletters) to challenge and promote spiritual growth.[473]

The organization also began to move the spiritual dynamic into its everyday communications and propagandas by revising the logo and website to reflect the holistic elements of serving the complete person (see logo below). In addition, the website brought to the front the organization's desire to point to Jesus Christ. For example, the "What We Do" page of the Total Health website includes the captions "We Stand for Healthy People," "We Stand for Combating Poverty," and "We Stand for Jesus."[474]

Figure 8. - Total Health Logo

An effective holistic mission points to Christ in all of its elements, whether it is in the service, the proclamation, or in these examples, the website and communications. These are tools to be used in the holistic mission of God. These tools serve as a means to make visible and noticeable God's transformative and reconciliatory work that he is doing in and through the lives of his people. This work

---

[472] Sider, Olson, and Unruh, 228.
[473] Excerpts taken from the Total Health mission and vision document drafted in 2017 and revised in 2018.
[474] Section headings in the website found at http://totalhealth.org/what-we-do/.

is fostered and made visible by the trusting horizontal relationships developed with others. Tizon places the pieces into perspective, noting "The church at its best makes visible the vertical, horizontal, and circular dimensions of reconciliation [holistic mission], made possible in Christ and by the power of the Spirit."[475] The mission partnership is a vessel for this work.

Summary

This chapter endeavored to answer the research question proposed in the case study regarding how Christian mission partnerships between churches and non-church organizations facilitate achievement of holistic mission. Holistic mission is effective when it promotes the spiritual formation and facilitates physical well-being of others. A Christian mission partnership facilitates this mission when it provides for a means of spiritual formation through evangelism and discipleship and a means of promoting physical well-being through service. The chapter examined three primary marks that make for such a Christian mission partnership.

First, the partnership drives practical benefits to each member. The diversity of the partners and the different gifts they bring to the relationship enhances each member's individual ministry and mission. In addition, each member is personally benefited and made better through mutual discipleship and service.

Secondly, there exists a vast myriad of relationships that provide for extended opportunities within the mission. These relationships offer unique evangelistic and service opportunities as well as a vast vehicle for spiritual formation and discipleship.

And finally, the partnership puts Christian unity on display for an unbelieving world. As these relationships are formed into various "missional communities" with a gospel intentionality, the world is given a glimpse of the love of Christ in many practical ways.

---

[475] Tizon, 89.

Chapter 5

Missiological Implications

Introduction

The instrumental case study of the partnership between Total Health and the GCLA church in La Ceiba, Honduras, was conducted in connection with research into the current literature of partnership and holistic mission. The study results suggest four pertinent categories of missiological implications regarding Christian mission partnerships as a facilitation vehicle for holistic mission.

1. There is a missiological need for a broadened perspective of both holistic mission and Christian mission partnership, specifically as it relates to the mission tasks that provide discipleship and spiritual formation.
2. There are unique missiological implications to the non-church organization involved in Christian mission partnerships with churches.
3. The U.S. context presents cultural challenges that impede successful Christian mission partnerships.
4. The relational nature of Christian mission partnerships provides a platform for expanded opportunities for relational and experiential discipleship and spiritual formation.

A Broadened Missiological Perspective

There is a missiological need for a broadened perspective of holistic mission and the related manner in which Christian mission partnership can facilitate the mission. The general view of holistic mission points narrowly to activities focused primarily on evangelistic proclamation combined with acts of service. Spiritual development and discipleship are noticeably absent from this narrow view. Void of spiritual development, other mission activities will present a much less effective Christian witness to the gospel, and at its worst, can lead to a distortion of the gospel message and an incomplete Christian conversion. The biblical call to make disciples of all nations and to teach them to obey all that Christ has commanded is a missiological void that exists in this narrow perspective.

This narrow view of holistic mission also leads to the much too narrow perspective that recognizes partnership solely as a means of adding resources in order to serve and evangelize more cost-effectively. A mission partnership creates a vast array of relationship groups (or community groups) that can exponentially expand the number of people impacted by the holistic mission tasks of evangelism, discipleship, and service. Most noticeable are the increased opportunity for relational discipleship. These communities of relationships give disciples other disciples from which they can learn (as well as teach) and provide a safe platform to actively put into practice the things they have learned.

Churches across the globe continue to search for better means of discipling their members. Discipleship has historically been approached as an intellectual learning experience with programs designed to entice church members to read their Bibles. These programs, however, lack the means to move disciples from knowing what they are to do onward to knowing how they are to do it. The question becomes, how can the mission replicate the discipleship transformation ("I learned to serve") as seen in the Total Health clinic staff? How can disciples be taught to love their neighbor?

In holistic discipling, Myers suggests,

> We must explore our assumptions about where discipling takes place. When discipling is treated solely as a spiritual activity, we tend to locate discipling in the church as a spiritual exercise. While it is this, it is also much more... Discipleship often happens on the periphery, the most frequent location of the risen Christ. A great number of my Christian friends testify to the fact that they learned far more about the true meaning of their faith and their Scripture working in dusty villages and squalid slums among the poor than they did in their comfortable churches.[476]

These relationships establish a form of community as they group together along lines of commonality. Flinn defines community for this purpose as "a self-organized neighborhood or network of people with a common purpose, cause, or interest."[477] The community is generally viewed as having some distinction from its surroundings, and people may belong to multiple communities. Those that have some direct involvement in the partnership can be considered a member of the partnership community. There are, however, within that partnership community many other smaller community groups. Examples of these communities within the partnership include, among others, the Total Health board of directors and the clinic staff. These are examples of small Christian community groups within the partnership that have come together in pursuit of the vision. Members of these groups, however, are also a member of other communities that include members that may or may not be members of the Total Health partnership community. For example, each of the members is also a member of his or her church community. In addition, the clinic staff are members of larger medical provider community of La Ceiba. This broadened perspective of the relational nature of Christian mission partnerships provides an extended platform of relationships that accommodates the broadened perspective of holistic mission inclusive of discipleship.

Implications of the Church – Non-Church Partnerships

The case study research specifically targets the missiological implications of churches partnering with non-church organizations. As churches begin to partner with non-church organizations, new opportunities to serve and evangelize begin to emerge. However, with these opportunities come ramifications. Both the church and the non-church organization must understand and take the appropriate steps to ensure that Christian values are maintained and that the mission activities point to Jesus Christ and his kingdom.

---

[476] Myers, *Walking with the Poor*, 228.
[477] Flinn, 172.

The literature suggests that much of the concern and practice of holistic mission flows through the domain of non-church organizations.[478] Churches partner with non-church organizations most often related to the holistic mission tasks of service and social responsibility. These partnerships give churches access to additional resources, allowing them to address needs that they otherwise may struggle to meet. The non-church organizations tend to be specialists in a specific task or aspect of holistic mission, such as healthcare or education and, as a result, can generally take advantage of a greater array of resources and reach an economy of scale that a single local church can seldom attain.

Holistic mission, however, is not simply about a more cost-effective or efficient delivery model of religious goods and services. A genuine mission partnership involved in the activities of holistic mission seeks to work together to transform lives both spiritually and physically by pointing to Jesus Christ. To do so requires the recognition that the non-church partner's specialty is viewed as an extension of the church and it requires an "equal yoking" of the church partner with the non-church partner.

Mission as an Extension of the Church

Each partner must recognize its responsibilities related to the holistic mission. This requires that the non-church organization recognize its responsibility as an extension of the church, facilitating the church's ability to fulfill its holistic mission. Padilla summarizes it, suggesting, "Service is better if it is integrated with other aspects of holistic mission, starting with the gospel of God's kingdom. Such integration frees the church to cooperate with secular entities for the common good, without neglecting Christian witnessing."[479] The Lausanne committee on church/parachurch relationships (LOP 24) states, "Service as an arm of the church is best."[480]

As noted earlier, the non-church element of holistic mission is generally found in some sort of service and social responsibility. It is important that these tasks are done as an arm of the church, not as another type of benevolent organization. First and foremost, service and compassion points to Christ when there is a recognizable link to the church.

In addition, when the service is done on or near the church complex, it gives people a reason to visit the church. It is analogous to Jesus' healing ministry in modern times. Jesus cared for them physically while taking the opportunity to care for them spiritually as well. Jesus cared for the physical ailment that was known to the "patient," while at the same time caring for the spiritual ailment which might not have been as obvious. This is exactly what Pastor Dago observed during those early medical brigades. There was an increase of people that came to the church complex to see the doctor, and he recognized that medical missions and healthcare would be a great opportunity to present the church and to reach a higher number of people with the gospel message.

Healthcare is but one example of a service element of holistic mission. Holistic mission can be tailored to the needs of the community. For example, in the U.S.,

---

[478] See Padilla, "Holistic Mission in Theological Perspective," and Ringma.
[479] Padilla, "Holistic Mission in Theolgical Perspective," 115.
[480] Lausanne Movement, "Cooperating in World Evangelism."

hundreds of communities of immigrants could be served by receiving English lessons. Many churches attempt to meet this challenge by offering some sort of classes. Like the healthcare example, this gives people a reason to come to the church.

The subject of this study, the Total Health partnership, provides an evangelist who attempts to speak with each clinic patient. This is not a requirement to receive care, but it is melded into the process in an unassuming manner. None of the patients interviewed expressed disappointment or a desire to not hear the gospel during their visit. However, on the contrary, almost every patient expressed how lovingly they are treated and suggested that hearing "about the Bible" is another way that the people at the clinic and the church show their love for the patients.

Christian Nature of the Non-Church Partner

The ultimate measure of holistic mission effectiveness is its ability to point to Jesus Christ in all elements of its tasks. Accordingly, this layers in a requirement that the non-church partner is a Christian or Christian organization, embracing all that comes with it. As Myers says, "We cannot witness to something that we are not."[481] This requirement stems from the concept of being "equally yoked" put forth by the Apostle Paul in one of his letters to the church in Corinth,

Don't **team up** with those who are unbelievers. How can righteousness be a **partner** with wickedness? How can light live with darkness? What harmony can there be between Christ and the devil? How can a believer be **a partner** with an unbeliever? (2 Cor. 6:14–15 NLT, emphasis added).[482]

The gravity of this passage is found in the ultimate goal of holistic mission, being a witness to the love of Christ. The underlying principle resides in the sanctity of the church's testimony. To the extent that the non-church partner could compromise the church's testimony, the relationship should be avoided.

This principle is germane to all partnerships, but with different "yoking" characteristics. In other words, a business partnership may be yoked by some other mutual characteristic such as a passion to provide a specific service or to beautify a community. The underlying principle remains the same. However, the nature of holistic mission requires a commitment to Christ as a minimum.

This does not mean that the non-church partner organization cannot be a secular organization. Total Health, for example, is considered a secular charity organization that provides medical care to the poor. However, it identifies also as a Christian organization, founded on Christian values.[483] As described in chapter four, Total Health's identity is found in its Christian values and as a partner in holistic mission.

This principle does not preclude a church or faith-based organization from doing specific actions of compassion or service alongside non-Christian organizations. For example, Christians in acts of disaster recovery, working alongside those of other faiths, attests to God's goodness. In addition, it adds to the

---

[481] Myers, Walking with the Poor, 221.
[482] The NIV translation uses the yoking term, "Do not be yoked together with unbelievers."
[483] Consistent with the concept of identity put forth by Kuitunen in his MTh dissertation regarding the missional identity of Christian development organizations.

potential relationships that could ultimately lead to a spiritual discussion and transformation.

Partnering in the U.S. Context

Livermore suggests that "The most common problems in ministry across different cultural contexts are not technical or administrative. The biggest challenges lie in miscommunication, misunderstanding, personality conflicts, poor leadership, and bad teamwork."[484] Certain negative elements of U.S. culture must be recognized and mitigated to avoid these challenges for an effective partnership model in the U.S. context. Specifically, individualism and cultural insensitivity can be significant impediments to the ability to productively participate in holistic mission collaboratively. To successfully partner in missions, these characteristics must be combatted, especially within the church.

Individualism

No national culture ranks as high on the individualism scale as the U.S.[485] Individualism is essentially the worship of one's self, and the importance of self becomes the lens through which all decisions are based. Manifestations of this can be seen within Christian service and testimony. Service projects become more about fulfillment of one's individual personal needs than about the service of others. A good deed is viewed as donating or signing up for a cause, especially a cause that might specifically help the donor or someone close to them.

Churches and their leaders are prone to the same fallacy. There is an unwillingness to collaborate or partner with others, whether it is other churches or non-church organizations. This unwillingness can stem from the individualistic need to be recognized or the need to have authority. An individualist seeks control in order to ensure that things are done "the right way," which is essentially the individualist's way.

In such a culture, partnership is difficult. However, if the church can see its way past its individualist tendencies toward that of collaboration, new service opportunities will emerge. With these come new opportunities to evangelize, to disciple, and to serve relationally. Sherman suggests, "As our service begins to be less sterile, less clinical, and more costly of our time, energy, and emotions, we grow in our appreciation of Jesus' servanthood, forbearance, and mercy."[486] This appreciation of Jesus' servanthood actively leads to an appreciation of what it means to love your neighbor.

Cultural Insensitivity and Misunderstanding

U.S. individualism also breeds into cultural insensitivity and misunderstandings. Individualism provokes a tendency to project one's own beliefs and values onto others. Today's U.S. society finds large people groups living in isolation from one another, in very different and unequal economic and social circumstances. However, this isolation prevents the groups from knowing and

---

[484] David A. Livermore. Cultural Intelligence: Improving Your CQ to Engage Our Multicultural World (Grand Rapids, MI: Baker Academic, 2009), 240.
[485] Becker, 122, and Hofstede, Hofstede, and Minkov, 95.
[486] Sherman, 231.

understanding one another. This lack of knowledge and understanding leads to a divisiveness within the society, the like of which the U.S. is experiencing today.

Elmer suggests that "If you try to serve people without understanding them, you are more likely to be perceived as a benevolent oppressor."[487] Bowman posits that cross-cultural partnerships help to mediate these tensions. He writes:

> By going to other cultures and nations in partnership with other believers, partners continue to mediate relational tensions. Before Christians enter into a new culture for the purpose of evangelism, discipleship, and church planting, they should already be engaging in cross-cultural partnerships with other believers. Therefore, cultural awareness and sensitivities develop before mission endeavors begin. Partners help each other understand diverse cultures and provide categories for understanding diverse cultures.[488]

Creating opportunities to serve others provides the opportunity to begin to understand others. As church members work with others, teaching immigrants English, for example, they invariably get to know them and develop a relationship with them. In the process, each person comes to the realization that though they are different in a number of ways, they are also remarkably similar.

Implication of Partnership Relationships on Discipleship

Discipleship is a relational experience that best happens in a relational community—not just a church community but in the communities involved in the everyday things of life.[489] Community fills the need for relational fellowship among the members while also serving the mission of the church. Disciple-making is meant to be experienced in relation with one another and happens as Christians share their kingdom life experiences (both good and bad) in the relational environment of the everyday actions of life. Within this community, disciples are provided growth opportunities in the same ways that the first disciples of Jesus experienced. They learn and grow, become more self-aware, and participate in God's mission in the loving relationship of the community.

In addition, communities with a holistic mission intent couple this means for discipleship and transformational growth with an intentional focus toward reaching and serving the growing number of those outside the church. The community becomes a safe place for those who are drawn to the winsome nature of the community to see and experience kingdom living expressed in the natural rhythms of the disciples' lives. A holistic mission-focused community provides a place for the post-modern culture to see, hear, and experience the gospel. It is a place for Christians to demonstrate that their faith is an integrated faith of believing and doing.

The mission partnership model as examined in the case study provides a platform of almost unlimited opportunities for relational and experiential

---

[487] Duane Elmer, *Cross-cultural Servanthood: Serving the World in Christlike Humility* (Downers Grove, IL: InterVarsity Press Books, 2006), 20.
[488] Bowman, 211.
[489] Flinn, 173.

discipleship. These opportunities allow disciples to move beyond intellectual learning to practical application of what they learn. Sherman writes,

Relational ministry also deepens our discipleship. It can help us to reveal prejudices that we need to confess and eschew. It can also "spur us on" to love those who are unlovely or exasperating. And how will we grow in the love Jesus calls us to—the love that surpasses "loving those who love us"—unless we pursue such stretching relationships?[490]

Discipleship is more than reading a book and discussing its ramifications. It requires practical application of the things Jesus commanded. Discipleship occurs holistically as Christians serve others and experience life on mission together.

Discipling Toward Cultural Understanding and Sensitivity

Cultural misunderstandings seem to be a significantly divisive element evident throughout today's society and culture, including the Christian Church. A concept of discipling in community provides a means of discipling toward cultural understanding. Members of the community come into relationships molded by their own cultural community experiences. These cultural experiences are many and need not be racial or ethnic. Differences stem from socio-economic differences, denominational differences, etc.

Christians who fear differences and isolate themselves lose the ability to relate to others, resulting in less effective witness, evangelism, and service. Living out their faith in a holistic mission community provides Christian disciples with a much better understanding of the culture, its needs, and its impact on the disciples' faith. It helps people develop what Daloz, *et al.*, describe as "cultural consciousness," or "more than a superficial tolerance by which one glibly confers value on another culture without engaging it. It requires acknowledging one's partial understanding of that culture, and tentatively presuming its worthwhile seeking to understand it better from the inside."[491] In the process, disciples often develop further self-awareness and insights into feelings about their own culture.

This also provides disciples with opportunities to integrate cultural understandings of the real world with biblical knowledge that they may have learned in the safety of a seminary or discipleship class. Wilkins highlights this discipleship importance, pointing out:

> We must develop our walk with Jesus in the real world... we all need to learn how to live with Jesus in the everyday world... He desires to walk with us in every circumstance of every day. We do not have to withdraw from the circumstances of life in order to be his disciples.[492]

Bowman suggests that Christians partnering cross-culturally can serve to mediate cross-cultural tensions. However, he suggests that before Christians enter into a new culture for the purpose of mission, "... they should already be engaging in cross-cultural partnership with other believers. Therefore, cultural awareness and sensitivities develop before mission endeavors begin."[493]

---

[490] Sherman, 231.
[491] Daloz, et al., Common Fire, 116.
[492] Wilkins, Following the Master, 142.
[493] Bowman, 211.

Christian disciples formed in this way can exist in the world's different cultures with confidence in God's Word and in their ability to live in such a way that will reflect positively the gospel message. These disciples remain steadfast in God's truths, while being a picture of Christlike love and grace. It is then that the true impact of the missional church can be realized outside its walls. By being in community together, fully equipped church "insiders" can begin to connect with church "outsiders" in the very community in which they both participate.

Discipleship While on Mission

Participating in missions with others, such as with the Total Health partnership, is a powerful method for discipleship and was central to how Jesus taught. Dwight J. Zscheile, Associate Professor of Congregational Mission and Leadership at Luther Seminary, points out that Jesus' disciples "learn what it means to follow Jesus as they experience ministry with him; their formation takes place in the context of mission."[494] Likewise, Zscheile suggests that transformation happens today as disciples participate in mission, "We are to go where Christ went in order to be formed in his likeness, to walk with others the ways of the world's forsakenness because we are found by him and find him there,"[495] (cf. "Whoever claims to live in him must live as Jesus did," 1 John 2:3–6).

One might argue that Jesus' method of disciple-making while on mission is not practical in today's society and culture. Jesus' closest disciples lived and traveled with him exclusively for three years. These exclusive arrangements generally do not happen today due to vocation and family commitments. Still, people long for relationship and involvement, and it is the commitment to a common cause that draws people together. This is found in the paradigm of community, offering belongingness and spiritual formation through a community drawn together for a common cause, a common mission.

Summary

Mission partnerships are a unique vehicle to provide the church with enhanced opportunities to serve their communities and their members holistically, with both physical care and spiritual care. Churches must be willing to look past a narrow view of partnership as solely a means of funding or adding a service, broadening their perspective to recognize the exponential missional relationships that exist within the sphere of these partnerships. This broadened perspective allows insights into the expanded opportunities for holistic mission, evangelism, discipleship, and service. In addition, as these missional relationships mature and branch out into the natural groups or communities of everyday life, they become greater witnesses to the goodness of Christ and begin evangelizing, discipling, and serving others.

---

[494] Dwight J. Zscheile, *Cultivating Sent Communities: Missional Spiritual Formation* (Grand Rapids, MI: Eerdmans, 2012), 24.
[495] Zscheile, 19.

Chapter 6

Conclusion

Christian partnership relationships in missions remain elusive. Western mission practices have seemed stuck in denominationalism or theological division and have been slow to move from traditional individualistic means of mission to evangelize and minister to the masses. At the same time, rapid globalization has shifted the "center of gravity" of the Christian church from the West to the Global South.[496] The unique missional challenges and opportunities created by this rapidly changing world require more effective mission. Stott called for innovation when he wrote, "What is needed now is the development of more innovative models of integrated mission, in which the Gospel, far from being silenced or marginalized by social involvement, is illuminated and enforced by it."[497]

This book endeavored to enter into the discussion by evaluating Christian mission partnerships as a means to facilitate holistic mission. The purpose of this instrumental case study is to describe and examine the mission partnership between Total Health and the GCLA church in La Ceiba, Honduras, to gain missiological insights and understandings about achieving holistic mission through partnerships between churches and non-church organizations. Specifically, the case study began with a goal to examine how these organizations created a mission partnership model that holistically integrated compassionate medical care with ongoing spiritual care and formation to serve the La Ceiba community and its residents.

Research findings from the qualitative instrumental case study suggest three primary marks or characteristics of a Christian mission partnership that facilitates the achievement of holistic mission. First, at its most basic level, the practical benefits of working together make the mission more effective. Reaching a conclusion that Christian mission partnerships facilitate holistic mission was not difficult from this perspective. The practical benefits of partnering in mission are readily apparent, and these benefits alone are sufficient motivations to partner. Organizations can work together to share resources and talents and accordingly make mission activities more widely available and cost effective. By partnering with a church, the non-church service specialist is able to mitigate many weaknesses, incremental costs, and additional risks that exist when performed outside the church or one's culture. Likewise, when the church partners with another organization, it gains access to valuable resources that allow it to serve the community in ways that it otherwise could not.

Second, there exists a myriad of relationships throughout the partnership and its constituents that promote opportunities for spiritual formation and transformation well beyond the observable purpose of the partnership. As the case study progressed, it became apparent that opportunities for holistic mission through Christian partnership extend well beyond supplying a more cost-effective

---

[496] Myers, Engaging Globalization, 197–98.
[497] Stott, "Twenty Years After Lausanne," 54.

delivery model of religious goods and services to the targeted community of the people in La Ceiba. These opportunities reside in the seemingly endless number of relationships that are ultimately impacted in some way by the partnership and the mission.

Mission is a relational function, and mission relationships start with the relationship of the Triune God and his people. God orchestrates and guides the mission with this vertical relationship, and his people carry out the mission horizontally. The horizontal relationships of mission are most often viewed as one-dimensional and outward flowing; there are the ones that through the power of the Spirit bring the mission and the ones that through the workings of the Spirit receive the mission. However, when considering the vast number of relational interactions within the structure and activities of a mission partnership, one comes away with a much different perspective of the breadth and depth of the potential reach and impact of the mission activities.

The observable goal of the mission partnership in this study is transforming hearts and lives by attending to the spiritual and physical well-being of those being served. The key to understanding the ultimate effectiveness of holistic mission is a true recognition of "those being served." The less obvious benefactors of the mission activities are these multitudes of relationships within and around the partnerships and the exponential impact these relationships can have on one another.

This perspective is most prevalent in the area of spiritual formation. Spiritual formation within holistic mission integrates evangelism, discipleship, and service into an organic relationship-building process. The partnership provides a platform for spiritual formation to occur as the mission tasks are being carried out. Essentially, the partnership creates a community of believers that evangelizes others, disciples one another and others, and serves one another and others. As this community of believers practice mission together, their discipleship is enhanced by the relational nature of the partnership. Through these relationships, they experience other believers to learn from, a constructive engagement with otherness (those culturally different than themselves in some manner), and a safe and practical place to put into practice what they have learned.

In addition to their own personal spiritual growth, the partnership provides unique, expanded evangelistic opportunities. As this community of transformed believers move out into other relational communities, new and different relationships are formed. These relationships can be formed with other Christians as well as non-Christians and often become the beginning of new discipleship relationships, thus allowing nonbelievers to see and experience Christlike behaviors and kingdom living. Halter and Smay refer to this aspect of discipleship as the "Discovery Zone," explaining:

The Discovery Zone is a sphere in which truth can be seen before it is spoken, where a new authority figure becomes trusted, and where people are able to weigh Christ's values over their own. In other words, where they can choose to "prefer" Christ's Kingdom ways over their own ways.[498]

The truth of the gospel becomes attractive as it is observed in the lives of others. This leads to the ultimate mark of holistic mission: the actions of the partnership through Christian witness service and its proclamation points to the

---

[498] Halter and Smay, 65.

gospel truth of Jesus Christ. In other words, it opens the door to the gospel discussion. An effective holistic mission points to Christ in all of its elements, whether it is in the service or the proclamation, the word or the deeds. These mission tasks are a means to serve and love others, making visible and noticeable God's transformative and reconciliatory work that he is doing in and through the lives of his people. This work is further made visible as maturing disciples share their lives through trusting relationships built with others.

Holistic mission is a subject of vast importance in order to serve and minister to this rapidly changing world. There is a growing understanding that the world's holistic mission needs will not be met by people or organizations working in isolation; to do so will leave the harvest plentiful but the workers few (Matt. 9:37). Individual interests are not lost in partnership with others; they are rather reshaped into greater common missional goals, allowing them to work together in order to share resources and yield a result greater than the simple sum of the two (Eccl. 4:9).

There is an old African proverb that says, "If you want to go fast, go alone. If you want to go far, go together" (author unknown). God has graciously invited Christians to partner with him in his mission. His mission is holistic as modeled by Jesus, and it is in partnership as modeled by the Trinity. It is only fitting the Triune God be honored by Christians who model mission after God's example by appropriately partnering with the many others whom he has invited.

APPENDIX 1 RESEARCH DESIGN AND METHODOLOGY

Introduction

This is an instrumental case study undertaken to describe and examine the mission partnership between the GCLA church in La Ceiba, Honduras, and Total Health, to evaluate and understand the missiological implications of mission partnerships between churches and non-church organizations specifically as they apply to holistic mission. The following sections describe the research methodology used in the study.

Methodological Design

The researcher adopted a qualitative research approach to complete this study. The research approach was guided by a list of defining characteristics of qualitative research created by Creswell and Cheryl N. Poth, faculty member of the Centre for Research and Applied Measurement and Evaluation, Department of Educational Psychology in the Faculty of Education at the University of Alberta:[499]

- The researcher is the key instrument to performing research activity.
- The study is performed in the natural setting or sites of the participants.
- Multiple data collection methods will be used to gather information.
- The research is context dependent, situated in the context of the participants.
- The research will present as much as possible a holistic account of the study.

Yin suggests that the design of the study is the "logical sequence that connects the empirical data to a study's initial research questions and, ultimately, to its conclusions."[500] This study was designed as an instrumental case study of the partnership between Total Health and the GCLA church in La Ceiba. The case is bounded by the partnership relationship of the two organizations involved, as well as the span of history of the partnership (2004–2018). An instrumental case study selects one bounded case to research in order to gain insights and understanding into the research questions proposed.[501] The case study design was guided by Yin's "components of research design; 1) study questions, 2) its propositions [theories] if any, 3) unit of analysis (case), 4) logic linking data to propositions, and 5) criteria for interpreting the findings."[502] The design was further guided by Creswell and Poth's "Defining Characteristics of Case Studies."[503]

Integrative Research Approach

The research was guided by Wan's emphasis on inter-disciplinary research. Inter-disciplinary research uses elements (e.g. theory, methodology) from one or more disciplines. It endeavors to combine and integrate biblical study, theology,

---

[499] Crewswell and Poth, 43–44.
[500] Yin, 28.
[501] Crewswell and Poth, 98; Stake, 3.
[502] Yin, 29.
[503] Crewswell and Poth, 97–98.

anthropology, demographics, statistics, etc., in order to achieve what Wan describes as a "high degree of coherence or unity in research and for the practice of Christian mission."[504] Table 2 below illustrates Wan's five-step methodology in priority sequence, acronym "STARS." that provides a framework for inter-disciplinary research in missiological studies.

Table 15. - Wan's Way of Integrative Research ("STARS")[505]

CRITERIA	*	EXPLANATION
1. Scripturally Sound	S	Not proof-text; but the "whole counsel of God" (Acts 20:26–27)
2. Theologically Supported	T	Not just pragmatism/expedience; but sound theology
3. Analytically Coherent	A	Not to be self-contradictory; but to be coherent
4. Relevantly contextual	R	Not to be out of place; but fitting for the context
5. Strategically practical	S	Not only good in theory; but can be strategically put into practice

Put into practice, Wan suggests that this methodology provides the means for missiological research to be "characteristically evangelical, doctrinally sound, and theologically grounded."[506]

Role of the Researcher

The researcher was the primary instrument for collecting, analyzing, and interpreting the data. The researcher has been associated with Total Health since its inception in 2004, first as its treasurer and member of the board of directors and more recently adding the responsibilities of Operations Officer. The researcher has traveled to the La Ceiba site on numerous occasions and is well known to the leaders of the GCLA church in La Ceiba and to those who work in the healthcare clinic. The interpretation and presentation of research findings as presented herein have been reviewed by the key constituents named in the partnership, notably, members of the Total Health board of directors and the former and current pastors and leaders at the GCLA La Ceiba church.

Data Collection

Yin suggests that a "major strength of case study data collection is the opportunity to use many different sources of evidence" and also that the "need to

---

[504] Enoch Wan, "Inter-disciplinary and Integrative Missiological Research: The 'What,' 'Why' and 'How,'" www.GlobalMissiology.org, July 2017.
[505] Wan, "Inter-disciplinary and Integrative Missiological Research."
[506] Wan, "Inter-disciplinary and Integrative Missiological Research."

use multiple sources of evidence [in case study research] far exceeds that in other research methods."[507] Adopting an integrative data collection methodology that uses multiple data sources allows the researcher to develop a broader and more in-depth understanding of the case and its missiological implications. Stake suggests that "all research is a search for patterns, for consistencies."[508] Likewise, multiple data sources provide what Yin calls "converging lines of inquiry."[509] These multiple sources provide converging themes that serve to corroborate findings throughout the research. These converging themes can then be triangulated into a cohesive set of observations and conclusions.

The researcher has used such an integrative research methodology illustrated in the diagram below. Data was collected primarily through observation (participant and direct), interviews, and review of organizational documents and archival records. The data was analyzed for consistent and convergent themes with observations and conclusions presented accordingly.

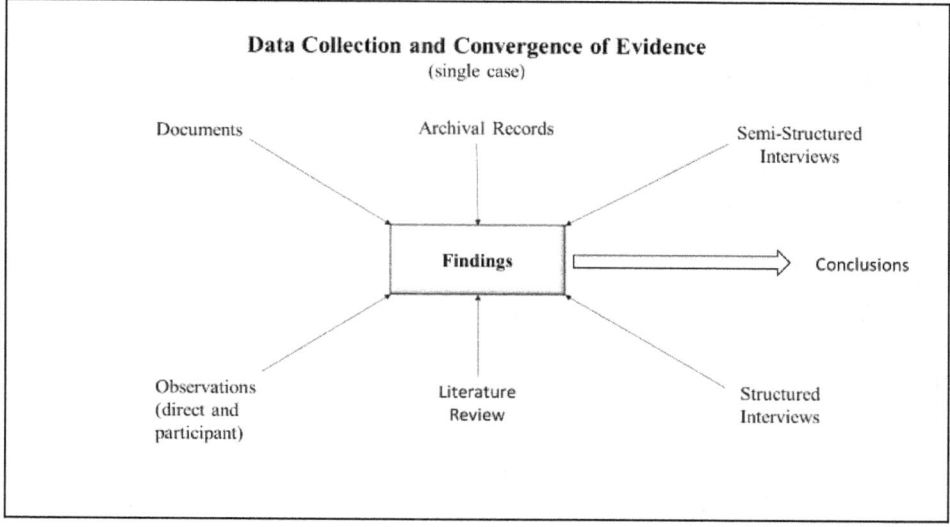

Figure 9. - Convergence of Multiple Data Sources into Thematic Conclusions[510]

Stake suggests that a "considerable proportion of all data is impressionistic, picked up informally as the researcher first becomes acquainted with the case."[511] The researcher's role within Total Health provided a unique opportunity to gather data as a participant-observer. During the study (as well as from the inception of the partnership), the researcher participated in the inner workings of the organization, including board meetings, site visits, and other related missional activities.

---

[507] Yin, 119.
[508] Stake, 44.
[509] Yin, 120.
[510] Adapted from Yin, 121.
[511] Stake, 49.

Participating in these activities provided access to thoughts, ideas, and critical partnership situations in real-time rather than learning about them after the fact via other data collection methods.

The researcher recognizes that such an insider status might bring a certain level of bias to the research. However, the researcher believes that the integrative approach of collecting data from multiple sources (other than the researcher's subjective experiences and observations) served as a mitigating factor to this insider bias. Accordingly, the research predominately reflects the finding from the data collected, though often corroborated by the researcher's firsthand experiences within the organization. Any data points used in the findings that reflect solely the participant-observer point of view have been noted appropriately.

A sizable portion of the research was collected via interviews of the study participants. Qualitative interviews "can be used to obtain in-depth information about a participant's thoughts, beliefs, knowledge, reasoning, motivations, and feelings about a topic."[512] The researcher's experience and history with the participants afforded a level of trust that provided some assurance that the participants were forthcoming with honest information despite cultural differences.

Structured interviews were conducted with both the paid and volunteer staff of the clinic (a total of eight interviews) in order to gather their thoughts and opinions regarding the holistic impact the partnership has had on the community. In addition, these interviews were used to illuminate and evaluate various missiological aspects of the partnership arrangement. Structured interviews were also conducted with thirty-two clinic patients to gather insights about the holistic impact to the individuals that attend and use the medical clinic. The patients interviewed were not targeted in any special way; they were simply the patients that showed up at the clinic on the days of the interviews and were willing to be interviewed. Patients included those that attended the adjacent church, those that indicated they attended a different church, as well as those that are not church attenders. The interviews included patients that had been coming to the clinic for many years as well as one patient for whom it was her first visit to the clinic.

Interviews of the leaders of the two organizations as well as other key partnership participants (non-patients) were generally conducted in an informal conversational and semi-structural style over a period of several months and several conversations. The researcher's participant-observer status allowed the researcher to conduct many of the interviews during normal organizational activities. This provided the opportunity for the interviews to be cumulative in nature and conversations directly related to the observations, the individuals, and the observed circumstances.

The interviews with patients and outsiders were more structured and consistent. The patient participants generally answered the same set of questions, with specific follow-up questions as needed. Additional data was collected via visual observation of this group of participants to corroborate the interviews and to determine the need for additional inquiry. Interview situations specifically designed for data collection (as opposed to participant observation data collection) were

---

[512] Johnson and Christensen, 235.

identified as such to the interview subject ensuring that they fully understood the value of their responses and the motivations of the researcher.

Data was also collected through the review of critical historical documents such as organizational records, correspondences, and minutes of past meetings. Yin suggests, "For case study research, the most important use of documents is to corroborate and augment evidence from other sources."[513] Archived organizational documents and correspondence were used to provide glimpses into the thoughts and feelings of the participants at strategic points in the organization's past. Such glimpses provided additional insights to the data collected through other sources.

Data collected that contains sensitive information has been preserved in either electronic format under password protection or preserved manually in secured files. Individual specific data has not been shared in this book unless properly authorized. For the record, both founders of the partnership, Jay E. Martin, MD and Pastor Dagoberto Irias (Dr. Martin and Pastor Dago),[514] have authorized the use of their names and specified comments and quotations attributed to them.

Data Interpretation and Presentation

Data is presented herein primarily in a narrative format. Consistent themes are highlighted and correlated to holistic mission and partnership theories. These themes are compared and contrasted to themes derived from other scholars and leaders identified through the review of the literature. These themes have been reviewed and validated by the leaders of both organizations.

Missiological implications for mission partnerships between a church and a non-church organization have been drawn from the data collected, its consistent themes, and related interpretations. These implications are summarized and presented herein.

Ethical Considerations

The researcher did not anticipate nor encounter significant ethical issues related to this study. Advance approval was obtained from the leaders of both organizations to perform the study and to use their respective background information. Others interviewed have not been identified by name without prior authorization. The researcher was experienced in this context and had observed the participants' willingness to participate in similar past interviews, allowing their stories, names, and faces to be used in newsletters and similar limited publications. Nonetheless, care was taken to ensure the privacy rights of the interviewees and only willing participants were interviewed. Finally, individual specific information gained through interview or observation has not been used in the presentation unless the information was specifically relevant and prior authorization was received.

---

[513] Yin, 107.

[514] Throughout this book, the two Total Health founders will be referred to as Dr. Martin and Pastor Dago. This is consistent with how they are referred to within the organization.

Bibliography

Addicott, Ernie. *Body Matters: A Guide to Partnership in Christian Mission.* Edmonds, WA: Interdev, 2005.

Ammerman, Nancy T. "Doing Good in American Communities: Congregations and Service Organizations Working Together." 2001. *Hartford Institute for Religious Research.* an online research project from the Organizing Religious Work Project. Accessed 3 August 2018. <http://hirr.hartsem.edu/orw/orw_cong-report.htm>.

Barnes, Jonathan S. *Power and Partnership: A History of the Protestant Mission Movement.* Eugene, OR: Pickwick Publications, 2013.

_____. "Whither Partnership? Reflections on the History of Mutuality in Mission," *Review and Expositor* Vol. 113 (1) (2016): 32–45.

Beard, Christopher. "Missional Discipleship: Discerning Spiritual-Formation Practices and Goals with the Missional Movement." *Missiology: An International Review* 43 (2) (2015): 175-194.

Becker, Thomas H. *Doing Business in the New Latin America: A Guide to Cultures, Practices, and Opportunities.* Westport, CT: Praeger Publishers, 2004.

Bediako, Kwame. "Theological Reflections." *Serving with the Poor in Africa: Cases in Holistic Ministry.* Ed. Tetsunao Yamamori, *et al.* Monrovia, CA: MARC, 1996. 181–192.

Bellah, Robert N. and Steven M. Tipton, *The Robert Bellah Reader.* Durham, NC: Duke University Press, 2006.

Borthwick, Paul. *A Mind for Missions: 10 Ways to Build Your World Vision.* Colorado Springs, CO: NavPress, 1987.

_____. *Six Dangerous Questions to Transform Your View of the World.* Downers Grove, IL: InterVarsity, 1996.

Bosch, David J. *Transforming Mission: Paradigm Shifts in Theology of Mission.* 20th Anniversary Edition. Maryknoll, NY: Orbis Books, 2011.

_____. *Witness to the World: The Christian Mission in Theological Perspective.* 1980 Reprint. Eugene, OR: Wipf&Stock, 2006.

Bowman, Joshua Stephen. *Cross-Cultural Mission Partnership: Mediating Relational, Cultural, and Hermeneutical Tensions for Mutual, Faithful Missional Engagement.* PhD Thesis, Southeastern Baptist Theological Seminary, September 2019.

Brookfield, Stephen D. "Transformative Learning as Ideology Critique." Jack Mezirow and Associates. *Learning as Transformation: Critical Perspectives on a Theory in Progress.* San Francisco, CA: Jossey-Bass, 2000. 125–148.

Burge, Gary M. *John: The NIV Application Commentary.* Grand Rapids, MI: Zondervan, 2000.

Bush, Luis. "In Pursuit of True Christian Partnership: A Biblical Basis from Philippians." *Partners in the Gospel: The Strategic Role of Partnership in World Evangelization*. Ed. James H. Kraakevik and Dotsey Welliver. Wheaton, IL: Billy Graham Center, 1992. 3–16.

Bush, Luis and Lorry Lutz. *Partnering in Ministry: The Direction of World Evangelism*. Downers Grove, IL: InterVarsity Press, 1990.

Butler, Phill. *Well Connected: Releasing Power, Restoring Hope Through Kingdom Partnerships*. Colorado Springs, CO: Authentic, 2006.

Butler, Phillip. "Kingdom Partnerships in the '90s: Is There a New Way Forward?" *Kingdom Partnerships for Synergy in Missions*. Ed. William D. Taylor. Pasadena, CA: William Carey Library, 1994. 9–30.

Carroll, Lewis. *Through the Looking Glass, and What Alice Found There*. London: MacMillan and Co, 1872.

Cheyne, John. "Strategies for Humanitarian Ministries." *Missiology: An Introduction to the Foundations, History, and Strategies of World Missions*. Ed. John Mark Terry, Ebbie Smith and Justice Anderson. Nashville, TN: Broadman & Holman, 1998. 515–525.

Corbett, Steve and Brian Fikkert. *When Helping Hurts: How to Alleviate Poverty without Hurting the Poor... and Yourself*. Chicago, IL: Moody, 2012.

Cotterell, Peter. *Mission and Meaninglessness: The Good News in a World of Suffering and Disorder*. London: SPCK, 1992.

Couto, Alva. "Latin American Social Contexts." *Serving with the Poor in Latin America: Cases in Holistic Ministry*. Ed. Tetsunao Yamamori, *et al*. Monrovia, CA: MARC, 1997. 87–99.

Creswell, John W. *Research Design: Qualitative, Quantitative and Mixed Methods Approaches*. Thousand Oaks, CA: Sage, 2014.

Crewswell, John W. and Cheryl N. Poth. *Qualitative Inquiry & Research Design: Choosing Among Five Approaches*. 4th edition. Thousand Oaks, CA: SAGE, 2018.

Daloz, Laurent A. Parks. "Transformative Learning for the Common Good." Mezirow, Jack and Associates. *Learning as Transformation: Critical Perspectives on a Theory in Progress*. San Francisco, CA: Jossey-Bass, 2000. 103–123.

Daloz, Laurent A. Parks, *et al*. *Common Fire: Leading Lives of Commitment in a Complex World*. Boston, MA: Beacon Press, 1996.

Davis, Charles A. *Making Disciples Across Cultures: Missional Principles for a Diverse World*. Downers Grove, IL: InterVarsity, 2015.

De Oliveira, Carlos Roberto. *Breaking Down the Resistance to the Gospel Through Holistic Medical Missions: A Strategy for Reaching Resistant Rural Towns in Mexico*. D.Min Thesis, Northern Baptist Theological Seminary, August 1999.

Elliston, Edgar J. *Introduction to Missiological Research Design*. Pasadena, CA: William Carey Library, 2011.

Elmer, Duane. *Cross-Cultural Conflict: Building Relationships for Effective Ministry*. Downers Grove, IL: InterVarsity Press Academic, 1993.

_____. *Cross-Cultural Connections: Stepping Out and Fitting in Around the World.* Downers Grove, IL: InterVarsity Press Academic, 2002.

_____. *Cross-Cultural Servanthood: Serving the World in Christlike Humility.* Downers Grove, IL: InterVarsity Press Books, 2006.

Engel, James F. and William A. Dyrness. *Changing the Mind of Missions: Where Have We Gone Wrong?* Downers Grove, IL: IVP, 2000.

Escobar, Samuel and John Driver. *Christian Mission and Social Justice.* Scottdale, PA: Herald Press, 1978.

Escobar, Samuel. *The New Global Mission: The Gospel from Everywhere to Everywhere.* Downers Grove, IL: IVP Academic, 2003.

Ferdinando, Keith. "Mission: A Problem of Definition." *Themelios* Volume 33.1 (2008): 46–59.

Flinn, John Jay. "Missional Community as Context for Disciple-Making: Theological and Theorectical Foundations." *Missional Disciple-Making: Disciple-Making for the Purpose of Mission.* Ed. Michael J. Breen and David M. Gustafson. Pawleys Island, SC: 3DM Publishing, 2019. 168–199.

Graham, Billy. "Why Lausanne?" *Let the Earth Hear His Voice.* Ed. J.D. Douglas. Minneapolis, MN: World Wide Publications, 1975. 22–36.

Griffiths, Michael. "Preface." *Kingdom Partnerships for Synergy in Missions.* Ed. William D. Taylor. Pasadena, CA: William Carey Library, 1994. vii–xi.

Guthrie, Stan. *Missions in the Third Millennium: 21 Key Trends for the 21st Century, Revised & Expanded Edition.* Milton Keynes: UK: Paternoster, 2014.

Halter, Hugh and Matt Smay. *The Tangible Kingdom: Creating Incarnational Community.* San Francisco, CA: Jossey-Bass, 2008.

Henry, Carl F.H. *The Uneasy Conscience of Modern Fundamentalism (1947).* 1947 Reprint. Grand Rapids, MI: Eerdmans, 2003.

Hesselgrave, David J. *Paradigms in Conflict: 10 Key Questions in Christian Missions Today.* Grand Rapids, MI: Kregel, 2005.

_____. "Redefining Holism." *Evangelical Missions Quarterly* Vol 35 (3) (1999): 278–84. Accessed 10 February 2017. <https://emqonline.com/node/632>.

Hiebert, Paul G. *Anthropological Insights for Missionaries.* Grand Rapids, MI: Baker Academic, 1985.

Hiebert, Paul G. and Monte B. Cox. "Evangelism and Social Responsibility." *Evangelical Dictionary of World Missions.* Ed. A. Scott Moreau. Grand Rapids, MI: Baker Academic, 2000. 344–346.

Hirsch, Alan. *The Forgotten Ways: Reactivating the Missional Church.* Grand Rapids, MI: Brazos Press, 2006.

Hofstede, Geert, Gert Jan Hofstede, and Michael Minkov. *Cultures and Organizations: Software of the Mind: Intercultural Cooperation and Its Importance for Survival.* Revised and Expanded 3rd Edition. New York, NY: McGraw Hill, 2010.

Horton, Michael. *The Christian Faith: A Systematic Theology for Pilgrims on the Way.* Grand Rapids, MI: Zondervan, 2011.

Hunter, James Davison. *To Change the World: The Irony, Tragedy, & Possibility of Christianity in the Late Modern World.* New York, NY: Oxford University Press, 2010.

IllustrationExchange. 13 July 2018. *Spilling Your Coffee.* Accessed 30 September 2019. <https://illustrationexchange.com/illustrations?category=91>.

Johnson, R. Burke and Larry Christensen. *Educational Research: Quantitative, Qualitative, and Mixed Approaches.* 6th edition. Thousand Oaks, CA: SAGE, 2017.

Keller, Timothy. *Center Church: Doing Balanced, Gospel-Centered Ministry in Your City.* Grand Rapids, MI: Zondervan, 2012.

Kirk, J. Andrew. *What Is Mission? Theological Explorations.* Minneapolis, MN: Fortress Press, 2000. Digital.

Kouzes, James M. and Barry Z. Posner. *The Leadership Challenge: How to Make Extraordinary Things Happen in Organizations.* 6th edition. Hoboken, NJ: Wiley, 2017.

Kraft, Charles H. *Anthropology for Christian Witness.* Maryknoll, NY: Orbis, 1996.

Labberton, Mark. *Called: The Crisis and Promise of Following Jesus Today.* Downers Grove, IL: InterVarsity Press, 2014.

Lausanne Committee for World Evangelism. *Lausanne Movement.* n.d. <www.lausanne.org>.

"Lausanne Movement." 8 October 2004. *Lausanne Occasional Paper No. 38 - Partnership and Collaboration.* Accessed 7 December 2015. <https://www.lausanne.org/content/lop/partnership-collaboration-lop-38>.

"Lausanne Movement." 12 June 1983. *Transformation: The Church in Response to Human Need.* Accessed 21 July 2018. <www.lausanne.org/content/statement/transformation-the-church-in-response-to-human-need>.

"Lausanne Movement." 2005. *Holistic Mission Lausanne Occasional Papr No. 33.* Accessed 5 December 2015. <https://www.lausanne.org/content/holistic-mission-lop-33>.

"Lausanne Movement." March 1983. *Cooperating in World Evangelism: A Handbook on Church/Para-Church Relationships - Lausanne Occasional Paper No 24.* Accessed 7 December 2015. <https://www.lausanne.org/content/lop/lop-24>.

"Lausanne Movement." 2011. *The Capetown Committment: A Confession of Faith and a Call to Action.* Accessed 22 April 2019. <https://www.lausanne.org/content/ctc/ctcommitment#capetown>.

"Lausanne Movement." July 1989. *The Manila Manefesto.* Accessed 26 Decemebr 2015. <https://www.lausanne.org/content/manifesto/the-manila-manifesto>.

"Lausanne Movement." 1 August 1974. *The Lausanne Covenant.* Accessed 5 December 2015. <https://www.lausanne.org/content/covenant/lausanne-covenant>.

Lederleitner, Mary T. *Cross-Cultural Partnerships: Navigating the Complexities of Money and Mission*. Downers Grove, IL: InterVarsity, 2010.

Lingenfelter, Sherwood G. *Leading Cross-Culturally: Covenant Relationships for Effective Christian Leadership*. Grand Rapids, MI: Baker, 2008.

Livermore, David A. *Cultural Intelligence: Improving Your CQ to Engage Our Multicultural World*. Grand Rapids, MI: Baker Academic, 2009.

Maggay, Melba Padilla. "Engaging Culture: Lessons from the Underside of History." *Missiology: An International Review* Vol. 33.no. 1 (2005): 62–70.

Mangalwadi, Vishal and Ruth Mangalwadi. *The Legacy of William Carey: A Model for the Transformation of a Culture*. Wheaton, IL: Crossway, 1999.

Merril, Tim, ed. *Honduras: A Country Study*. Washington D.C.: GPO for the Library of Congress, 1995.

Meyer, Peter J. "Honduras: Background and U.S. Relations." 22 July 2019. *U.S. Department of State, Congressional Research Service Reports (CRS) and Issue Briefs*. Accessed 10 October 2019. <https://www.fas.org/sgp/crs/row/RL34027.pdf>.

Mezirow, Jack. "Learning to Think Like an Adult: Core Concepts of Transformation Theory." Mezirow, Jack and Associates. *Learning as Transformation: Critical Perspectives on a Theory in Progress*. San Francisco, CA: Jossey-Bass, 2000.

Moberg, David O. *The Great Reversal: Reconciling Evangelism and Social Concern*. Eugene: OR: Wipf & Stock, 2006.

Moreau, A. Scott. "Mission and Missions." *Evangelical Dictionary of World Missions*. Ed. A. Scott Moreau. Grand Rapids, MI: Baker, 2000. 636–638.

Myers, Bryant L. "Another Look at 'Holistic Mission': A Response." *Evangelical Missions Quarterly* Vol. 35(3) (1999): 285–87. Accessed 10 February 2017. <https://www.emqonline.com/node/631>.

_____. "At the End of the Day." *Serving with the Poor in Asia*. Ed. Tetsunao Yamamori, Bryant L. Myers and David Conner. Monrovia, CA: Marc, 1995. 195–201.

_____. *Engaging Globalization: The Poor, Christian Mission, and Our Hyperconnected World*. Grand Rapids, MI: Baker Academic, 2017.

_____. "The Holistic Practitioner." *Serving With the Poor in Latin America*. Ed. Tetsunao Yamamori, *et al*. Monrovia, CA: MARC, 1997. 129–36.

_____. *Walking With the Poor: Principles and Practices of Transformational Development*. Revised and Expanded Edition. Maryknoll, NY: Orbis Books, 2011.

Myers, Bryant L., Erin Dufault-Hunter, and Isaac B. Voss. *Health Healing and Shalom: Frontiers and Challenges for Christian Health Missions*. Pasadena, CA: William Carey Library, 2015.

Neill, Stephen. *A History of Christian Mission: The Penguin History of the Church 6*. New York, NY: Penguin Books, 1990.

_____. *Creative Tensions: The Duff Lectures, 1958*. London: Edinburgh House Press, 1959.

Newbigin, Lesslie. "Can the West be Converted." *The Princeton Seminary Bulletin* (1985): 25–37.

_____. "Cross-Currents in Ecumenical and Evangelical Understandings of Mission." *International Bulletin of Missionary Research* Vol. 6 (4) (1982): 146-151.

_____. *The Gospel in a Pluralist Society*. Grand Rapids, MI: William B. Erdmans Publishing Company, 1989.

_____. *The Open Secret: An Introduction to the Theology of Mission*. Revised Edition. Grand Rapids, MI: William B. Eerdmanns Publishing, 1995.

_____. *A Word in Season: Perspectives on Christian World Missions*. Grand Rapids, MI: Eerdmans Publishing, 1994.

Nida, Eugene A. *Understanding Latin Americans: With Special Reference to Religious Values and Movements*. Pasadena, CA: William Carey Library, 1974.

Ott, Craig and Stephen J. Strauss. *Encountering Theology of Mission: Biblical Foundations, Historical Developments, and Contemporary Issues*. Grand Rapids, MI: Baker Academic, 2010.

Padilla, C. René. "Holistic Mission in Theological Perspective." *Serving With the Poor in Latin America: Cases in Holistic Ministry*. Ed. Tetsunao Yamamori, *et al.* Monrovia, CA: Marc Publications, 1997. 100–118.

_____. "Integral Mission and its Historical Development." *Justice, Mercy and Humility: Integral Mission and the Poor*. Ed. Tim Chester. Waynesboro, GA: Paternoster, 2002. 42–58.

_____. *Mission Between the Times: Essays on the Kingdom*. Grand Rapids, MI: William B. Eerdmans Publishing, 1985.

Peters, George W. *A Biblical Theology of Missions.* 1972. New Edition. Chicago, IL: Moody Press, 1984.

Plueddemann, James E. *Leading Across Cultures: Effective Ministry and Mission in the Global Church*. Downers Grove, IL: InterVarsity, 2009.

Pocock, Michael, Gailyn Van Rheenen and Douglas McConnell. *The Changing Face of World Missions: Engaging Contemporary Issues and Trends*. Grand Rapids, MI: Baker Academic, 2005.

Priest, Robert J. and Joseph Paul Priest. "They See Everything, and Understand Nothing: Short-Term Mission and Service Learning." *Missiology: An International Review* Vol. XXXVI.no. 1 (2008): 53-73.

Pue, Carson. *Mentoring Leaders: Wisdom for Developing Character, Calling, and Competency*. Grand Rapids, MI: Baker Books, 2005.

Rankin, Jerry A. "The Present Situation in Missions." *Missiology: An Introduction to the Foundations, History, and Strategies of World Missions*. Ed. John Mark Terry, Ebbie Smith and Justice Anderson. Nashville, TN: Broadman & Holman, 1998. 30–50.

Rauschenbusch, Walter. *Christianity and the Social Crisis*. London: The Macmillan Company, 1914.

Rickett, Daniel. *Building Strategic Relationships: A Practical Guide to Partnering with Non-Western Missions*. Third Edition. Minneapolis, MN: Stem Press, 2008.

_____. *Making Your Partnership Work*. Third edition. Roswell, GA: Daniel Rickett, 2014.

Ringma, Charles. "Holistic Ministry and Mission: A Call for Reconceptualization." *Missiology: An International Review* Vol. XXXII No. 4 (2004): 431–48.

Robbins, Richard H. and Rachel Dowty. *Cultural Anthropology: A Problem-Based Approach*. Seventh Edition. Boston, MA: Cengage Learning, 2016.

Russel, Mark. "Christian Mission is Holistic." *International Journal of Frontier Missiology* Volume 25:2 (Summer 2008): 93–98.

Schaeffer, Francis A. *The Mark of the Christian*. Downers Grove, IL: InterVarsity Press, 1970.

Sherman, Amy L. *Restorers of Hope: Reaching the Poor in Your Community with Church-based Ministries that Work*. 1997 Reprint. Eugene, OR: Wipf & Stock, 2004.

Sider, Ronald J., et al. *Linking Arm, Linking Lives: How Urban Partnerships Can Tranform Communities*. Grand Rapids, MI: Baker, 2008.

Sider, Ronald J., Philip N. Olson, and Heidi Rolland Unruh. *Churches That Make a Difference: Reaching Your Community with Good News and Good Works*. Grand Rapids, MI: Baker, 2002.

Smith, Ebbie. "Introduction to the Strategy of Missions." *Missiology: An Intrduction to the Foundations, History, and Strategies of World Missions*. Ed. John Mark Terry, Ebbie Smith and Justice Anderson. Nashville, TN: Broadman & Holman, 1998. 434–449.

Smither, Edward L. *Mission in the Early Church: Themes and Reflections*. Eugene, OR: Cascade, 2014.

Spitters, Denny and Matthew Ellison. *When Everything Is Missions*. BottomLine Media, 2017.

Stake, Robert E. *The Art of Case Study Research*. Thousand Oaks, CA: SAGE, 1995.

Stearns, Richard. *The Hole in our Gospel*. Nashville, TN: Thomas Nelson, 2009.

Stetzer, Ed. "Involving All of God's People in All of God's Mission, Part 2." 1 June 2010. *Christianity Today*. Accessed 4 June 2019. <https://www.christianitytoday.com/edstetzer/2010/june/involving-all-of-gods-people-in-all-of-gods-mission-part-2.html>.

_____. "Responding to "Mission Defined and Described' and the Four Respondents." *Mission Shift: Global Mission Issues in the Third Millenium*. Ed. David J. Hesselgrave and Ed Stetzer. Nashville, TN: B&H Academic, 2010. 71–81.

Stott, John R.W. *Christian Mission in the Modern World: What the Church Should Be Doing Now!* Downers Grove, IL: InterVarsity Press, 1975.

_____. ed. *Making Christ Known: Historic Mission Documents from the Lausanne Movement 1974–1989*. Grand Rapids, MI: William B. Eerdmans Publishing, 1996.

_____. "Twenty Years After Lausanne: Some Personal Reflections." *International Bulletin of Missionary Research* (1995): 50–55.

Taylor, Edward W. "Analyzing Research on Transformative Learning." Ed., Jack Mezirow and Associates. *Learning As Transformation: Critical Perspectives on a Theory in Progress*. San Francisco, CA: Jossey-Bass, 2000. 285–328.

Taylor, William D., ed. *Kingdom Partnerships for Synergy in Missions*. Pasadena, CA: William Carey Library, 1994.

Tizon, Al. *Whole & Reconciled: Gospel, Church, and Mission in a Fractured World*. Grand Rapids, MI: Baker Academic, 2018.

U.S. Department of State. *2018 Report on International Religious Freedom: Honduras*. Accessed 19 October 2019. <https://www.state.gov/reports/2018-report-on-international-religious-freedom/honduras/>.

_____. *International Religious Freedom Report 2005: Honduras*. 2005. Accessed 29 December 2015. <http://www.state.gov/j/drl/rls/irf/2005/51644.htm>.

United Nations Economic Commission for Latin America and the Carribean. "Honduras: Assessment of the Damage Caused by Hurricane Mitch, 1998." *United Nations Economic Commission for Latin America and the Carribean*. Accessed 29 December 2015. <http://www.cepal.org/publicaciones/xml/6/15506/L367-1-EN.pdf>.

Vanier, Jean. *Community and Growth*. Revised Edition. Mahwah, NJ: Paulist Press, 1989.

Visser 't Hooft, William A. *The Background of the Social Gospel in America*. St Louis, MO: Bethany, 1928.

Wallis, Jim. *The Call to Conversion: Why Faith Is Always Personal but Never Private*. San Francisco, CA: HarperCollins, 2005.

_____. *Faith Works: Lessons from the Life of an Activist Preacher*. New York, NY: Random House, 2000.

Wan, Enoch. "Diaspora Missiology and International Student Ministry (ISM)." *Diaspora Missions to International Students*. Ed., Enoch Wan. Portland, OR: Western Seminary Press, 2019.

_____. *Diaspora Missiology: Theory, Methodology, and Paractice* 2nd Edition. Portland, OR: Institute of Diaspora Studies of USA, Western Seminary, 2014.

_____. "IE707 ICE: What, Why & How." Western Seminary, May 2019. Pre-publication Material.

_____. "Inter-disciplinary and Integrative Missiological Research: The "What", "Why" and "How"." July 2017. *Global Missioolgy*. Accessed 18 July 2019. <http://ojs.globalmissiology.org/index.php/english/article/viewFile/2019/4514>.

_____. "Mission Amid Global Crisis: Holistic Mission to Diaspora Groups." Toronto, Canada, 8 March 2019. Paper presented at Tyndale University College & Seminary.

_____. "The Pardigm of 'Relational Realism'." *Occasional Bulletin of the Evangelical Missiological Society* Spring 2006.

_____. "Relational Theology and Relational Missiology." *Occasional Bulletin of the Evangelical Missiological Society* Spring 2007.

_____. "Rethinking the Great Commission for the African Context: A Proposal for the Paradigm of Relational Missiology (Part 1)." April 2019. *Global Missiology*. Accessed 15 July 2019. <http://ojs.globalmissiology.org/index.php/english/article/view/2234>.

Wan, Enoch and Kevin P. Penman. "The Trinity: A Model for Partnership in Christian Missions." 1 April 2010. *Global Missiology*. Accessed 1 October 2015. <http://ojs.globalmissiology.org/index.php/english/article/view/138>.

_____. "The "Why." "How" and "Who" of Partnership in Christian Mission." 1 April 2010. *Global Missiology.* Accessed 1 October 2015. <http://ojs.globalmissiology.org/index.php/english/article/view/61>.

Wan, Enoch and Mark Hedinger. *Relational Missionary Training.* Skyforest, CA: Urban Loft, 2017.

Warren, Max. *Partnership: The Study of an Idea.* London: SCM Press LTD, 1956.

Wells, David F. *Above all Earthly Pow'rs: Christ in a Postmodern World.* Grand Rapids, MI: Eerdmans, 2005.

White, James Emery. *The Rise of the Nones: Understanding and Reaching the Religiously Unaffiliated.* Grand Rapids, MI: Baker Books, 2014.

Whitehead, Evelyn Eaton and James D. Whitehead. *The Promise of Partnership: A Model for Collaborative Ministry.* Lincoln, NE: iUniverse.com, 2000.

Wilkins, Michael J. "Disciple, Discipleship." *Evangelical Dictionary of World Missions.* Ed. A. Scott Moreau. Grand Rapids, MI: Baker, 2000. 278-80.

_____. *Following the Master: A Biblical Theology of Discipleship.* Grand Rapids, MI: Zondervan, 1992.

_____. *Matthew: The NIV Application Commentary.* Grand Rapids, MI: Zondervan, 2004.

Willard, Dallas. *The Great Omission: Reclaiming Jesus's Essential Teachings on Discipleship.* New York, NY: Harper, 2006.

Wright, Christopher J.H. *The Mission of God: Unlocking the Bible's Grand Narrative.* Downers Grove, IL: IVP Academic, 2006.

_____. *The Mission of God's People: A Biblical Theology of the Christian Mission.* Grand Rapids, MI: Zondervan, 2010.

Yin, Robert K. *Case Study Research: Design and Methods.* 5th edition. Thousand Oaks, CA: SAGE, 2014.

Zscheile, Dwight J, ed. *Cultivating Sent Communities: Missional Spiritual Formation.* Grand Rapids, MI: Eerdmans, 2012.